The SuperCalc® Program Made Easy

Chris Wood

Osborne/McGraw-Hill
Berkeley, California

Published by
Osborne/McGraw-Hill
2600 Tenth Street
Berkeley, California 94710
U.S.A.

For information on translations and book distributors outside of the U.S.A, please write to Osborne/McGraw-Hill at the above address.

The SuperCalc® Program Made Easy

1234567890 DODO 8987654

ISBN 0-931988-88-8

Judy Ziajka, Acquisitions Editor
Richard Katz, Technical Editor
Ted Gartner, Copy Editor
Yashi Okita, Cover Design

CONTENTS

To my daughters,
Emily and Melinda

Introduction

SuperCalc Made Easy is a tutorial guide for learning to use the SuperCalc programs. The rudimentary skills you need to use SuperCalc are explained in a series of lessons in Chapters 1 through 3. When you have completed these "hands-on" lessons, you will have a basic understanding of how to use SuperCalc.

Chapters 4 through 12 give in-depth coverage of the complete program. Each command and function in SuperCalc and SuperCalc^2 is explained through the use of examples. You are encouraged to try the examples on your own computer. Chapter 12 describes SuperCalc^3.

Chapter 11 discusses special techniques for applying SuperCalc to a problem. When you finish this book, you will be able to make good use of SuperCalc, no matter what your application may be.

This is not a book of "canned" worksheets; rather, it teaches by example. When you have read this book, you will know how to make your own worksheets, and you will be able to adapt "canned" worksheets easily to your own applications.

You can also refer to Appendixes A and B for details about each command and function.

Introducing SuperCalc

SuperCalc is an electronic spreadsheet program. Its nearest equivalent in pencil and paper is the ubiquitous accountant's ruled worksheet. In the simplest terms, SuperCalc replaces the paper worksheet with an electronic worksheet on the computer screen. In SuperCalc, the rows and columns are labeled. The intersections of rows and columns are separate locations on the worksheet, which are called *cells*. You can enter information into any cell on the SuperCalc worksheet just as you would pencil in a number on an accounting worksheet. The similarity quickly fades, however, when the calculations begin. SuperCalc automatically makes whatever calculations are required instantly and repeatedly. And SuperCalc can recalculate the entire worksheet when changes are made to the initial values. It recalculates automatically every time you make a change.

But SuperCalc is more than an electronic accountant's worksheet: it also has scientific and engineering capabilities including mathematical, trigonometric, and logic functions.

SuperCalc is not limited to the size of a piece of paper. The SuperCalc worksheet contains 64 columns and 254 rows. The computer's screen acts as a window that can be moved to any position on this extended worksheet.

With SuperCalc you can create "template" worksheets that contain all the calculations of a particular task but with none of the data. This would be analogous to using a printed form. You fill in the template as you would a blank form, and SuperCalc does the required calculations automatically. Templates are ideal for applications that are used many times like daily sales analyses or monthly inventories. SuperCalc has the ability to *protect* locations on the worksheet that you do not want accidentally changed. This avoids the problem of a template being damaged by an error when the worksheet is used by someone else.

SuperCalc can display numbers and text in many different *formats*, allowing you to produce reports that are easy to understand and easy to read. Because SuperCalc has the flexibility to format and position numbers and text, it is possible to produce highly sophisticated reports. With SuperCalc, you can also arrange a report in a different sequence, format currency amounts with commas, and display dates.

SuperCalc also contains many built-in calculations called *functions* that simplify turning calculations into formulas.

Once you have created a worksheet, you can save it on disk for future use, modification, or updating. And at any time, all or part of the worksheet can be printed.

You can easily modify your worksheets with SuperCalc's ability to insert, delete, or move complete columns or rows of information. You can expand your worksheets with SuperCalc's ability to make copies of any part of a worksheet.

SuperCalc is a powerful program that can assist you in budgeting, scheduling, and even engineering calculations. As you progress through this book, you will learn of SuperCalc's many capabilities.

There are actually several different versions of the SuperCalc program, and each has different capabilities. These versions are shown in Table I-1.

Each version has slightly different prompts and options. Throughout this book, the prompts shown will be those of SuperCalc^2. If you are using a different version of SuperCalc, the prompts you see as you operate your program will vary slightly from what is shown.

Program Version	*Release Date*	*Major Enhancements*
SuperCalc 1.01	1981	Original version of SuperCalc for the CP/M operating system
SuperCalc 1.10	1982	Version for MS-DOS. Added the /eXecute command and the /Save Part option
SuperCalc 1.12	1982	Same as 1.10 for CP/M
SuperCalc^2	1983	Added sorting (/Arrange command), formats with embedded commas (U1 through U8), consolidation, calendar date functions, the ROUND and MOD functions, resume execute (&), and the data conversion program SDI
SuperCalc^3	1983	Added screen, plotter, and printer graphics (/View), data management (//Data), entering text without double quote, plus Internal Rate of Return (IRR) and other functions

Table I-1.

Versions of SuperCalc

Getting the Most From This Book

When you use this book, work along with the examples. To make it easy to follow the examples, everything that you need to enter is set in **boldface** type.

The lessons in Chapters 1 through 3 present the first example for learning the SuperCalc program. You are encouraged to follow these lessons in order. However, you may want to save your work before completing these chapters. If you do not want to work through all of these lessons in one session, you can skip ahead to Chapter 3, Lesson 12: "Saving a Worksheet" so that you can save the work you have completed. When you resume, start with Lesson 15: "Loading a Worksheet," and then continue where you left off.

Every computer keyboard has a key on it that is like the carriage return key on a typewriter. This return key has various names: Return, Enter, End of Line, or maybe it's just marked with a downward and back arrow ↵ . In this book, the return key will always be referred to as <RET>.

In SuperCalc, you often press <RET> to tell the program that you have finished entering information. There are two terms that we use to direct you to enter information into your computer. The first is *type*, as in "Type: **345**". The word type is used when you should just type the characters given without pressing <RET> (unless <RET> is one of the things you are told to type). The word *enter*, as in "Enter **345**", means to type the characters given and then press **<RET>**. The distinction between these two terms is not something you need to keep constantly in mind. In most situations, it will be obvious which is required. The word *press* tells you to press a key, as in "press the letter **A** or press the **right arrow** key."

With SuperCalc, you use the arrow keys to move around the worksheet. However, some keyboards do not have arrow keys. This is not a problem because you can use some other keys that *are* on your keyboard instead. This is explained in Chapter 1; however, throughout this book we will speak of the arrow keys.

As new concepts or technical terms are introduced, they will be shown in *italics*. You can refer to the Glossary in Appendix D for definitions of these terms.

Computers That Run SuperCalc

SuperCalc is available for computers that use the CP/M, CP/M-86, MS-DOS, or PC-DOS operating systems. If your computer uses one of these operating systems, you can probably obtain SuperCalc for it.

SuperCalc is also being sold under the name of PeachCalc by Peachtree Software. There are versions of PeachCalc for many computers, including the Epson QX-10.

Getting Started With SuperCalc

To operate SuperCalc, you must have a disk that has both the operating system and the SuperCalc program on it. (SuperCalc consists of three program files, SC.COM, SC.OVL, and SC.HLP, as shown in Table I-2.) The SuperCalc program may need to be tailored to your particular computer. It must be set up for your keyboard, display screen, and printer.

If you have already successfully operated SuperCalc on your computer, these conditions have been met. If you are just getting started, use the documentation furnished with the SuperCalc program entitled "Installing the SuperCalc Program" to accomplish this now.

Before you begin, be sure that you have several blank, *formatted* diskettes available to store the worksheets that you create. With most computers that will run SuperCalc, you use a command called "FORMAT" to prepare a blank diskette for use. Your operating system manual will tell you how to make formatted diskettes.

To start the SuperCalc program, place the disk with the program on it in drive A of your computer. The prompt on the screen tells you which drive is your *default* drive; if the prompt is "A>" then drive A is the default drive. If the prompt is *not* "A>", change the default drive by typing **A:** and press

	SuperCalc	***SuperCalc***^{2}	***SuperCalc***^{3}
To start the program enter	A>**SC**	A>**SC2**	A>**SC3**
Files needed on disk A			
Main program	SC.COM	SC2.COM	SC3.COM
Overlays	SC.OVL	SC2.OVL	SC3.OVL
Help file		SC2.HLP	SC3.HLP
Data Conversion program	(not available)	SDI.COM SDI.OVL	SDI.COM SDI.OVL

Table I-2.

SuperCalc Program Modules

<RET>. The prompt will change to "A>", telling you that drive A is now the system drive.

Throughout this book we will assume that the SuperCalc program diskette is in drive A and a diskette for storing worksheets is in drive B.

SuperCalc will run on any drive you have loaded it into as long as it is in the default drive. SuperCalc keeps part of the program on the disk all the time to conserve memory. When it needs a part of the program that is on the disk, it always loads it from the default drive. This flexibility allows you to run SuperCalc from a hard disk or a RAM disk emulator. Appendix C describes how to operate SuperCalc from a hard disk or a RAM disk. However, if SuperCalc is not on the system drive, the program will not work.

To start SuperCalc type **SC** and press **<RET>**. If you are using SuperCalc^2 (or SuperCalc^3), you need to type **SC2** (or **SC3**) and press **<RET>**. Wait a few seconds and the program title page will be on the display. If you get a display that looks something like Figure I-1, you have started the program correctly.

On many computers, starting SuperCalc is even easier. Some operating systems allow you to create a file that tells the computer to start a program automatically. This feature is furnished on the SuperCalc disk for the Osborne 1 and IBM PC computers. With these computers all you need to do is install the operating system on the SuperCalc program disk, put the disk in drive A, and reset or "boot" the computer. If you are using an Osborne 1, turn the power on *before* placing a disk in drive A. The Osborne 1 requires you to press <RET> to tell it that the disk is in position.

```
                    SuperCalc2(tm)
                    Version  1.00
                    TeleVideo  950
                     CPU: 8080
                  S/N-002405 CP/M 2.2

                    Copyright 1983
                     SORCIM CORP.
                     San Jose, CA.



Enter "?" for HELP or "return" to start.
```

Figure I-1.

Opening screen of the SuperCalc program

Other computers also have the ability to start SuperCalc automatically when they are turned on. The specific procedure varies, so you will have to look in the manual that came with your operating system to see how to start SuperCalc automatically with your computer.

NOTE: It is a good idea to make a working copy and backup copy of the SuperCalc disk before you use the program. To do this, follow the procedure in the installation guide which the manufacturer supplies with the software. If your version of SuperCalc did not include an installation guide, you can request one from Sorcim Corporation by writing to them at 2310 Lundy Avenue, San Jose, CA 95131, or by calling them at (408) 942-1727.

Versions of SuperCalc

The SuperCalc program has evolved over time. The original version of SuperCalc was released in the summer of 1981. Since then, Sorcim has improved the program in many ways. If you have one of the later versions, SuperCalc^2 or SuperCalc^3, you will find that the program has become very powerful and that it is more useful and applicable to a wider range of business problems. Exploring the graphics or data selection capabilities of SuperCalc^3 can keep you occupied for several days.

As of this writing, there are three major versions of SuperCalc, plus revisions of the original SuperCalc program in which Sorcim has included major enhancements. These are shown in Table I-1. All versions are able to read model files that were created by previous versions of SuperCalc, so you can upgrade from one version to the next without changing or reentering a model or the data.

In this book the lessons in Chapters 1 through 3 are written assuming that you have the original SuperCalc and SuperCalc^2. The SuperCalc^3 program will operate approximately the same for these lessons. However, if you have SuperCalc^3, take a quick look at the first section of Chapter 12, which describes entering text in SuperCalc^3. This will make it slightly easier for you to use the program.

CHAPTER ONE

Entering Data Into the Worksheet

When you first start the SuperCalc program, you are presented with the title page (see Figure I-1). This page shows the copyright notice, the version of SuperCalc you are using, and the serial number of your disk.

Press the RETURN key (<RET>). The display will change from the title page to an empty worksheet. This screen will appear like the worksheet shown in Figure 1-1. The letters A to H across the top of the display screen identify the columns of the worksheet. The numbers 1 to 20 down the left side of the screen identify the rows of the worksheet.

In combination, the column letters and row numbers define locations on the worksheet called *cells.* The name of any particular cell is created by combining the letter of its column with the number of its row. The cell in the upper-left corner of the display screen is A1. The cell directly to the right of A1 is B1, and the cell directly below B1 is B2. If you are using an 80-column display, the cell in the lower-right corner of the initial screen is H20. Figure 1-2 shows some of the cells on the initial worksheet.

```
  |    A    ||    B    ||    C    ||    D    ||    E    ||    F    ||    G    ||    H    |
 1|
 2|
 3|
 4|
 5|
 6|
 7|
 8|
 9|
10|
11|
12|
13|
14|
15|
16|
17|
18|
19|
20|
> A1
Width:  9  Memory: 27 Last Col/Row:A1      ? for HELP
   1>
```

Figure 1-1.

The worksheet

```
  |    A    ||    B    ||    C    ||    D    ||    E    ||    F    ||    G    ||    H    |
 1| A1        B1         C1         D1         E1         F1         G1         H1
 2| A2        B2         C2         D2         E2         F2         G2         H2
 3| A3        B3         C3         D3         E3         F3         G3         H3
 4| A4        B4         C4         D4         E4         F4         G4         H4
 5| A5        B5         C5         D5         E5         F5         G5         H5
 6| A6        B6         C6         D6         E6         F6         G6         H6
 7| A7        B7         C7         D7         E7         F7         G7         H7
 8| A8        B8         C8         D8         E8         F8         G8         H8
 9| A9        B9         C9         D9         E9         F9         G9         H9
10| A10       B10        C10        D10        E10        F10        G10        H10
11| A11       B11        C11        D11        E11        F11        G11        H11
12| A12       B12        C12        D12        E12        F12        G12        H12
13| A13       B13        C13        D13        E13        F13        G13        H13
14| A14       B14        C14        D14        E14        F14        G14        H14
15| A15       B15        C15        D15        E15        F15        G15        H15
16| A16       B16        C16        D16        E16        F16        G16        H16
17| A17       B17        C17        D17        E17        F17        G17        H17
18| A18       B18        C18        D18        E18        F18        G18        H18
19| A19       B19        C19        D19        E19        F19        G19        H19
20| A20       B20        C20        D20        E20        F20        G20        H20
v A1          Form=A1
Width:  9  Memory: 23 Last Col/Row:J20      ? for HELP
   1>
```

Figure 1-2.

Cells of the visible worksheet

Look at the highlighted bar in the upper-left corner of Figure 1-1. Notice that this highlighting is over the cell that is in row 1, column A (which is cell A1). This highlighted cell is where you can currently enter information, and it is referred to as the *active cell.* The active cell may be highlighted in one of several ways depending on your terminal; it may appear as a white bar in reverse video, it may be underlined, or it may be enclosed with the angular brackets < and >.

At the bottom of the screen are three lines of program status information called the *status line,* the *prompt line,* and the *entry line,* as shown in Figure 1-3. The status line always shows the location of the active cell. The prompt line displays questions and options when SuperCalc prompts you to enter something. The entry line is where information appears as you enter it.

The display on your screen should be similar to Figure 1-3, although there are two things that may be different on your display. Some versions of SuperCalc have an additional line at the bottom of the screen that explains how to use function keys that are particular to that version. The number after the word "Memory" on the prompt line shows how much *memory* your computer has available for SuperCalc worksheets. This number may be different on different computers.

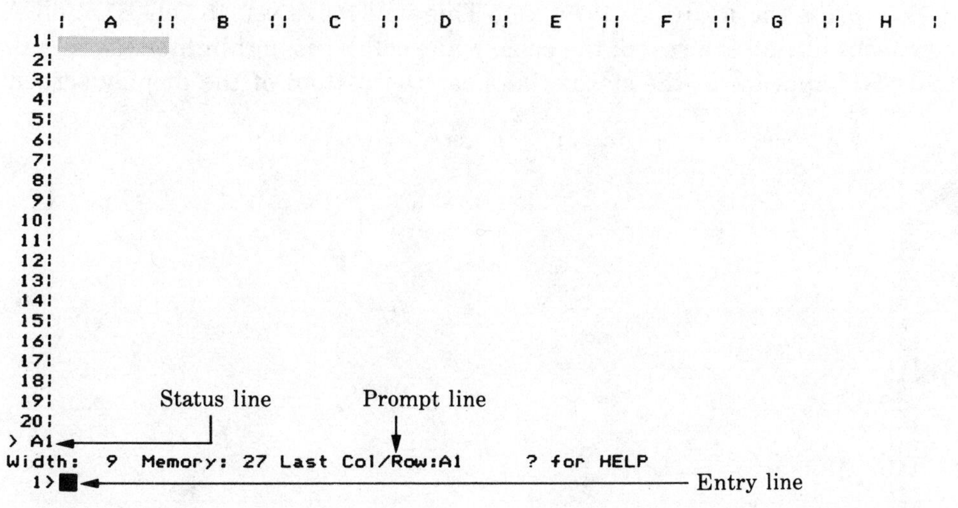

Figure 1-3.

The program status lines

Lesson 1: Moving Around the Worksheet

The arrow keys are used to move the active cell around the worksheet. If your terminal does not have arrow keys, you need to use the letters E, S, D, and X with the CTRL key instead. Pressing the CTRL key and the letter E simultaneously will function as the up arrow. Likewise, CTRL-X functions as the down arrow, CTRL-S, the left arrow, and CTRL-D functions as the right arrow. Notice that these keys are laid out in a diamond pattern on the keyboard and that the relative positions of the keys indicate their functions.

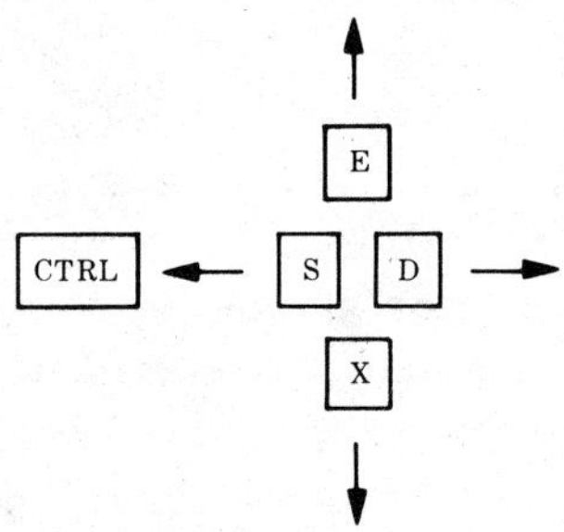

Now press the **RIGHT ARROW** key. This will move you to cell B1. Cell A1 now looks like all the rest of the cells, while cell B1 is highlighted. Notice also that "B1" appears in the status line near the bottom of the display screen.

```
      |    A    ||    B    ||    C    ||    D    ||    E    ||    F    ||    G    ||    H    |
    1|
    2|
    3|
    4|
    5|
    6|
    7|
    8|
    9|
   10|
   11|
   12|
   13|
   14|
   15|
   16|
   17|
   18|
   19|
   20|
> B1
Width:  9  Memory: 27 Last Col/Row:A1        ? for HELP
  1>
```

Press the **RIGHT ARROW** key a few more times until you reach the column at the right edge of the display.

```
   :   A   ::   B   ::   C   ::   D   ::   E   ::   F   ::   G   ::   H   :
  1:
  2:
  3:
  4:
  5:
  6:
  7:
  8:
  9:
 10:
 11:
 12:
 13:
 14:
 15:
 16:
 17:
 18:
 19:
 20:
> H1
Width:  9  Memory: 27 Last Col/Row:A1      ? for HELP
  1>
```

Now press the **RIGHT ARROW** key one more time.

```
   :   B   ::   C   ::   D   ::   E   ::   F   ::   G   ::   H   ::   I   :
  1:
  2:
  3:
  4:
  5:
  6:
  7:
  8:
  9:
 10:
 11:
 12:
 13:
 14:
 15:
 16:
 17:
 18:
 19:
 20:
> I1
Width:  9  Memory: 27 Last Col/Row:A1      ? for HELP
  1>
```

The highlighted cell stays in the same location on the display, but the letters across the top of the screen move to the left. Column A is no longer on the display, but the next column to the right is now visible. Moving the worksheet one column at a time is called *scrolling.* Scrolling keeps the active cell visible on the screen.

Scrolling is made easier on terminals with a "repeat" capability. With some terminals you can repeat a key by simultaneously pressing a REPEAT key and the key that you want to repeat. On terminals without a REPEAT key, you can usually repeat a key by holding it down; after a slight delay, it will repeat until you release it. Experiment with your computer to see how its repeat function works. While you are holding down the **RIGHT ARROW** key (and possibly the **REPEAT** key), watch the status line at the bottom of the screen. The cell name shown indicates where the active cell is located. As you move the active cell the information in the status line changes. This is a handy reference for quickly noting where you are on the worksheet.

Continue to press the **RIGHT ARROW** key until the active cell is just past cell Z1.

```
    :  T  ::  U  ::  V  ::  W  ::  X  ::  Y  ::  Z  ::  AA  :
  1:
  2:
  3:
  4:
  5:
  6:
  7:
  8:
  9:
 10:
 11:
 12:
 13:
 14:
 15:
 16:
 17:
 18:
 19:
 20:
> AA1
Width:  9  Memory: 27  Last Col/Row:A1     ? for HELP
  1> ■
```

The worksheet has 63 columns identified with the letters A through Z, AA through AZ, and BA through BK. The next cell is AA1. The remaining cells to the right continue as AB1, AC1, and so on until AZ1 and then BA1 to BK1. If you like, you can scroll the active cell to cell BK1. Just continue to press or hold down the **RIGHT ARROW** key. When the active cell is in cell BK1, continue to press the **RIGHT ARROW** key. This is the rightmost end of the worksheet. You can't move to the right of column BK, but there is no harm in trying.

The **LEFT ARROW** key, as you might imagine, does the opposite of the **RIGHT ARROW** key. It moves one cell to the left each time it is pressed. Press and hold the **LEFT ARROW** key (and the **REPEAT** key if necessary) to return to cell A1. Don't worry about going past column A; SuperCalc won't let you run off the worksheet.

Press the **DOWN ARROW** key and you move down to cell A2. Continue moving the active cell down until the worksheet scrolls vertically. You can also scroll to the bottom of the worksheet if you like, but you may wish to wait until you learn a quicker method of moving long distances, since there are 254 rows on the worksheet.

The worksheet consists of 63 × 254, or 16,002 cells. Relatively few of these cells can be seen on the display screen at any one time. However, by moving to different locations on the worksheet, any particular group of cells can be seen. The display screen acts as a mobile window through which you can see a part of the total worksheet, as shown in Figure 1-4.

Lesson 2: Moving Long Distances Quickly

Scrolling the worksheet to move long distances can be quite time-consuming. However, you can move long distances quickly with the *Go to* function. The Go to function provides a way to move to a named cell quickly.

To start the Go to function, press the equal sign (=). SuperCalc displays a stylized arrow on the entry line that looks like this:

```
   |  A  ||  B  ||  C  ||  D  ||  E  ||  F  ||  G  ||  H  |
  1|
  2|
  3|
  4|
  5|
  6|
  7|
  8|
  9|
 10|
  .
  .
  .
 14|
 15|
 16|
 17|
 18|
 19|
 20|
 21|
> A21
Enter cell to jump to.
  3>=> █
```

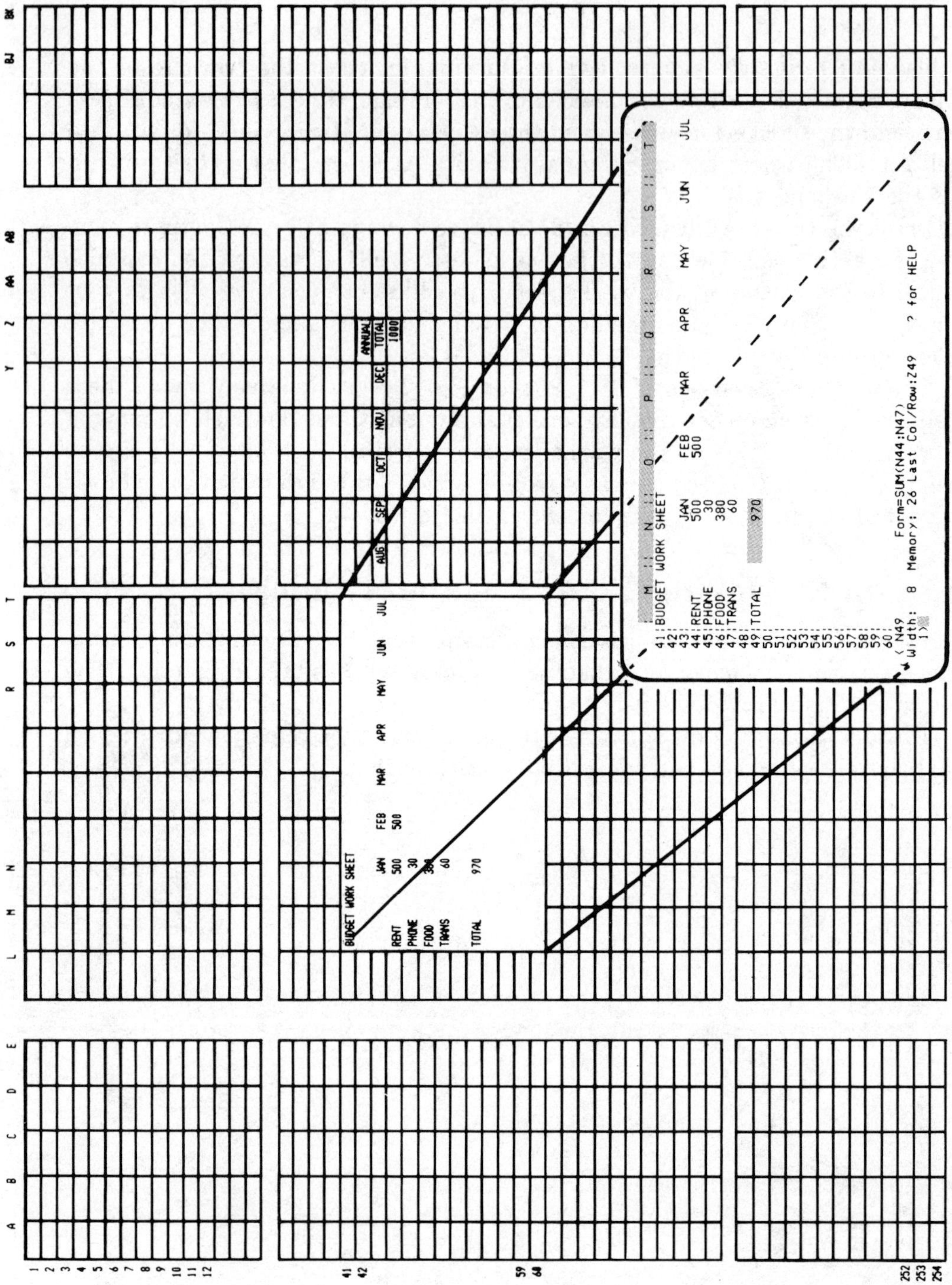

Figure 1-4.

The display screen is a window to the worksheet

Also notice that the prompt line asks you to "Enter cell to jump to".

Enter the name of the cell where you wish to go (for this example enter **A1**) and press **<RET>**. No matter where you were before, you are now at cell A1 in the upper-left corner of the worksheet.

Now "Go to" cell E18 by entering **=E18 <RET>**. The active cell moves to cell E18. Now "Go to" cell E21 (**=21 <RET>**).

```
    :    E    ::    F    ::    G    ::    H    ::    I    ::    J    ::    K    ::    L    :
  21:
  22:
  23:
  24:
  25:
  26:
  27:
  28:
  29:
  30:
  31:
  32:
  33:
  34:
  35:
  36:
  37:
  38:
  39:
  40:
> E21
Width:   9  Memory: 27 Last Col/Row:A1      ? for HELP
   1> █
```

If the new cell is visible on the screen when the Go to function is initiated, the active cell is just moved to the destination location. But if the destination cell is not visible when you enter the "=" sign, the new active cell is placed in the upper-left cell position on the screen.

The Go to function can also be used to place the current active cell in the upper-left position of the screen. This is done by entering the "=" without a cell destination.

To try this, move the active cell to H30, which now should be at about the middle of the display. Press = and press **<RET>**, and H30 will be moved to the upper-left position of the display. Finally, enter **=A1 <RET>**. The screen returns to its original position, and the active cell returns to A1.

Lesson 3: Entering Numbers

Now that you are comfortable moving around the worksheet, you will learn how to enter information. We will create a simple Budget Worksheet (shown in Figure 2-3) as we learn about SuperCalc.

Using the **DOWN ARROW** key, move the active cell to cell A6. Then press the **RIGHT ARROW** key once to move to cell B6.

Now watch the entry line (the third status line at the bottom of the display screen). As you enter data, it will appear on this line.

Press the **1** key on the top row of the keyboard. Notice that the number 1 appears in the entry area. Type **000** to make the number 1000. The bottom lines on your screen should look like this:

```
    :    A    ::    B    ::    C    ::    D    ::    E    ::    F    ::    G    ::    H    :
  1:
  2:
  3:
  4:
  5:
  6:
  7:
  8:
  9:
 10:
 11:
  •
  •
  •
 17:
 18:
 19:
 20:
> B6
Width:  9  Memory: 27 Last Col/Row:A1      ? for HELP
  5>1000 █
```

Press **<RET>** and several things happen. The number 1000 appears in cell B6 and the entry line is cleared, the highlighted active cell moves to location C6, and C6 appears on the status line.

```
    :    A    ::    B    ::    C    ::    D    ::    E    ::    F    ::    G    ::    H    :
  1:
  2:
  3:
  4:
  5:
  6:               1000 ░░░░░░░░
  7:
  8:
  9:
 10:
 11:
  •
  •
  •
 17:
 18:
 19:
 20:
> C6
Width:  9  Memory: 26 Last Col/Row:B6      ? for HELP
  1>█
```

It is reasonable to expect the number you have entered to be placed in cell B6 because B6 is where the active cell was. But why did the active cell move to C6? Look at the first character on the status line (the first of the program status lines at the bottom of the screen). It is a greater than symbol ">" pointing to the right. Each time you press <RET> the active cell advances one location. The direction this character points determines the direction you will move each time <RET> is pressed.

Enter the following numbers and press **<RET>** after each entry (for the present, ignore any errors you may make):

Cell	*Entry*
C6	**1000**
D6	**1000**
E6	**1050**
F6	**1050**
G6	**1050**

Each time you press <RET> the active cell advances one cell to the right. When these entries are complete, your worksheet should like this:

```
    :   A   ::   B   ::   C   ::   D   ::   E   ::   F   ::   G   ::   H   :
  1:
  2:
  3:
  4:
  5:
  6:              1000      1000      1000      1050      1050      1050
  7:
  8:
  9:
 10:
 11:
  .
  .
  .
 17:
 18:
 19:
 20:
> H6
Width:  9  Memory: 26 Last Col/Row:G6      ? for HELP
  1>
```

This *automatic advance* feature makes entering large amounts of data very easy. What the automatic advance feature does is similar to what the automatic carriage advance does on a typewriter except that you choose the direction of advance. However, until you are used to it, you may find it slightly confusing. To use the automatic advance effectively, you have to move into the cell going the same direction you wish to exit.

Try the same procedure going in other directions. Press **<RET>** without entering a number to avoid entering extraneous information on your worksheet. Press an arrow key to change direction and press **<RET>** again. The auto advance will work in any of the four directions. Using the **LEFT ARROW** key, move the active cell to B6, and then use the **DOWN ARROW** key to move to B9. Look at the direction arrow now; it is pointing down. Enter **500** and press **<RET>**. The active cell will advance to cell B10.

Figure 1-5 shows the worksheet you have been building with the addition of three columns of numbers. Using the skills you have just learned, enter the numbers shown in cells B9 through B12, C9 through C12, and D9 through D12 in this figure. You will use these entries in the next few lessons. When you are finished, compare your worksheet to Figure 1-5. (Again, as you enter the numbers just ignore any errors. You will learn how to correct them in the next lesson.)

```
    |    A    ||    B    ||    C    ||    D    ||    E    ||    F    ||    G    ||    H    |
  1|
  2|
  3|
  4|
  5|
  6|                1000       1000       1000       1050       1050       1050
  7|
  8|
  9|                 500        500        500
 10|                 280        280        280
 11|                  90         90         90
 12|
 13|                 120        120        120
 14|
 15|
 16|
 17|
 18|
 19|
 20|
< A12
Width:  9  Memory: 26 Last Col/Row:G12    ? for HELP
 1> 
```

Figure 1-5.

The worksheet after entering data in rows 9 through 12

Lesson 4: Correcting Mistakes

It is important to be able to correct your errors while you are making entries on the worksheet. There are three types of errors that need to be considered.

Incorrect Cell Entries

The first type of error is an incorrect entry in a cell. In this case, the solution is simple: just move back to the cell, reenter the data correctly, and press **<RET>**. The new entry will replace the old incorrect entry.

Errors on the Entry Line

The second type of error is an error on the entry line. One way to correct this is to clear the entry line and start over by pressing **CTRL-Z** when you discover the error. To do this, hold down the **CONTROL** (or **CTRL**) key and press the Z key.

Type **123456** on the entry line, but do not press <RET>. To remove this from the entry line, press CTRL-Z. The entry line will clear. On the IBM PC, you can use the F2 function key instead. It has the same effect as CTRL-Z.

Removing Unwanted Cell Entries (/Blank)

By now you may have noticed that although you can change cell entries by reentering different information, you cannot clear a cell by "entering" nothing. SuperCalc ignores this and moves on to the next cell. But SuperCalc does have a command called the /Blank command that clears all the information from a cell. For now you will learn to use the /Blank command to clear individual cells, although you will later learn how to use it to clear many cells at once.

First move to cell A2, enter the number **9999**, and press **<RET>**. You will use the /Blank command to remove this entry.

Move back to cell A2. Now press the slash key /. The slash tells SuperCalc that what follows is a command and not information to be entered into a cell. All SuperCalc commands must be preceded by a slash. Look at the prompt line (the second line at the bottom of your screen). It has changed to look like this:

```
   :   A   ::   B   ::   C   ::   D   ::   E   ::   F   ::   G   ::   H   :
 1:
 2:     9999
 3:
 4:
 5:
 6:            1000      1000      1000      1050      1050      1050
 7:
 8:
 9:             500       500       500
10:             280       280       280
11:              90        90        90
12:             120       120       120
13:
 •
 •
17:
18:
19:
20:
v A2          Form=9999
Enter A,B,C,D,E,F,G,I,L,M,O,P,Q,R,S,T,U,W,X,Z,?
  2>/ █
```

This row of letters indicates the first letter of each of the SuperCalc commands. This prompt lets you know that SuperCalc is waiting for you to enter a command. Press the letter **B**, the first letter of the word "Blank." The status lines at the bottom of your screen will change to look like this:

```
   :   A   ::   B   ::   C   ::   D   ::   E   ::   F   ::   G   ::   H   :
 1:
 2:     9999
 3:
 4:
 5:
 6:            1000      1000      1000      1050      1050      1050
 7:
 8:
 9:             500       500       500
10:             280       280       280
11:              90        90        90
12:             120       120       120
13:
 •
 •
20:
v A2          Form=9999
Enter Range
  8>/Blank, █
```

SuperCalc has spelled out the word "/Blank," for you on the entry line, and the prompt now reads "Enter Range". Since you are only trying to blank the cell you are in, you can use a shortcut that SuperCalc provides. Whenever SuperCalc requests you to "Enter Range", you can press <RET> to tell SuperCalc to act only on the cell you are in. Press **<RET>** now to blank cell A2.

Use the /Blank command to remove any other entries that may be in the wrong places on your worksheet. Use Figure 1-5 for checking.

Lesson 5: Entering Text

Headings, comments, and labels have a very important function in a worksheet. You can build complex and sophisticated worksheets, but without labels and comments you will have a hard time explaining them to others. Indeed, some time later even you may have trouble figuring it out.

Entering text with SuperCalc is very easy. You can enter any characters you want in text entries. To inform the program that what you are entering is text, you begin an entry with a double quote character ("). The double quote character signals the program that what follows is text. The double quote is not displayed in the cell after you have entered it.

Move to cell B3 of the Budget Worksheet that you started in Lesson 3. Since you are creating a monthly budget worksheet, you need to label the months across the top and also income and expense categories down the left side. Enter the characters **"JAN** and press **<RET>**. JAN is displayed in cell B3 and, as predicted, the double quote character is not displayed.

This is a good time to investigate what happens if you forget to precede text entries with the double quote character. Move to cell C3 and type **FEB <RET>** without preceding it with the double quote character. Note that the message "Formula ERROR" has appeared at the right end of the status line, and your entry has not been entered into cell C3.

NOTE: If you are using SuperCalc^3, you do not need to enter the double quote and the message "Formula ERROR" will not occur. Instead SuperCalc^3 will recognize any entry as text which is not clearly a number or a formula. For more information turn to Chapter 12 and read the section called "Entering Data."

Why should SuperCalc display "Formula ERROR" when you are trying to enter text? To SuperCalc there are only two types of entries: formulas and text. (Numbers are simple formulas to SuperCalc.) The way SuperCalc distinguishes text entries is to look at the first character. If the first character of an entry is anything but a double quote or a single quote, as you will see shortly, SuperCalc assumes it is a formula.

Since SuperCalc cannot calculate FEB as a formula, it displays the message "Formula ERROR" and will not enter the text into a cell. You must correct your entry before proceeding.

To remove the offending entry from the input line, press CTRL-Z. The error message will disappear, and the entry line will be cleared.

Continue labeling your worksheet by making the following entries:

Cell	*Entry*
C3	**"FEB**
D3	**"MAR**
E3	**"APR**
F3	**"MAY**
G3	**"JUN**
H3	**"Y.T.D.**
A5	**"INCOME:**
A6	**"SALARY**
A8	**"EXPENSES**
A9	**"RENT**
A10	**"FOOD**
A11	**"UTIL**
A12	**"AUTO**
A14	**"TOTAL**

If you enter information into a cell incorrectly, just back up to the cell with the error and reenter the text correctly. The new entry will replace the old entry. If you make an entry in a cell that should remain empty, use the /Blank command to remove it.

When these entries are completed, the month names will not line up very well with the numbers that are already entered, but you will find out how to fix this in Chapter 2. Your worksheet should appear as follows:

```
  !   A   !!   B   !!   C   !!   D   !!   E   !!   F   !!   G   !!   H   !
 1!
 2!
 3!         JAN       FEB       MAR       APR       MAY       JUN      Y.T.D
 4!
 5!INCOME:
 6!SALARY         1000      1000      1000      1050      1050      1050
 7!
 8!EXPENSES:
 9!RENT            500       500       500
10!FOOD            280       280       280
11!UTIL             90        90        90
12!AUTO            120       120       120
13!
14!TOTAL
15!
16!
 :
20!
v A15
Width:  9  Memory: 26 Last Col/Row:H14     ? for HELP
  1>
```

Long Text Entries

Now we are going to provide a title for the worksheet that we are creating. Cell A1 is a good place to put a title because SuperCalc will display this entry as a title when it shows you a directory of the worksheets on disk. Move to cell A1, enter "**Simple Budget Worksheet**, and press **<RET>**. Notice that this label crosses over the width of cell A1 and into the adjoining cells. The top of your worksheet should look like this:

```
  !   A   !!   B   !!   C   !!   D   !!   E   !!   F   !!   G   !!   H   !
 1!Simple Budget Worksheet
 2!
 3!         JAN       FEB       MAR       APR       MAY       JUN      Y.T.D
 4!
 5!INCOME:
 6!SALARY         1000      1000      1000      1050      1050      1050
 7!
 8!EXPENSES:
 9!RENT            500       500       500
10!FOOD            280       280       280
11!UTIL             90        90        90
12!AUTO            120       120       120
13!
14!TOTAL
15!
 :
20!
 A1          Text="Simple Budget Worksheet
Width:  9  Memory: 26 Last Col/Row:H14     ? for HELP
  1>
```

Text entries will display over adjoining cells if those cells are empty. This makes entering long names easier because a careful count of characters is not required. Note however that the overlapping label is not entered into the adjoining cells; it is only displayed over them. Entering data into one of the cells that is covered by text will cut off the display of the label at the left side of that cell. Move to cell B1, enter **1**, and press **<RET>** to see how the entry in cell A1 is cut off.

```
   !    A    !!    B    !!    C    !!    D    !!    E    !!    F    !!    G    !!    H    !
  1!Simple Bu          1
  2!
  3!          JAN       FEB       MAR       APR       MAY       JUN      Y.T.D
  4!
  5!INCOME:
  6!SALARY          1000      1000      1000      1050      1050      1050
  7!
  8!EXPENSES:
  9!RENT             500       500       500
 10!FOOD             280       280       280
 11!UTIL              90        90        90
 12!AUTO             120       120       120
 13!
 14!TOTAL
 15!
 16!
 17!
 18!
 19!
 20!
> C1
Width:  9  Memory: 26 Last Col/Row:H14     ? for HELP
  1>
```

Now move back to B1 and use the /Blank command to remove this entry. Then move to cell B2 so that the entire title is visible once more.

Repeating Text Entries

Another form of text is called *repeating text*. This type of entry is used to form lines and borders on the worksheet. To make a repeating text entry, begin with the single quote (') instead of the double quote. The characters you enter after the single quote are repeated over and over to form a line across the worksheet. A repeating text entry will display across empty cells just like a normal text display, except that a repeating text entry will display to the edge of the worksheet if it finds no occupied cells. There are no limits on the type or number of characters used in a repeating text entry. The most often used character is probably the hyphen, which is typically used to form a line under a column of numbers.

Move to cell A13 and enter '- and press **<RET>**. A horizontal line will be formed across the worksheet below the columns of numbers. Move the active cell to A4 and enter '= **<RET>**. A double line is formed across the worksheet below the column headings. Make another double line across your worksheet starting in cell A7 by entering '= **<RET>**. When these entries are finished, your worksheet should appear as follows:

```
   :  A   ::  B   ::  C   ::  D   ::  E   ::  F   ::  G   ::  H  :
  1:Simple Budget Worksheet
  2:
  3:       JAN      FEB      MAR      APR      MAY      JUN     Y.T.D
  4:=================================================================
  5:INCOME:
  6:SALARY       1000     1000     1000     1050     1050     1050
  7:=================================================================
  8:EXPENSES:
  9:RENT          500      500      500
 10:FOOD          280      280      280
 11:UTIL           90       90       90
 12:AUTO          120      120      120
 13:-----------------------------------------------------------------
 14:TOTAL
 15:
 16:
 17:
 18:
 19:
 20:
v A8           Text="EXPENSES:
Width:  9  Memory: 26 Last Col/Row:H14     ? for HELP
  1> █
```

Repeating text always begins in the cell in which it is entered and extends to the right edge of the worksheet unless it encounters an occupied cell. To keep a repeating text entry from continuing farther than you wish, you can stop it with an empty text entry. To make an empty text entry, you enter just the double quote ("). This is a valid entry, and it stops a repeating text entry without displaying anything itself.

Move to cell E4 and enter " **<RET>**. This entry will stop the double horizontal line at the right edge of cell D4. Now move back to E4 and enter **/B** **<RET>**. Notice that this restores the line.

Lesson 6: Getting Help With the ?

SuperCalc provides an on-screen "Help" function to supplement the manual. You can obtain explanations and other reference information at any time by pressing the question mark (?). The help screens are reminders that describe what options or keys are available. At times, you may find them somewhat cryptic, and they may not seem like much help at first.

To try an experiment with the help screen, be sure your entry line is clear (use **CTRL-Z** to clear it), press the ?, but do not press <RET>. (Remember to use the shift to get the question mark, if it is required on your keyboard.) The worksheet display will be replaced with a screen of information (similar to Figure 1-6) about special keys. Much of the information on this screen—the arrow keys, the quote keys, the = key, and CTRL-Z—has been explained in this chapter. Review the information on the screen quickly; the rest will be covered in later chapters. Press **<RET>** to return to the worksheet display.

SuperCalc has several different help screens. Type a number on the entry line (such as **23**) and then press the ?. As you can see, the information has changed to inform you about how to enter and edit information with SuperCalc, as shown in Figure 1-7. Press **<RET>** to return to the worksheet. Now clear the entry line (**CTRL-Z**) and press the slash (/). As mentioned previously, the slash tells SuperCalc that what follows is a command instead of data. Now press the ? again. A list of the available commands similar to the list in Figure 1-8 will appear. Return to the worksheet again by pressing **<RET>** and clear the entry line with **CTRL-Z**.

```
SuperCalc2    AnswerScreen Initial Character Meanings:

 /  -- Starts a command entry.
 "  -- Starts text entry.
 '  -- Starts Repeating Text entry.
 =  -- Specifies a cell to jump to.
 !  -- Forces recalculation.
 ;  -- Puts cursor in other window.
 &  -- Resumes Execute (.XQT) file control.

 Four arrow keys move the Spreadsheet Cursor.
 Four CTRL+Key combinations also move the cursor:
        CTRL/E    CTRL/X    CTRL/S    CTRL/D
        UP        DOWN      LEFT      RIGHT

 Any other character starts formula entry.




     Press any key to continue
```

Figure 1-6.

Help from the ? key

```
SuperCalc2     AnswerScreen Entry/Edit Options:

 The first character determines whether you are entering a formula or a text
string (label).  A quote mark (") starts a text string. An apostrophe (')
starts a repeating text string. Any other character starts a formula.

 While entering data, the arrow keys (which normally scroll around the
spreadsheet) become editing keys:
      Left arrow   - Backspace one character.
          (or CTRL/S)
      Right arrow - Move right one character.
          (or CTRL/D)
      Up arrow     - Insert one blank.
          (or CTRL/E)
      Down arrow   - Delete one character.
          (or CTRL/X)
 Other keys also aid in editing the entry line:
      [TAB]   - Moves the Entry Cursor to the beginning or alternately to the
end of the entry.
      [ESC]   - Enters the location of the Spreadsheet Cursor in the entry.
After pressing [ESC], the arrow keys can move the Spreadsheet Cursor to the
desired cell, and any other key (such as +,-,*,/,etc.) fixes that current cell
position in the entry.  To leave this mode, press [ESC] again and edit the line
    Press any key to continue
```

Figure 1-7.

Pressing ? while entering data

```
SuperCalc2     AnswerScreen   Slash Commands:
   A(rrange)--- Sorts cells in ascending or descending order.
   B(lank)----- Removes (empties) contents of cells.
   C(opy)------ Duplicates contents and display format of cells.
   D(elete)---- Erases entire rows or columns.
   E(dit)------ Allows editing of cell contents.
   F(ormat)---- Sets display format at Entry, Row, Column, or Global levels.
   G(lobal)---- Changes global display or calculation options.
   I(nsert)---- Adds empty rows or columns.
   L(oad)------ Reads spreadsheet (or portion) from disk into the workspace.
   M(ove)------ Inserts existing rows or columns at new positions.
   O(utput)---- Sends display or cell contents to printer, screen or disk.
   P(rotect)--- Prevents future alteration of cells.
   Q(uit)------ Ends the SuperCalc2 program.
   R(eplicate)- Reproduces contents of partial rows or columns.
   S(ave)------ Stores the current spreadsheet on disk.
   T(itle)----- Locks upper rows or left-hand columns from scrolling.
   U(nprotect)- Allows alteration of protected cells.
   W(indow)---- Splits the screen display.
   X(eXecute)-- Accepts commands and data from an .XQT file.
   Z(ap)------- Erases spreadsheet and format settings from workspace.


      Press any key to continue
```

Figure 1-8.

Help from /?

You can ask for help at almost any point in the program and get a more or less relevant response. Since there are only a limited number of help messages provided, you will find that they may not always completely fit the situation that you are in.

If you wish to stop working with SuperCalc now, turn to Chapter 3, Lessons 12 through 15. These lessons show you how to save your worksheet onto a disk, exit from SuperCalc, and reload your worksheet later. You can then continue with the next chapter at your convenience. In Chapter 2 you will learn how to make SuperCalc perform calculations that turn the data you have just entered into a complete budget sheet.

CHAPTER TWO

Performing Calculations

After making the entries in the previous lessons, you should have the beginnings of a Budget Worksheet with several columns of numbers and some labels. This worksheet is designed to total year-to-date and monthly expenses. This lesson teaches you how to use SuperCalc to calculate these totals.

Lesson 7: Entering Simple Formulas

First we'll show you how some simple formulas work. Move the worksheet so that cell A25 is in the upper-left corner. (Enter **=A25** and press **<RET>**.) We will use this cell so that the trial formulas you are about to enter will not interfere with what has already been entered. Enter **5+9** into cell A25.

```
   :  A  ::  B  ::  C  ::  D  ::  E  ::  F  ::  G  ::  H  :
 25:     14
 26:
 27:
 28:
 29:
 30:
 31:
 32:
 33:
 34:
 35:
 36:
 37:
 38:
 39:
 40:
 41:
 42:
 43:
 44:
< A25         Form=5+9
Width:  9  Memory: 26 Last Col/Row:H27    ? for HELP
  1>
```

SuperCalc evaluates this entry as a formula and displays the result 14. Move to cell B25 and enter **14−9**. The plus (+) and the minus (−) are two of the arithmetic operators. They do just what you might expect, add and subtract.

In cell C25 enter **14−9+5−6+23**. The answer 27 is displayed in cell C25.

You can calculate the results of very complicated formulas with SuperCalc. However, its usefulness comes from its ability to have formulas use the contents of other cells. For instance, you can create a formula to add two cells together. Move down and left to cell A27 and enter **A25+B25**.

```
   :  A  ::  B  ::  C  ::  D  ::  E  ::  F  ::  G  ::  H  :
 25:     14        5       27
 26:
 27:     19
 28:
 29:
 30:
 31:
 32:
 33:
 34:
 35:
 36:
 37:
 38:
 39:
 40:
 41:
 42:
 43:
 44:
< A27         Form=A25+B25
Width:  9  Memory: 26 Last Col/Row:H27    ? for HELP
  1>
```

Cell A25 contains 14 and cell B25 contains 5. Thus 19, the sum of cells A25 and B25, is now displayed in cell A27. Now move to cell A25 and enter **50**. Notice that as soon as you make this entry, the value of cell A27 changes to 55. SuperCalc automatically recalculates the formulas as you enter new numbers.

Move to cell C27 and enter **A27+B25**. Now change the value in cell A25 to **10**, and both cells A27 and C27 are affected.

```
    !    A    !!    B    !!    C    !!    D    !!    E    !!    F    !!    G    !!    H    !
 24!
 25!       10         5        27
 26!
 27!       15                  20
 28!
 29!
 30!
 31!
 32!
 33!
 34!
 35!
 36!
 37!
 38!
 39!
 40!
 41!
 42!
 43!
  A25            Form=10
 Width:   9  Memory: 26 Last Col/Row:H27     ? for HELP
  1>
```

The formula in cell A27 uses cell A25, and the formula in cell C27 uses cell A27 to make its calculations. These formulas are shown in Figure 2-1.

A formula can refer to any cell that contains a number or another formula, and there is no limit to the number of formulas that can refer to the same cell.

Now that you have an idea of what formulas can do, let's use some in the Budget Worksheet. But first, use the /Blank command (/B) to remove the entries in cells A25, B25, C25, A27, and C27.

Move back to cell A1 so that the entire Budget Worksheet is on the screen.

You now know enough to total the expenses by month. Enter the column totals as follows:

Cell	*Entry*
B14	**B9+B10+B11+B12**
C14	**C9+C10+C11+C12**
D14	**D9+D10+D11+D12**

```
   !  A   !!  B   !!  C   !!  D   !!  E   !!  F   !!  G   !!  H   !
 24!
 25! 10        14-9      14-9+5-6+23
 26!
 27! A25+B25             A27+B25
 28!
 29!
 30!
 31!
 32!
 33!
 34!
 35!
 36!
 37!
 38!
 39!
 40!
 41!
 42!
 43!
  A25         Form=10
Width:  9  Memory: 26 Last Col/Row:H27    ? for HELP
  1>
```

Figure 2-1.

Cell C27 depends on A27 which depends on A25

As these entries are made, the results of the formulas will show in the cells. When the entries are complete, move back to cell B14, and your worksheet will appear as follows:

```
   !  A   !!  B   !!  C   !!  D   !!  E   !!  F   !!  G   !!  H   !
  1!Simple Budget Worksheet
  2!
  3!         JAN      FEB      MAR      APR      MAY      JUN     Y.T.D
  4!=====================================================================
  5!INCOME:
  6!SALARY       1000     1000     1000     1050     1050     1050
  7!=====================================================================
  8!EXPENSES:
  9!RENT          500      500      500
 10!FOOD          280      280      280
 11!UTIL           90       90       90
 12!AUTO          120      120      120
 13!---------------------------------------------------------------------
 14!TOTAL         990      990      990
 15!
 16!
 17!
 18!
 19!
 20!
v B14         Form=B9+B10+B11+B12
Width:  9  Memory: 26 Last Col/Row:H27    ? for HELP
  1>
```

SuperCalc keeps track of what kind of information is in each cell. With the active cell on B14, look at the status line at the bottom of the screen (the topmost line of the three program status lines). At the center of the line is the word "Form=" followed by the formula that is in the active cell. The word "Form=" means that the cell contains a formula. Labels display the word "Text=", and repeating entries display the word "Rtxt=". In this way the status line provides a means to check the actual contents of any cell. Look at the contents of other cells on your worksheet by moving the active cell to C14, D14, and other locations.

Change some of the expenses (in the area between B9 and D12), and watch the column totals change. As new values are entered, SuperCalc displays the new totals on the screen.

Lesson 8: Totals Made Easy (SUM)

In Lesson 6 you learned how to add and subtract cell values. With that skill, you added some of the columns of a worksheet. The formulas that were developed were simple; only four entries were required in each formula. But what if you had a model with many rows and many columns? Using addition, the formulas would become extremely long and unwieldy.

SuperCalc provides several built-in calculations called *functions*, which you use to reduce the complexity of formulas. One of these is the *SUM* function. As its name implies, the SUM function will sum, or add, a group of cells.

Continuing the Budget Worksheet, make the following entry in cell H6: **SUM(B6:G6)**. This tells SuperCalc to add up the cells from B6 to G6. The result (6150) is the same as if you had entered a formula that added all six of these cells.

The SUM function requires a *range* of cells to act on. You will use ranges often in SuperCalc. You specify ranges both in many of the functions, such as SUM, and in some of the commands. To SuperCalc, a *range* is a series of cells. It is defined by entering the first cell in the series, then a colon, and then the last cell in the series. The range you specified (B6:G6) includes all the cells from cell B6 to cell G6; thus, SUM(B6:G6) is the same as B6+C6+D6+E6+F6+G6.

There are various shapes that a range can take. The four most common ranges are a single cell, a partial row, a partial column, and a block. Figure 2-2 illustrates the shapes of these ranges.

```
  :    A    ::    B    ::    C    ::    D    ::    E    ::    F    ::    G    :
 1:Examples of Ranges
 2:
 3:
 4:          :============== B4:E4 =================:
 5:
 6:
 7:                          ------
 8:                            ::
 9::== A9 ==:                  ::                 ::=========================::
10:                            ::                 ::                         ::
11:                            ::                 ::                         ::
12:                          C7:C17               ::                         ::
13:                            ::                 ::                         ::
14:                            ::                 ::          E9:G19         ::
15:                            ::                 ::                         ::
16:                            ::                 ::                         ::
17:                          ------               ::                         ::
18:                                               ::                         ::
19:                                               ::=========================::
20:
< A2
Width: 10  Memory: 26 Last Col/Row:G19     ? for HELP
 1>
```

Figure 2-2.

Common range shapes

To define a partial row as a range, you enter the left end cell, a colon, and the right end cell. The number part of these cells is the same; for example, in the range B6:G6, both cells are on row 6.

To define a partial column as a range, enter the top cell, a colon, and the bottom cell. The letter part of these cells is the same, for example, C7:C17.

A rectangle, or block of cells, can be defined by entering the upper-left cell, a colon, and the lower-right cell. Both the letter and number parts of these cells are different, for example, E9:G19. All the cells in the rectangle formed by cells E9, G9, G19, and E19 are included in this range.

The smallest range that can be specified is a single cell. While using a range of a single cell would not be useful with the SUM function, it can be useful with other functions. To define a range of a single cell, only the single cell need be entered, for example, A9.

Make the following entries, using the SUM function, to your worksheet:

Cell	*Entry*	*Type of Range*
H9	**SUM(B9:G9)**	SUM of a row
H14	**SUM(B9:G12)**	SUM of a block
G14	**SUM(G9:G12)**	SUM of a column

The result in G14 is (0) since there are no entries in cells G9 through G12. Finally, reenter the formula in B14 as **SUM (B9:B12)**. When these entries are made, your worksheet should appear as follows:

```
  !  A   !!  B   !!  C   !!  D   !!  E   !!  F   !!  G   !!  H   !
 1!Simple Budget Worksheet
 2!
 3!      JAN       FEB       MAR       APR       MAY       JUN       Y.T.D
 4!=================================================================
 5!INCOME:
 6!SALARY       1000      1000      1000      1050      1050      1050      6150
 7!=================================================================
 8!EXPENSES:
 9!RENT          500       500       500                                    1500
10!FOOD          280       280       280
11!UTIL           90        90        90
12!AUTO          120       120       120
13!-----------------------------------------------------------------
14!TOTAL         990       990       990                             0      2970
15!
16!
17!
18!
19!
20!
v A14          Text="TOTAL
Width:  9  Memory: 26 Last Col/Row:H27     ? for HELP
 1>■
```

While the results are no different than they would be if you used addition (+) in these formulas rather than the SUM function, the usefulness of the worksheet is increased. The entries are simpler, the worksheet is more general, and the specific number of cells being added is no longer important.

Lesson 9: Aligning Labels With Numbers (/Format)

There is one thing about the Budget Worksheet that so far is not right: the column headings are not aligned with the numbers in the columns. Now we are going to find out how to fix that.

In SuperCalc, the /Format command provides us with the ability to change the way many things are displayed on the worksheet. In this lesson we will explore only one of the many functions of the /Format command: how to align column headings with the numbers in the columns.

To initiate the /Format command press the slash (/) and then the letter **F**. SuperCalc spells out the word "/Format," and the prompt line changes to look like this:

```
   !  A   !!   B   !!   C   !!   D   !!   E   !!   F   !!   G   !!   H   !
  1!Simple Budget Worksheet
  2!
  3!        JAN      FEB      MAR      APR      MAY      JUN     Y.T.D
  4!=========================================================================
  5!INCOME:
  6!SALARY         1000     1000     1000     1050     1050     1050     6150
  7!=========================================================================
  8!EXPENSES:
  9!RENT            500      500      500                                1500
 10!FOOD            280      280      280
 11!UTIL             90       90       90
 12!AUTO            120      120      120
 13!-------------------------------------------------------------------------
 14!TOTAL           990      990      990                          0     2970
 15!
  :
 20!
v A14          Text="TOTAL
Enter Level: G(lobal), C(olumn), R(ow), E(ntry) or D(efine)
  9>/Format,
```

SuperCalc is asking if we want to change the display format of the entire worksheet (Global), a column, a row, or an entry. The column headings of the Budget Worksheet are all in row 3, so enter **R** for "Row". The word "Row" is added to the entry line, and the prompt asks you for a "Row Number". Enter **3** since that is the row that contains the column headings, and press **<RET>**. Your status lines should now look like this:

```
   !  A   !!   B   !!   C   !!   D   !!   E   !!   F   !!   G   !!   H   !
  1!Simple Budget Worksheet
  2!
  3!        JAN      FEB      MAR      APR      MAY      JUN     Y.T.D
  4!=========================================================================
  5!INCOME:
  6!SALARY         1000     1000     1000     1050     1050     1050     6150
  7!=========================================================================
  8!EXPENSES:
  9!RENT            500      500      500                                1500
 10!FOOD            280      280      280
 11!UTIL             90       90       90
 12!AUTO            120      120      120
 13!-------------------------------------------------------------------------
 14!TOTAL           990      990      990                          0     2970
 15!
  :
 20!
v A14          Text="TOTAL
Define Formats: (I,G,E,$,R,L,TR,TL,*,U(1-8),H,D)
 15>/Format,Row,3,
```

This prompt line presents us with the various format options available. The option we are interested in is "Text Right", which will move the column heads to the right edge of their cells. To use this option, press **T** ("Text" is spelled out) and then **R** ("Right" is spelled out).

```
  :  A   ::   B   ::   C   ::   D   ::   E   ::   F   ::   G   ::   H   :
 1:Simple Budget Worksheet
 2:
 3:         JAN         FEB         MAR         APR         MAY         JUN         Y.T.D
 4:===========================================================================
 5:INCOME:
 6:SALARY          1000        1000        1000        1050        1050        1050        6150
 7:===========================================================================
 8:EXPENSES:
 9:RENT             500         500         500                                            1500
10:FOOD             280         280         280
11:UTIL              90          90          90
12:AUTO             120         120         120
13:---------------------------------------------------------------------------
14:TOTAL            990         990         990                                   0        2970
15:
16:
17:
18:
19:
20:
v A14           Text="TOTAL
Define Formats: (I,G,E,$,R,L,TR,TL,*,U(1-8),H,D)
 25>/Format,Row,3,TextRight,█
```

Finally, press <**RET**> to execute the command. All your column headings should now align with the numbers in the columns as shown in the following screen:

```
  :  A   ::   B   ::   C   ::   D   ::   E   ::   F   ::   G   ::   H   :
 1:Simple Budget Worksheet
 2:
 3:                 JAN         FEB         MAR         APR         MAY         JUN       Y.T.D
 4:===========================================================================
 5:INCOME:
 6:SALARY          1000        1000        1000        1050        1050        1050        6150
 7:===========================================================================
 8:EXPENSES:
 9:RENT             500         500         500                                            1500
10:FOOD             280         280         280
11:UTIL              90          90          90
12:AUTO             120         120         120
13:---------------------------------------------------------------------------
14:TOTAL            990         990         990                                   0        2970
15:
16:
17:
18:
19:
20:
v A14           Text="TOTAL
Width:  9  Memory: 25 Last Col/Row:H19    ? for HELP
  1>█
```

Lesson 10: A Cross-Totaling Worksheet (/Replicate)

The word replicate means to copy, and that is what the /Replicate command does; it makes multiple copies of a cell. We will use this ability to copy cells to complete the worksheet that we have been building.

The formulas in row 14 that total the columns are all very similar. Each calculates the sum of the entries above it. The /Replicate command uses this similarity when it copies formulas; it automatically adjusts the formulas so they make the same calculations in their new location that the original formula did. The formula in cell B14 calculates the sum of four entries above it. When you replicate the formula in B14 to other cells, the formulas created will also calculate the sum of the four entries above them.

Move the active cell to B14. You should find the formula SUM(B9:B12) in this cell. Type **/R**. SuperCalc will complete the word "/Replicate," and prompt you for a "From?" range.

```
   !  A   !!  B   !!  C   !!  D   !!  E   !!  F   !!  G   !!  H   !
  1!Simple Budget Worksheet
  2!
  3!               JAN     FEB     MAR     APR     MAY     JUN   Y.T.D
  4!=================================================================
  5!INCOME:
  6!SALARY        1000    1000    1000    1050    1050    1050    6150
  7!=================================================================
  8!EXPENSES:
  9!RENT           500     500     500                            1500
 10!FOOD           280     280     280
 11!UTIL            90      90      90
 12!AUTO           120     120     120
 13!-----------------------------------------------------------------
 14!TOTAL          990     990     990                       0    2970
 15!
 16!
 17!
 18!
 19!
 20!
< B14          Form=SUM(B9:B12)
From? (Enter Range)
 12>/Replicate,█
```

The range you will be replicating is the single cell B14. Since B14 is where you have located the active cell, simply press **<RET>**. Just as you used the /Blank command in Lesson 4, pressing <RET> when you are asked for a range tells SuperCalc that the range you want is only the active cell. When you do this, the cell B14 appears on the entry line followed by a comma, and the prompt changes to ask for a "To?" range. The range that requires formulas similar to the formula in B14 is the range of cells from C14 to G14. Enter **C14:G14**.

```
 :   A   ::   B   ::   C   ::   D   ::   E   ::   F   ::   G   ::   H   :
 1:Simple Budget Worksheet
 2:
 3:              JAN       FEB       MAR       APR       MAY       JUN    Y.T.D
 4:=========================================================================
 5:INCOME:
 6:SALARY       1000      1000      1000      1050      1050      1050     6150
 7:=========================================================================
 8:EXPENSES:
 9:RENT          500       500       500                                  1500
10:FOOD          280       280       280
11:UTIL           90        90        90
12:AUTO          120       120       120
13:-------------------------------------------------------------------------
14:TOTAL         990       990       990                           0     2970
15:
 •
 •
20:
< B14        Form=SUM(B9:B12)
To? (Enter Range), then Return; or "," for Options
 23>/Replicate,B14,c14:g14 █
```

Now press **<RET>**. After pressing <RET>, the formula in cell B14 is copied, automatically adjusted, and reproduced in each of the destination cells. Move the active cell across row 14, stopping in each cell. Look at the formulas and verify that they have been adjusted correctly.

To complete the cross-totaling you need to replicate the formula in cell H9 down column H. First position the active cell to H9 and then enter the following:

- **/R** (The word "/Replicate" will be spelled out.)
- Press **<RET>** (This selects H9 as the "From" range.)
- Type **H10:H12** (This defines the "To" range.)
- Press **<RET>** (This will execute the command.)

```
 :   A   ::   B   ::   C   ::   D   ::   E   ::   F   ::   G   ::   H   :
 1:Simple Budget Worksheet
 2:
 3:              JAN       FEB       MAR       APR       MAY       JUN    Y.T.D
 4:=========================================================================
 5:INCOME:
 6:SALARY       1000      1000      1000      1050      1050      1050     6150
 7:=========================================================================
 8:EXPENSES:
 9:RENT          500       500       500                                  1500
10:FOOD          280       280       280                                   840
11:UTIL           90        90        90                                   270
12:AUTO          120       120       120                                   360
13:-------------------------------------------------------------------------
14:TOTAL         990       990       990         0         0         0     2970
15:
 •
 •
20:
> H9         Form=SUM(B9:G9)
Width:  9  Memory: 26 Last Col/Row:H27    ? for HELP
  1>█
```

The formulas for this worksheet are now complete. Now you can enter the expenses for the remaining four months. If the budget for a row is the same from month to month, you can use the /Replicate command to copy the information from the first column to the remaining columns in that row. For instance, you can replicate the RENT amount in cell B9 across the open cells in row 9. To do this, enter **/R B9 <RET> C9:G9 <RET>**. After this, replicate cells B10, B11, and B12 to columns E, F, and G in the same way.

Your worksheet should look like Figure 2-3. If you have changed some of the numbers in earlier lessons, take a few moments now to change them back so that your worksheet is like Figure 2-3. We will be using this worksheet again, and it will be easier if all the numbers are the same.

Lesson 11: Using the Arrow Keys to Enter Cell Ranges

Rather than typing the cells you want to use to define a range, you can use the arrow keys to point to the cells that you want to use. To notify SuperCalc that you want to use this feature, you press the Escape (ESC) key. When you

```
  :  A  ::  B  ::  C  ::  D  ::  E  ::  F  ::  G  ::  H  :
 1:Simple Budget Worksheet
 2:
 3:            JAN      FEB      MAR      APR      MAY      JUN    Y.T.D
 4:=======================================================================
 5:INCOME:
 6:SALARY     1000     1000     1000     1050     1050     1050     6150
 7:=======================================================================
 8:EXPENSES:
 9:RENT        500      500      500      500      500      500     3000
10:FOOD        280      280      280      280      280      280     1680
11:UTIL         90       90       90       90       90       90      540
12:AUTO        120      120      120      120      120      120      720
13:-----------------------------------------------------------------------
14:TOTAL       990      990      990      990      990      990     5940
15:=======================================================================
16:
17:
18:
19:
20:
< B9          Form=500
Width:  9  Memory: 25 Last Col/Row:H15    ? for HELP
  1>█
```

Figure 2-3.

Complete cross-totaling Budget Worksheet

do this, SuperCalc displays the current location of the active cell on the input line. Then you can use the arrow keys to move the active cell around the screen and "point to" any cell you wish. As you move around the screen, the name of the cell displayed on the entry line changes accordingly. In SuperCalc, the ESC key is referred to as the *current cell key*. You can use it anytime SuperCalc prompts you to enter a range.

To illustrate how this works, we will add a cumulative savings analysis to the Budget Worksheet that you have been constructing. We will put this section in rows 15 through 19, as is shown in Figure 2-4. To begin, enter the labels and the double lines in cells A16, A17, A18, and A19 as they appear in Figure 2-4.

Move to cell B17 and enter the formula **B6−B14** (savings is income minus expenses). Now we will replicate this formula across row 17 for the remaining months. But this time we will use the ESC key and the arrow keys to set the ranges for the /Replicate command. First enter **/R**. Now press the **ESC** key. The active cell now appears on the entry line. Use the arrow keys to move back to cell B17 if you are not already there. This cell contains the

```
  |   A    ||   B    ||   C    ||   D    ||   E    ||   F    ||   G    ||   H    |
 1|Simple Budget Worksheet
 2|
 3|               JAN       FEB       MAR       APR       MAY       JUN     Y.T.D
 4|=============================================================================
 5|INCOME:
 6|SALARY        1000      1000      1000      1050      1050      1050      6150
 7|=============================================================================
 8|EXPENSES:
 9|RENT           500       500       500       500       500       500      3000
10|FOOD           280       280       280       280       280       280      1680
11|UTIL            90        90        90        90        90        90       540
12|AUTO           120       120       120       120       120       120       720
13|-----------------------------------------------------------------------------
14|TOTAL          990       990       990       990       990       990      5940
15|=============================================================================
16|SAVINGS:
17|MONTHLY         10        10        10        60        60        60       210
18|CUMM.           10        20        30        90       150       210
19|=============================================================================
20|
v H14          Form=SUM(B9:G12)
Width:  9  Memory: 25 Last Col/Row:H19    ? for HELP
 1>█
```

Figure 2-4.

Budget Worksheet with accumulated savings

formula that we want to replicate. The cell on the entry line will change as you move. The entry line will look like this:

```
/Replicate,B17
```

Press **<RET>**. SuperCalc adds a comma to the entry line to show that the "From" range is completed and returns the active cell to the position from which it started. Now press the ESC key again to enter the "To" range. Again the active cell is added to the entry line. The range will be C17 to H17. Use the arrow keys to move the active cell to cell C17. Now press the colon (:) to show that this is the first cell of a range. The colon is added to the entry line and then the name of the active cell is repeated. The entry line will look like this:

```
/Replicate,B17,C17:C17
```

Now move the active cell to the right to cell H17. The last cell on the entry line has changed to H17 so that the complete entry looks like this:

```
/Replicate,B17,C17:H17
```

Press **<RET>** to complete the replication. SuperCalc will copy the formula from B17 to all the cells from C17 to H17 and return the active cell to the position from which it originally started.

NOTE: When you are using the current cell key functions, you can turn off the current cell function by pressing the ESC key a second time. This will return the active cell to where you started and allow you to use the arrow keys for their editing functions.

Now move to cell B18 to begin the cumulative savings line. The cumulative total through the first month is just the total for the first month, so in cell B18 enter **B17**. In cell C18 enter **B18+C17**. (The cumulative total for any month except the first is the cumulative total for the preceding month plus the current month's total.) Replicate the formula in cell C18 across row 18 to cells D18 through G18. Use whichever method you prefer. (If you are having trouble, enter **/R C18 , D18:G18 <RET>**.)

This completes our basic Budget Worksheet. But do not turn your computer off. The next lessons will show you how to print and how to save the Budget Worksheet so that you can retrieve it for future use.

CHAPTER THREE

Saving and Printing The Worksheet

If you have done the lessons in Chapters 1 and 2, you have mastered the fundamentals of building a worksheet. But the worksheet you have built exists only inside the memory of your computer. To make use of this worksheet you need to know how to print it on the printer, how to save it for future use, and how to retrieve it later. The lessons in this chapter explain how to do these things.

If you have already turned off the computer, the Budget Worksheet is gone. In this case, you need to spend a few minutes reentering it. The lessons in this chapter will teach you how to save your worksheet so that you will not have to reenter it again.

Lesson 12: Saving a Worksheet (/Save)

This lesson will show you how to save the worksheet on disk so that you can use it again at a later time. First, take out one of the formatted disks you prepared earlier and insert it in drive B.

When you store a worksheet on disk, you must assign it a name to identify it. This name will appear in the disk directory, and you can refer to it later when you wish to reload the worksheet. The name must be a *file name* that is valid for your computer's operating system. Most computer systems that will run SuperCalc use file names of the following format:

d:filename.ext

where *d:* is a letter that designates the disk drive, such as A, B, C, and so on. This letter tells SuperCalc on which drive to store the file. For this example use B. You must name a disk drive if you want to save your worksheet on a disk other than the *default* disk. (The default disk is the one that has the SuperCalc program on it; it is usually drive A.)

The *filename* is the name of the file. A file name may include as many as eight characters. These characters can be any combination of letters or numbers.

.ext is the file name *extension*. The extension is generally used to tell what kind of information is stored in the file. You don't need an extension on your file names because the SuperCalc program automatically adds the extension ".CAL" to identify all worksheet files as containing SuperCalc worksheets.

To save your worksheet, enter **/S**. SuperCalc will complete the word "/Save," and prompt you for a file name. Enter the file name **B:FIRSTTRY**. After you have entered the file name, press **<RET>**. Since file names can be different lengths, you need to press <RET> to tell SuperCalc that you have finished entering the file name.

SuperCalc now displays the prompt, "A(ll), V(alues) or P(art)?" You are being asked if you want to save "All" the information contained in your worksheet, including formulas and format information, just the current "Values" of the cells of your worksheet, or only "Part" of the cells on the worksheet.

Older versions of SuperCalc do not have the "Part" option. This option was added to accommodate worksheets too big to fit on one disk.

Most of the time you should select "All" if you want to reload and continue to work with the worksheet later. If you save "Values" only, you will not be saving the formulas on the worksheet, and you will not be able to modify it and recalculate the results. Later you will see why you might want to save just the current values from a worksheet or only part of the cells on the worksheet.

At this point, the bottom of your screen should look like this:

```
  :   A    ::    B    ::    C    ::    D    ::    E    ::    F    ::    G    ::    H   :
 1:Simple Budget Worksheet
 2:
 3:              JAN        FEB        MAR        APR        MAY        JUN     Y.T.D
 4:==========================================================================
 5:INCOME:
 6:SALARY        1000       1000       1000       1050       1050       1050      6150
 7:==========================================================================
 8:EXPENSES:
 9:RENT           500        500        500        500        500        500      3000
10:FOOD           280        280        280        280        280        280      1680
11:UTIL            90         90         90         90         90         90       540
12:AUTO           120        120        120        120        120        120       720
13:--------------------------------------------------------------------------
14:TOTAL          990        990        990        990        990        990      5940
15:==========================================================================
16:SAVINGS:
17:MONTHLY         10         10         10         60         60         60       210
18:CUMM.           10         20         30         90        150        210
19:==========================================================================
20:
< A16         Text="SAVINGS:
A(ll), V(alues), or P(art)?
 18>/Save,B:FIRSTTRY,█
```

Press the letter **A** to save "All" of the worksheet. After you press the "A" key, the /Save command will be executed and the file will be saved on disk B:.

Now let's try to save the file again. This time, however, a new complication is going to arise. First enter the following:

/S B:FIRSTTRY <RET>

This time you will see a prompt that says "File already exists: C(hange name), B(ackup) or O(verwrite)?". SuperCalc is checking to make sure that you do not replace an existing file unknowingly. You cannot have two files with the same name on the same disk. Saving a file with a file name that already exists on the disk will destroy the existing file.

You are given three options. "Change name" gives you the opportunity to edit the file name you have just entered. You would press "C" if you had entered the wrong file name and wanted to change it. You could then reenter the file name or just press CTRL-Z to cancel the /Save command.

You would select the "Backup" option when you have modified your worksheet and want to save it, but also want to preserve the unmodified version. When you use the Backup option, SuperCalc will first change the file name extension of the existing disk file to ".BAK" and then save the current worksheet in a disk file with the normal ".CAL" extension. The second time you do this to the same file, the first backup file will be erased.

Use the "Overwrite" option if you have complete faith in your changes. This option first deletes the existing disk file and then saves the worksheet.

WARNING: Be careful when using the Overwrite option. It is possible to delete the existing disk file and *not* save the worksheet, leaving you with no disk file at all. If you select the Overwrite option, *do not abort the /Save command* (by pressing CTRL-Z on the next prompt). The existing disk file is deleted when you choose the Overwrite option. Your new file is not created until the /Save command is finished.

Select the Backup option by pressing **B**. After selecting the Backup option, the command returns to the "A(ll), V(alues) or P(art)?" prompt previously discussed. Press **A** for "All" to save another complete copy of your worksheet.

Lesson 13: Printing the Worksheet (/Output)

The purpose of the /Output command is to make printed copies of worksheets on your computer's printer.

To start the /Output command, type **/O**. SuperCalc will spell out the word "/Output," and ask you if you wish a "D(isplay) or C(ontents) report?" The Display option will print the worksheet as you see it on the screen, with rows and columns of information. The Contents option lists the actual formulas, numbers, or text in each cell, one line at a time.

Press **D** for "Display." SuperCalc then prompts "Enter Range". Enter **A1:H20** and press **<RET>**. You will be prompted to select an output device. If you do not have a printer attached to your computer, press C. (Otherwise, if you press "P", the computer will go into a loop waiting for the printer to become ready. Since no printer exists, it will wait forever. You will then need to press RESET, but you will lose your worksheet when you do.)If you have a printer attached to the computer, press **P** for "Printer." The worksheet will then be printed on your printer. The printout should appear just as it does in Figure 3-1. When the report is finished, SuperCalc displays the message "End of Report – type any key". Press **<RET>** to return to the worksheet.

On some computers, if the printer is not ready when you start the /Output command, SuperCalc may respond with an error message that reports that the printer is not ready or is out of paper. You will then have the choice of making the printer ready and pressing the space bar to continue, or entering CTRL-Z to cancel the command. If you do not see one of these error messages, even pressing CTRL-Z won't do any good.

You can also use /Output to preview a portion of a report on the display screen. To try this, let's "print" the range A8:G14 of your worksheet onto the screen. To do this, enter **/O D A8:G14 <RET> C**. Your screen will change from a normal worksheet to look like the following:

```
  :  A   ::  B   ::  C   ::  D   ::  E   ::  F   ::  G   :
 8:EXPENSES:
 9:RENT        500     500     500     500     500     500
10:FOOD        280     280     280     280     280     280
11:UTIL         90      90      90      90      90      90
12:AUTO        120     120     120     120     120     120
13:-------------------------------------------------------
14:TOTAL       990     990     990     990     990     990

End of Report...Press a key to continue
```

Again, a line at the bottom tells you that you may press any key to return to the worksheet. Press **<RET>** (more than once, if necessary) to return to the worksheet when you have finished looking at the report.

You can print any part of the worksheet, from a single cell to the entire worksheet. The range specification "All" may be used to print the entire worksheet.

When you are printing a large worksheet, SuperCalc will stop at the end of each page to allow you to change paper. SuperCalc also remembers how wide your printer is, and it will automatically break up a report into sections to make it fit. For instance, if your printer is 80 characters wide, the first section of the report will be the first 80-character width of the worksheet. When this is finished, the next width of 80 characters will be printed, and so on, until the entire report is finished. All you have to do is to connect the sections together to make a complete report. You can also change the page length and printer width. This is explained in Chapter 11.

```
  :   A   ::   B   ::   C   ::   D   ::   E   ::   F   ::   G   ::   H   :
 1:Simple Budget Worksheet
 2:
 3:                JAN      FEB      MAR      APR      MAY      JUN    Y.T.D
 4:=========================================================================
 5:INCOME:
 6:SALARY         1000     1000     1000     1050     1050     1050     6150
 7:=========================================================================
 8:EXPENSES:
 9:RENT            500      500      500      500      500      500     3000
10:FOOD            280      280      280      280      280      280     1680
11:UTIL             90       90       90       90       90       90      540
12:AUTO            120      120      120      120      120      120      720
13:-------------------------------------------------------------------------
14:TOTAL           990      990      990      990      990      990     5940
15:=========================================================================
16:SAVINGS:
17:MONTHLY          10       10       10       60       60       60      210
18:CUMM.            10       20       30       90      150      210
19:=========================================================================
20:
```

Figure 3-1.

Printout of the Budget Worksheet

Lesson 14: Clearing the Whole Worksheet (/Zap and /Quit)

There are two commands that clear the entire worksheet. They are the /Zap and /Quit commands. /Zap and /Quit are the two simplest commands to execute, but they have the greatest potential for destroying information and a lot of hard work. Both of these commands completely destroy all the information on the worksheet when they are executed. It's a good idea to gain a full understanding of these commands before trying too many experiments.

The /Zap command completely clears the worksheet, destroying whatever is on it and leaving you with a blank worksheet. The active cell is returned to A1, and all worksheet parameters are set to their default values, It is identical to the worksheet you see when you first start SuperCalc.

Cell protection means nothing to this command; it "Zaps" protected and unprotected cells alike. (Cell protection is a special SuperCalc feature that is explained in Chapter 4.) If you use the /Zap command but have not saved your worksheet on a disk, it's gone forever.

/Quit has much the same effect. It destroys the entire worksheet, but it goes one step further: it places your computer back under control of the operating system. When you execute a /Quit command, the screen clears and you see the "A>" prompt.

Now that you are fully aware of the havoc that can be wreaked by these commands, you may wonder what they are used for. /Zap is usually used when you have finished one worksheet and wish to work on another. First you save the worksheet if you will need it again, "Zap" the worksheet to clear it, and then load or input the next worksheet that you want to use.

Try the /Zap command by typing **/Z**; SuperCalc will complete the phrase "/Zap – ENTIRE – Worksheet?" and prompt you to enter Y (for "Yes") to continue or N (for "No") if you don't wish to continue. This gives you a last chance to change your mind. You must press either "Y" or "N". Any other entry will be ignored until you do. You have saved your worksheet and also have a backup copy, so enter **Y** to "Zap" it. The worksheet will clear to an initial worksheet.

/Quit is used when you are done with SuperCalc and wish to use your computer for other things. It stops the SuperCalc program and returns you to the operating system. To restart SuperCalc, type "SC" ("SC2" if you have SuperCalc^2 or "SC3" if you have SuperCalc^3) at the "A>" prompt.

To try the /Quit command enter **/Q**. SuperCalc will complete the word "/Quit" and prompt you to enter Y (for "Yes") to quit SuperCalc or N (for "No") if you do not want to quit. If you are using SuperCalc^2, you may also enter "T" (for "To") and specify the program you want to run. Any other entry will be ignored. Press **Y** to quit. Your screen will clear, and you will be left with the "A>" prompt of your operating system on your screen. To reenter SuperCalc, enter **SC** (or **SC2** or **SC3**) **<RET>**. The SuperCalc title page will reappear on your screen. Press **<RET>** to return to the initial worksheet.

```
    |  A  ||  B  ||  C  ||  D  ||  E  ||  F  ||  G  ||  H  |
  1|
  2|
  3|
  4|
  5|
  6|
  7|
  8|
  9|
 10|
 11|
 12|
 13|
 14|
 15|
 16|
 17|
 18|
 19|
 20|
> A1
Width:  9  Memory: 27 Last Col/Row:A1      ? for HELP
  1>■
```

Lesson 15: Loading a Worksheet (/Load)

The /Load command is used to "load" a worksheet from a disk file. It is important to clear your worksheet with the /Zap command before loading another worksheet because /Load does not clear an existing worksheet—it just loads over whatever is there. This could easily cause unexpected problems on your worksheet.

/Load works very much like /Save. Enter **/L**. SuperCalc completes the word "/Load" and asks for a file name. The same rules for file names apply here as apply to the /Save command. To reload the worksheet that you saved in Lesson 12, enter **B:FIRSTTRY <RET>**.

SuperCalc now poses a question that looks much like the prompt for /Save:

```
A(ll) or P(art)?
```

The prompt "A(ll) or P(art)?" is asking if you wish to reload "All" of the worksheet or "Part" of the worksheet. "Part" of the worksheet refers to a range of cells on the worksheet. For now, load "All" of your worksheet (press the letter **A**). The "Part" option of the /Load command will be discussed in more detail in Chapter 10.

Your worksheet should reload just as it was when you saved it.

You probably noticed that the prompts for both the /Save and /Load commands included the phrase "(or <RETURN> for directory)" when they were requesting a file name. To see what this means, type **/L <RET>**.

The top half of your screen should look something like this:

```
SuperCalc2 Directory Display
Current Work Disk is A:
Current working file is : B:FIRSTTRY.cal

 OPTIONS:
    C(hoose) alternate disk drive
    D(isk) directory, All files
    S(uperCalc) format files only
    E(nter) filename

 CTRL-Z to abort command.█




Type C(hoose), D(isk), S(uperCalc), or E(nter)
  7>/Load,
```

This is a menu of directory options. The second line shows you from which disk you will get the directory. This is the default drive (usually drive A) unless you change it each time you want a directory. The second line shows the last file that you attempted to load. If you have not attempted to load a file, this will read "NONE."

Below this are the directory options. "C(hoose) alternate disk drive" allows you to get a directory of a disk that is not in the system disk drive. Press **C** for "Choose"; this line changes to "Drive to use:". A one-letter entry is all that is required to select a drive. Press **B** for drive B. Notice that the top line now says that the work disk is "B".

Now press **D** for "Disk directory, All files". This will get a complete directory of all the files on the work disk. The disk directory will look something like this:

```
Directory of files on Disk:

  FIRSTTRY.bak  FIRSTTRY.cal
 •
 •
 •
 <CTRL-Z>=abort, <SP>=more...■
    7>/Load,
```

The message at the bottom of the screen indicates that pressing the space bar will list the rest of the directory (if there is more) or return you to the directory menu (if the complete directory has been displayed). Continue to press the **space bar** until you are back at the directory menu.

The third option in the menu, "S(uperCalc) format files only", produces a directory of the files on the working disk with the ".CAL" file name extension. Press **S** to see this directory. This directory shows the name of each of the files and also the contents of cell A1. This is why cell A1 is a good place to put a descriptive title on your worksheets.

```
Directory of SuperCalc2 Files:
Filename      Version/Title

FIRSTTRY.CAL  SuperCalc ver.  1.00
Simple Budget Worksheet
•
•
•
<CTRL-Z>=abort, <SP>=more...■
  7>/Load,
```

A directory of the SuperCalc[2] sample model files is shown in Figure 3-2. Press the **space bar** until you are back to the directory menu again.

When you have finished reviewing the directory, you can return to the worksheet with the command on the entry line just as it was by pressing **E** (on older versions of SuperCalc, press **CTRL-Z**). Now you can enter the name of the file you want to load. However, for this demonstration, press **CTRL-Z** again to cancel the /Load command.

If you attempt to load a file that does not exist, SuperCalc will respond with the message "File NOT on disk" and give you a chance to correct the file name. If there is a problem with the disk drive or the disk itself, you will see one of several messages, depending on your operating system. CP/M usually responds with "BDOS ERROR...", while other operating systems respond with an error such as "Command aborted due to disk error". Make sure that the proper disk is in the proper disk drive. If this error persists, it may indicate either a bad diskette or a malfunctioning disk drive. If you attempt to save a file onto a diskette that is full, you will see the message "Disk Full". You can replace the diskette with one that is not full and try again.

```
Directory of SuperCalc2 Files:
Filename       Version/Title

BRKEVN  .CAL  SuperCalc ver.  1.00
     Break Even Analysis
CHECKS  .CAL  SuperCalc ver.  1.00
Check Register
SAMPLE  .CAL  SuperCalc ver.  1.00
THIS IS A SAMPLE SUPERCALC WORKSHEET
TENMIN  .CAL  SuperCalc ver.  1.00

BUDGET  .CAL  SuperCalc ver.  1.00
SAMPLE BUDGET




<CTRL-Z>=abort, <SP>=more...█
  7>/Load,
```

Figure 3-2.

Directory of SuperCalc^2 files

CHAPTER FOUR

A Look at How SuperCalc Works

If you have followed the examples up to this point, you know how to operate a bit of the SuperCalc program. Now it is time to explore the functions of the program in more detail. In the rest of this book, each SuperCalc command will be explained in detail and demonstrated through examples.

Editing Capabilities

It is important to be able to correct your errors while you are making entries on the worksheet. Until now you have had two ways to correct errors, both of which required you to retype the entire entry. If you entered incorrect information into a cell, you could replace it with a corrected entry. If you made a mistake before you pressed <RET>, you could use CTRL-Z to clear the entry line and start over. But what about correcting errors while you are typing?

The Entry Line Editor

SuperCalc provides editing capabilities to correct errors as you type. The entry line editor uses the four arrow keys for editing. By pressing the LEFT and RIGHT ARROW keys you move the cursor left and right along the entry line. The cursor does not change the characters in the entry line as it moves past them. You can make corrections by backspacing to the incorrect character and simply retyping the correct one over it. The newly typed character will replace the old character.

You can also insert additional characters in the middle of the line. To do this you press the UP ARROW key. The UP ARROW key inserts a space to the left of the cursor each time you press it. You can then enter new characters in these spaces. Pressing the DOWN ARROW key will delete the character where the cursor is positioned.

To see how this works, move to cell A1 of an empty worksheet and type the following intentionally misspelled label: **"Simple bugget wrksheeet**. Don't press <RET> yet, because you are going to correct this entry before it's entered onto the worksheet.

```
    |  A  ||  B  ||  C  ||  D  ||  E  ||  F  ||  G  ||  H  |
  1|
  2|
  3|
  4|
  5|
  6|
  7|
  8|
  9|
 10|
 11|
 12|
 13|
 14|
 15|
 16|
 17|
 18|
 19|
 20|
> A1
Width:  9  Memory: 27 Last Col/Row:A1      ? for HELP
 25>"Simple bugget wrksheeet █
```

Use the **LEFT ARROW** key to move the cursor back to the middle "e" in the word "wrksheeet".

```
    |  A  ||  B  ||  C  ||  D  ||  E  ||  F  ||  G  ||  H  |
  1|
  2|
  3|
  4|
  5|
  6|
  7|
  8|
  9|
 10|
 11|
 12|
 13|
 14|
 15|
 16|
 17|
 18|
 19|
 20|
> A1
Width:  9  Memory: 27 Last Col/Row:A1      ? for HELP
 22>"Simple bugget wrksheeet
```

Press the **DOWN ARROW** key to delete the letter.

```
    |  A  ||  B  ||  C  ||  D  ||  E  ||  F  ||  G  ||  H  |
  1|
  2|
  3|
  4|
  5|
  6|
  7|
  8|
  9|
 10|
 11|
 12|
 13|
 14|
 15|
 16|
 17|
 18|
 19|
 20|
> A1
Width:  9  Memory: 27 Last Col/Row:A1      ? for HELP
 22>"Simple bugget wrksheet
```

Now move the cursor left to the "r" and press the **UP ARROW** key.

```
   |    A    ||    B    ||    C    ||    D    ||    E    ||    F    ||    G    ||    H    |
  1|
  2|
  3|
  4|
  5|
  6|
  7|
  8|
  9|
 10|
 11|
 12|
 13|
 14|
 15|
 16|
 17|
 18|
 19|
 20|
> A1
Width:  9  Memory: 27 Last Col/Row:A1      ? for HELP
 17>"Simple bugget w rksheet
```

This inserts a space to the left of the "r." Type an **o** to complete correcting this word. Now move the cursor to the first "g" in "Bugget".

```
   |    A    ||    B    ||    C    ||    D    ||    E    ||    F    ||    G    ||    H    |
  1|
  2|
  3|
  4|
  5|
  6|
  7|
  8|
  9|
 10|
 11|
 12|
 13|
 14|
 15|
 16|
 17|
 18|
 19|
 20|
> A1
Width:  9  Memory: 27 Last Col/Row:A1      ? for HELP
 11>"Simple bugget worksheet
```

Type a **d** to correct this word; the "d" replaces the "g."

```
  |  A  ||  B  ||  C  ||  D  ||  E  ||  F  ||  G  ||  H  |
 1|
 2|
 3|
 4|
 5|
 6|
 7|
 8|
 9|
10|
11|
12|
13|
14|
15|
16|
17|
18|
19|
20|
> A1
Width:  9  Memory: 27 Last Col/Row:A1      ? for HELP
 12>"Simple budget worksheet
```

To complete the entry, just press **<RET>**. You don't have to move the cursor to the end of the entry. All the characters on the line will be entered into the cell no matter where the cursor is located.

On most computers you can use the backspace key just like the LEFT ARROW key to move the cursor to the left. On the IBM PC, Compaq, and similar computers, the "Del" key, the "Ins" key, and the "F2" key have special editing functions. The "Del" key works just like the DOWN ARROW key and deletes the character over the cursor. The "Ins" key provides a true insert function to the editor. When you press the "Ins" key, it activates an insert mode that allows characters to be inserted directly to the left of the cursor by just typing them in. Pressing the "Ins" key again turns the insert mode off. When you are in the insert mode, the word "INSERT" is displayed at the right end of the bottom line on the display screen.

On all computers the entire contents of the entry line can be erased by pressing CTRL-Z. On the IBM PC the "F2" key does the same thing.

NOTE: If you try to backspace past the left end of the entry line, SuperCalc will erase the entire entry. So watch out! When you are trying to edit the first several characters, be sure of where the cursor is located. You can move the cursor under the first character, but do not attempt to move it any farther left or the whole line will be erased.

Editing Cell Contents (/Edit)

With the /Edit command you can edit information that is already in a cell. The easiest way to learn how to use the /Edit command is to try it. Start this exercise with an empty worksheet (enter **/ZY** to clear the worksheet). Move to cell A1 and type **"THIS IS A TEST <RET>**. Move the active cell back to A1 if the auto-advance moved you ahead. Now type /**E** to start the /Edit command. SuperCalc will prompt you "From? Enter cell".

```
   :  A  ::  B  ::  C  ::  D  ::  E  ::  F  ::  G  ::  H  :
  1:THIS IS A TEST
  2:
  3:
  4:
  5:
  6:
  7:
  8:
  9:
 10:
 11:
 12:
 13:
 14:
 15:
 16:
 17:
 18:
 19:
 20:
< A1          Text="THIS IS A TEST
From? Enter cell
 26>/Edit(into current cell),█
```

With the /Edit command you can copy information from any cell to the entry line, edit it, and then enter it into the active cell. For this example, press **<RET>**. This indicates that you want to edit "from" cell A1, which is where the active cell is currently located. The entry from cell A1 will appear on the entry line at the bottom of the screen.

```
  :   A   ::   B   ::   C   ::   D   ::   E   ::   F   ::   G   ::   H   :
 1:THIS IS A TEST
 2:
 3:
 4:
 5:
 6:
 7:
 8:
 9:
10:
11:
12:
13:
14:
15:
16:
17:
18:
19:
20:
< A1            Text="THIS IS A TEST
Width:  9  Memory: 26 Last Col/Row:A1       ? for HELP
 16>"THIS IS A TEST█
```

You can now use the SuperCalc editing capabilities to change this entry. For example, change the word "IS" to "WAS". Move the cursor to the "I" in "IS" using the **LEFT ARROW** key.

```
  :   A   ::   B   ::   C   ::   D   ::   E   ::   F   ::   G   ::   H   :
 1:THIS IS A TEST
 2:
 3:
 4:
 5:
 6:
 7:
 8:
 9:
10:
11:
12:
13:
14:
15:
16:
17:
18:
19:
20:
< A1            Text="THIS IS A TEST
Width:  9  Memory: 26 Last Col/Row:A1       ? for HELP
  7>"THIS IS A TEST
```

Press the **DOWN ARROW** key twice to delete the word "IS".

```
   :   A   ::   B   ::   C   ::   D   ::   E   ::   F   ::   G   ::   H   :
  1:THIS IS A TEST
  2:
  3:
  4:
  5:
  6:
  7:
  8:
  9:
 10:
 11:
 12:
 13:
 14:
 15:
 16:
 17:
 18:
 19:
 20:
< A1           Text="THIS IS A TEST
Width:  9  Memory: 26 Last Col/Row:A1      ? for HELP
  7>"THIS█A TEST
```

Press the **UP ARROW** key three times to insert three spaces. Now type **WAS** to complete the change.

```
   :   A   ::   B   ::   C   ::   D   ::   E   ::   F   ::   G   ::   H   :
  1:THIS IS A TEST
  2:
  3:
  4:
  5:
  6:
  7:
  8:
  9:
 10:
 11:
 12:
 13:
 14:
 15:
 16:
 17:
 18:
 19:
 20:
< A1           Text="THIS IS A TEST
Width:  9  Memory: 26 Last Col/Row:A1      ? for HELP
 10>"THIS WAS█A TEST
```

When all the changes are made, press **<RET>** to enter the revised entry into the active cell. As before, no matter where the cursor is on the entry line, the entire entry is entered into the active cell.

You can also copy and change an entry in one operation. Move the active cell down to cell A4, type /**E**, and then type **A1 <RET>** to define the source cell (the cell you want to edit from) as cell A1. The active cell is A4, yet the entry from cell A1 is displayed on the entry line. You can edit this before you enter it into cell A4. Move the cursor left so that it is on the letter "I" in the word "THIS" and type **AT**. Now press **<RET>** and the label will be stored into cell A4.

```
   |   A   ||   B   ||   C   ||   D   ||   E   ||   F   ||   G   ||   H   |
  1|THIS WAS A TEST
  2|
  3|
  4|THAT WAS A TEST
  5|
  6|
  7|
  8|
  9|
 10|
 11|
 12|
 13|
 14|
 15|
 16|
 17|
 18|
 19|
 20|
^ A4          Text="THAT WAS A TEST
Width:  9  Memory: 26 Last Col/Row:A4      ? for HELP
  1>█
```

You can also copy a cell without changing it. Move the active cell to A8. Type /**E**, and define a source cell of **A1 <RET>**. Now just press **<RET>**, and cell A1 will be copied into cell A8 with no changes.

While only text entries have been used in these examples, the /Edit command can also be used to change formulas and numbers. Note, however, that if you use the /Edit command to copy a formula from one cell to another, the formula will not be automatically adjusted as it is when you use the /Replicate command. This is not necessarily a problem, but you should be aware of it. To illustrate this, make the following entries on your worksheet:

Cell	*Entry*
C1	**10**
C2	**20**
C4	**C1+C2**
D1	**1**
D2	**2**

Move the active cell to D4, type **/E C4 <RET>**, and then press **<RET>** again. Look at the entry that is now in cell D4. It is exactly like the entry in cell C4 and is therefore giving a sum of the numbers in column C. If this were an application like the Budget Worksheet, the formula in D4 would probably be wrong. However, there are times where an exact copy of a formula is what is needed, and the /Edit command can be used to make it.

```
   :    A    ::    B    ::    C    ::    D    ::    E    ::    F    ::    G    ::    H    :
  1:THIS WAS A TEST              10          1
  2:                             20          2
  3:
  4:THAT WAS A TEST              30         30
  5:
  6:
  7:
  8:THIS WAS A TEST
  9:
 10:
 11:
 12:
 13:
 14:
 15:
 16:
 17:
 18:
 19:
 20:
v D4           Form=C1+C2
Width:  9  Memory: 26 Last Col/Row:D8      ? for HELP
   1>█
```

Here is a quick summary of the SuperCalc editing capabilities:

1. As you enter information on the entry line, the functions of the arrow keys change. Instead of moving the active cell around the screen, they become the editing control keys.

2. To edit information that you have already entered into a cell on the worksheet, move the active cell to that cell, type **/E**, and press **<RET>**. The cell contents will be placed on the entry line where you can edit them.
3. The LEFT and RIGHT ARROW keys move the cursor back and forth in the entry line. You can make corrections by backspacing with the LEFT ARROW (or BACKSPACE) key until the cursor is under the character that needs correcting. Then when you type the correct character it will replace the incorrect character.
4. The UP and DOWN ARROW keys also work differently during editing. The UP ARROW key inserts spaces into the line in the position just to the left of the cursor. If you need to insert one or more characters, use the UP ARROW key to insert a sufficient number of blanks where the characters need to go, and then back up and type over the blanks to change them to the characters you want.
5. The DOWN ARROW key deletes the character that is over the cursor. Use it to remove unwanted characters from the entry line.
6. You can press <RET> with the cursor anywhere in the line, and the whole line will be entered—even information to the right of the cursor.

How Commands Are Entered

All SuperCalc commands are entered in the same way. We will take some time now to look at the way commands are entered so that when we look at particular commands we can concentrate on their functions. First clear the worksheet (enter /**ZY**.)

All SuperCalc commands begin with a "/" (slash) character. This character notifies the program that what you are about to type is a command, and it is not intended to be entered as data into a cell.

All commands are identified by a one-word descriptive name. When selecting a command, you just enter the first letter of the command name. SuperCalc will finish the name for you and add a comma at the end. SuperCalc will also prompt you with a message telling you what to enter next. These prompts have a consistent structure which makes them easy to interpret.

SuperCalc commands have basically three kinds of prompts: option prompts, information prompts, and range prompts.

Option prompts ask you to choose from a list of options. The options will appear as a list of words with the initial letter capitalized and all but the initial letter in parentheses. To make your selection, press the initial letter of the word describing the option you want. SuperCalc will again complete the word for you.

Information prompts request specific information from you, like the prompt for a file name in the /Save and /Load commands.

A range prompt asks for a range. The idea of a "range" is the same in all of the commands as it was in the SUM function and the /Replicate command. In most commands, a range can be entered as any of the following:

1. A single cell (such as "A5").
2. A partial row, which is defined by a pair of cells separated by a colon (such as "A5:G5").
3. A partial column, which is defined by a pair of cells separated by a colon (such as "A5:A12").
4. A rectangle or block of cells, which is defined by a pair of cells separated by a colon (such as "A5:G12").
5. A complete column or complete row (such as "A"). In SuperCalc^2 some commands permit you to specify a range of complete rows or columns such as "A:D", which means columns A through D, or "5:10", meaning rows 5 through 10.
6. The word "All," which defines the whole worksheet as the range.

With many commands, pressing <RET> or the comma (,) enters the current active cell as the range. You can also use the arrow keys to select cells by first pressing the ESC key, as was explained in Chapter 2.

The /Format command will be used as an example to demonstrate command syntax. First press the slash key (/). The prompt line changes to show you the initial letters of all the commands.

```
    :    A    ::    B    ::    C    ::    D    ::    E    ::    F    ::    G    ::    H    :
  1:
  2:
  3:
  4:
  5:
  6:
  7:
  8:
  9:
 10:
 11:
 12:
 13:
 14:
 15:
 16:
 17:
 18:
 19:
 20:
> A1
Enter A,B,C,D,E,F,G,I,L,M,O,P,Q,R,S,T,U,W,X,Z,?
  2>/ █
```

Press the letter **F** for "Format." Note that as you do this, the word "/Format," is spelled out on the entry line. The prompt now shows the options: "Enter Level: G(lobal), C(olumn), R(ow), E(ntry) or D(efine)". This prompt is asking you to select one of these five options.

```
    :    A    ::    B    ::    C    ::    D    ::    E    ::    F    ::    G    ::    H    :
  1:
  2:
  3:
  4:
  5:
  6:
  7:
  8:
  9:
 10:
 11:
 12:
 13:
 14:
 15:
 16:
 17:
 18:
 19:
 20:
> A1
Enter Level: G(lobal), C(olumn), R(ow), E(ntry) or D(efine)
  9>/Format, █
```

Press the letter **E** for "Entry"; the prompt changes to a range prompt: "Enter range". Enter the range **A1:B3**, but don't press <RET>.

```
    !   A   !!   B   !!   C   !!   D   !!   E   !!   F   !!   G   !!   H   !
  1!
  2!
  3!
  4!
  5!
  6!
  7!
  8!
  9!
 10!
 11!
 12!
 13!
 14!
 15!
  •
  •
  •
> A1
Enter Range
 20>/Format,Entry,A1:B3█
```

You are now in the middle of entering a command. However, you can edit the command and correct it before you enter it, just as you can edit data on the entry line.

For instance, press the **LEFT ARROW** key to move the cursor to the left so that it is on the "B". Press the **DOWN ARROW** key to delete the "B". Now press the **UP ARROW** key to insert a space, and finally type the letter **C** to replace the space with a "C". This works just like editing a data entry.

```
    !   A   !!   B   !!   C   !!   D   !!   E   !!   F   !!   G   !!   H   !
  1!
  2!
  3!
  4!
  5!
  6!
  7!
  8!
  9!
 10!
 11!
 12!
  •
  •
  •
> A1
Enter Range
 19>/Format,Entry,A1:C3
```

However, SuperCalc's entry-line editing capabilities work differently in other parts of the command. When you back the cursor to the comma at the end of any word that SuperCalc finishes after you enter the first letter, the whole word is erased and the prompt is changed back to the previous prompt.

To try this, move the cursor a few more spaces to the left so it is positioned on the comma after the word "Entry".

```
9>/Format, █
```

Now the range and the entire word "Entry" are gone. This is how command words are edited in SuperCalc; it takes one keystroke to enter them and one backspace to remove them. Notice how SuperCalc is prompting you now.

```
   :  A  ::  B  ::  C  ::  D  ::  E  ::  F  ::  G  ::  H  :
  1:
  2:
  3:
  4:
  5:
  6:
  7:
  8:
  9:
 10:
 11:
 12:
 13:
 14:
 15:
 16:
 17:
 18:
 19:
 20:
v A1
Enter Level: G(lobal), C(olumn), R(ow), E(ntry) or D(efine)
  9>/Format,█
```

SuperCalc has gone back to the "Enter Level" prompt and expects you to enter a G, C, R, E, or D. To reenter the word "Entry," just press **E**. This time, instead of entering a range, press **<RET>**. The location of the active cell is entered as a range; this is a quick method of entering a range for commands that affect only the cell where you are currently located. Finally, clear the command by typing CTRL-Z.

SuperCalc recognizes both uppercase and lowercase letters interchangeably. Occasionally you will notice that SuperCalc will change lowercase letters to uppercase ones. For instance, the initial letter of all command words is changed to uppercase when the command word is displayed. When you enter a range or formula, lowercase letters are not changed to uppercase, but they will be recognized properly. This means that you can keep your keyboard in lowercase to enter readable text on your worksheet and not be concerned about capitalizing letters entered for commands.

Changing Display Formats (/Format)

You will realize the versatility of a spreadsheet program when you are able to make information display in a manner that is meaningful to your particular application. SuperCalc has a variety of display options for you to choose from, and they can be implemented on various levels. The /Format command changes the width of columns and allows you to specify the format of a cell, a group of cells, a row, a column, or the entire worksheet with one command.

Changing Column Widths

With the /Format command you can adjust the width of individual columns to suit your needs. When you first start SuperCalc, all columns are 9 character positions wide. Columns can be set to any width from 0 to 126 characters. This makes it possible to build usable and attractive worksheets. Columns for descriptive text entries can be set wide, and columns that contain small numbers can be set narrow.

Clear the worksheet if necessary and load the Budget Worksheet that you saved as B:FIRSTTRY (Enter **/L B:FIRSTTRY <RET> A**). The columns on this worksheet are all 9 characters wide. This width is all right as long as the descriptions in column A are short and cryptic. But you may need longer descriptions. For instance, to include rent figures for two different properties, it might be hard to identify the two properties with only 9 characters. If this column were 15 characters wide, it would be easier to make this distinction.

To change the column widths in the Budget Worksheet enter /**F C** to specify a Column level format command. Enter **A <RET>** to identify column A, and then enter **15 <RET>** to adjust the column width to 15 characters. The width of column A will adjust to 15 characters, thus allowing longer descriptions. One other thing happened when the width of column A was increased: column H disappeared from the display. There is no longer any room for column H because column A is now so much wider. Of course, you can scroll the worksheet to see column H, but when column H comes into view, column A disappears. Later you will learn how to lock parts of the worksheet on the display so that they will not scroll off. However, you can also change column widths in order to see the whole budget model on the screen.

Type /**F G** to define a Global level format. Now type **8 <RET>** to specify a column width of 8 characters. All the columns except column A are reduced to 8 characters, and column H again appears on the display. The width of column A is not changed because it was defined using a Column level format, and this format has priority over a Global level format. Everything now fits on the display as shown in the following illustration:

```
  :       A       :: B :: C :: D :: E :: F :: G :: H :
 1:Simple Budget Worksheet
 2:
 3:                  JAN     FEB     MAR     APR     MAY     JUN   Y.T.D
 4:=====================================================================
 5:INCOME:
 6:SALARY           1000    1000    1000    1050    1050    1050    6150
 7:=====================================================================
 8:EXPENSES:
 9:RENT              500     500     500     500     500     500    3000
10:FOOD              280     280     280     280     280     280    1680
11:UTIL               90      90      90      90      90      90     540
12:AUTO              120     120     120     120     120     120     720
13:---------------------------------------------------------------------
14:TOTAL             990     990     990     990     990     990    5940
15:=====================================================================
16:SAVINGS:
17:MONTHLY            10      10      10      60      60      60     210
18:CUMM.              10      20      30      90     150     210
19:=====================================================================
20:
^ A9        Text="RENT
Width: 15  Memory: 25 Last Col/Row:H19     ? for HELP
 1>█
```

You will notice that the last prompt for the /Format command is slightly different depending on which level you select.

The prompt for a Global or Column level (after you enter the column letter) is

```
Define Formats: (I,G,E,$,R,L,TR,TL,*,U(1−8),H,D,column width)
```

And the prompt for Row or Entry level is

```
Define Formats: (I,G,E,$,R,L,TR,TL,*,U(1−8),H,D)
```

As you look through these prompt lines, you can see letters for the various format options: Integer, General, Exponential, $ (Dollar), Right, Left, Text Right, Text Left, * (Graphic), User Defined, Hide, and Default. If you are using an older version of SuperCalc, the U(1−8) and H options will not appear in this prompt. Default is actually not a format option. When you specify a default format, you are removing any explicit format specifications and letting the format revert to a lower priority level, or back to the general formats if no other format levels have been defined.

Numeric Display Formats

When you start SuperCalc, the display formats are set according to certain *defaults*. The *General* format is the default. This means that numbers will be displayed as decimal fractions (for example 10.29). In General format, numeric entries are displayed flush right. If the number is too long to fit in the width of the column, it will be displayed in *exponential notation*, which is a way of abbreviating a number for a narrow column width.

Exponential notation shortens the display of a number by representing the number along with its magnitude (power of ten). For example, the number 3000 in exponential notation is 3e3, which means 3 × 10 to the third power (10 × 10 × 10) or 3 × 1000. The number 3,000,000 could be represented as 3e6 or 3 × 10 to the sixth power or 3 × 1,000,000. Thus the seven-digit number 3,000,000 requires a column width of only 3 character spaces when expressed in exponential notation.

Numeric entries can be displayed in General, Integer, Exponential, Dollar, or Graphic formats. Integer format displays all numbers rounded to the nearest whole number with no decimal point. If the format is set to Dollar or

Integer and the number won't fit in the cell width, the program displays a row of greater than symbols (>>>>>>>>>>) to show you that there is a value that will not fit.

Dollar format rounds all values off to two decimal places, which is to the nearest cent if you are using dollars. It displays numbers with two decimal places even if both decimal digits are zeros. No dollar sign is displayed, even though this is called Dollar format. It can also be used for numbers that do not represent money.

Exponential format scales all numbers into exponential or scientific notation. In SuperCalc you can work with numbers as large as 10 to the 63rd power and as small as 10 to the −63rd power; that is 1 and 63 zeros, either before or after the decimal point. Table 4-1 shows some examples of exponential notation.

Graphic format displays numbers as rows of asterisks. The value is truncated to the nearest whole number, and that many asterisks are displayed if the column is wide enough. The program does not do any scaling of values. It is left to you to ensure that the numbers you enter will fit into the columns.

Any of the numeric formats except Graphic can be displayed either *right-justified* or *left-justified* in the cell. This means that either the right ends of the numbers are aligned at the right edge of the cell, or the left ends of the numbers are aligned at the left cell edge. The default for numbers is right-justified, which provides proper alignment of Dollar and Integer formatted numbers.

The number you enter	The number displayed in exponential format
.000000035467	3.5467e−8
.035467	3.5467e−2
.35467	3.5467e−1
3.5467	3.5467e0
35.467	3.5467e1
3546700000	3.5467e9

Table 4-1.

Exponential Format

```
  |       A       ||    B    ||    C    ||    D    ||    E    ||           F            |
 1|Numeric Formats
 2|
 3|
 4| What you enter   General   Integer Exponent    Dollar                         Graphic
 5|=====================================================================================
 6|             .9        .9         1     9e-1       .90
 7|              1         1         1      1e0      1.00 *
 8|            1.8       1.8         2    1.8e0      1.80 *
 9|           2.35      2.35         2   2.35e0      2.35 **
10|       8.997532  8.997532         9 8.9975e0      9.00 ********
11|             15        15        15    1.5e1     15.00 ***************
12|        1000.75   1000.75      1001 1.0008e3   1000.75 ************************
13|         100000    100000    100000      1e5 >>>>>>>>> ************************
14|    83000000000    8.3e10 >>>>>>>>>   8.3e10 >>>>>>>>> ************************
15|
 •
 •
 •
20|
v A15
Width: 15  Memory: 25 Last Col/Row:F14    ? for HELP
 1>■
```

Figure 4-1.

Numeric formats

The example in Figure 4-1 shows the five numeric formats. The same value has been placed across each row; only the formatting has been changed. Clear your worksheet (enter **/Z Y**) and create this example by making the following entries:

Cell	*Entry*
B6	**A6**
	/R B6 , B7:B14 <RET>
	/R B6:B14 , C6:F6 <RET>
	/F C A , 15 <RET>
	/F C C , I <RET>
	/F C D , E <RET>
	/F C E , $ <RET>
	/F C F , * 24 <RET>
	/F R 4 , TR <RET>
A1	**"Numeric Formats**
A4	**"What you enter**
B4	**"General**
C4	**"Integer**
D4	**"Exponent**
E4	**"Dollar**
F4	**"Graphic**

A5	**'=**
G5	**"**
A6	**.9**
A7	**1**
A8	**1.8**
A9	**2.35**
A10	**8.997532**
A11	**15**
A12	**1000.75**
A13	**100000**
A14	**83000000000**

Column A shows the numbers as you entered them. Column B shows the same numbers in General format. This is the format that displays numbers as they best fit the cell. The numbers are displayed as normal decimal fractions, meaning that if you enter 2.30, it shows up as 2.3 with the extra zero taken out. If the values get so large that they don't fit the cells, General format automatically switches to Exponential format to give you the most information in the available space (cell B14).

Integer format, as shown in column C, always displays whole numbers. The original value you entered is shown rounded to the closest whole number. This rounding is well illustrated by rows 6 through 9, where all of the values in A6 through A9 are different, but the Integer format in C6 through C9 only displays two different numbers. Notice in cell C14 that when the number is too large for Integer format it does not switch to another format, it just gives up. The series of greater than symbols is SuperCalc's way of letting you know that the value is too large to display in the cell, given the current column width.

Exponential format, in column D, displays a number between 1 and 10 multiplied by a power of ten. The power of ten is separated from the number by the letter "e" for exponent. This format will display as many significant digits to the right of the decimal as it has room for.

The Dollar format (Column E) always rounds to two decimal places. Like Integer format, when Dollar format runs out of room, the display changes to a series of greater than symbols. In spite of being called Dollar format, this format is useful for many things besides dollars. Any number that you want to represent with two significant decimal digits can use this format.

The last column of Figure 4-1 demonstrates the Graphic format. This format displays one asterisk for each whole number in the value to be represented. Notice that there are no asterisks in cell F6 because the value (0.9) is less than one. As cells F12 through F14 demonstrate, Graphic display format doesn't report that it has run out of room, it just shows you what it can. As you can see, it doesn't take long to exceed the capacity of even rather wide columns, so it's important to take this into consideration when using graphic displays.

Figure 4-2 displays the same values as Figure 4-1, but with all displays left-justified. Do this by entering **/F G L <RET>**. All the numbers are now displayed at the left side of the cells. For certain applications this is useful, but for most it probably makes the display confusing. This is especially true with Dollar formatted displays. The Graphic formatted column hasn't changed; there is no left or right for this format, it always starts at the left side. Now change your worksheet so that the numbers are lined up on the right again by entering **/F G R <RET>**.

```
   :       A       ::   B    ::   C    ::   D    ::   E    ::           F           :
  1:Numeric Formats
  2:
  3:
  4: What you enter  General  Integer Exponent  Dollar                      Graphic
  5:===============================================================================
  6: .9              .9       1        9e-10A .90
  7: 1               1        1        1e0     1.00      *
  8: 1.8             1.8      2        1.8e0   1.80      *
  9: 2.35            2.35     2        2.35e0  2.35      **
 10: 8.997532        8.997532 9        8.9975e0 9.00     ********
 11: 15              15       15       1.5e1   15.00     ***************
 12: 1000.75         1000.75  1001     1.0008e3 1000.75  **********************
 13: 100000          100000   100000   1e5     >>>>>>>>  **********************
 14: 83000000000     8.3e10   >>>>>>>> 8.3e10  >>>>>>>>  **********************
 15:
 16:
 17:
 18:
 19:
 20:
v A15
Width: 15  Memory: 25 Last Col/Row:F14    ? for HELP
  1>█
```

Figure 4-2.

Left-justified numbers

If you are using SuperCalc² or SuperCalc³, you may have noticed the characters "U(1-8)" appear in the format options prompt. These characters represent some additional ways to display numbers, which are called the "User Defined" formats. These formats are useful for formatting amounts of money. To see what they do, enter the following (skip over this if you have an older version of SuperCalc):

Cell	*Entry*
F4	**"User Defined 1**
	/F C F , U1 <RET>

```
  :      A       ::    B    ::    C    ::    D    ::    E    ::           F            :
 1:Numeric Formats
 2:
 3:
 4: What you enter   General   Integer Exponent    Dollar           User Defined 1
 5:=====================================================================================
 6:               .9       .9         1     9e-1       .90                       $.90
 7:                1        1         1      1e0      1.00                      $1.00
 8:              1.8      1.8         2    1.8e0      1.80                      $1.80
 9:             2.35     2.35         2   2.35e0      2.35                      $2.35
10:         8.997532 8.997532         9 8.9975e0      9.00                      $9.00
11:               15       15        15    1.5e1     15.00                     $15.00
12:          1000.75  1000.75      1001 1.0008e3   1000.75                  $1,000.75
13:           100000   100000    100000      1e5 >>>>>>>>                $100,000.00
14:      83000000000   8.3e10 >>>>>>>>   8.3e10 >>>>>>>>         $83,000,000,000.00
15:
16:
17:
18:
19:
20:
> F4            Text="User Defined 1
Width: 24  Memory: 25 Last Col/Row:F14     ? for HELP
  1>■
```

In Figure 4-2, column F shows the numbers you entered displayed in format U1, the first of the eight User Defined formats. Initially, format U1 and the other seven User Defined formats (U2, U3, ... U8) are all set to display numbers as dollars and cents with a floating dollar sign and commas just as the numbers now appear in column F. However, you can customize the User Defined formats to display numbers in other ways. This will be explained in Chapter 8.

Format Priority Levels

When you enter /F, the word "/Format," is completed and you are requested to enter a "Level." To tell SuperCalc how much of the worksheet you want to affect by the /Format command, you select "Global," "Column," "Row," or "Entry." This "Level" not only defines which cells the command will affect, but it also represents a priority level of format specifications.

We will now create an example to investigate how priority levels interact. Clear your worksheet (enter **/ZY**) and enter **12.333** in cell A1. Replicate this across row 1 to column H by typing **/R A1 <RET> B1:H1 <RET>**. Now replicate this row down column A by typing **/R A1:H1 <RET> A2:A20 <RET>**. The entire visible worksheet should now have 12.333 in every cell, as follows:

```
   :    A   ::    B   ::    C   ::    D   ::    E   ::    F   ::    G   ::    H   :
  1:  12.333   12.333   12.333   12.333   12.333   12.333   12.333   12.333
  2:  12.333   12.333   12.333   12.333   12.333   12.333   12.333   12.333
  3:  12.333   12.333   12.333   12.333   12.333   12.333   12.333   12.333
  4:  12.333   12.333   12.333   12.333   12.333   12.333   12.333   12.333
  5:  12.333   12.333   12.333   12.333   12.333   12.333   12.333   12.333
  6:  12.333   12.333   12.333   12.333   12.333   12.333   12.333   12.333
  7:  12.333   12.333   12.333   12.333   12.333   12.333   12.333   12.333
  8:  12.333   12.333   12.333   12.333   12.333   12.333   12.333   12.333
  9:  12.333   12.333   12.333   12.333   12.333   12.333   12.333   12.333
 10:  12.333   12.333   12.333   12.333   12.333   12.333   12.333   12.333
 11:  12.333   12.333   12.333   12.333   12.333   12.333   12.333   12.333
 12:  12.333   12.333   12.333   12.333   12.333   12.333   12.333   12.333
 13:  12.333   12.333   12.333   12.333   12.333   12.333   12.333   12.333
 14:  12.333   12.333   12.333   12.333   12.333   12.333   12.333   12.333
 15:  12.333   12.333   12.333   12.333   12.333   12.333   12.333   12.333
 16:  12.333   12.333   12.333   12.333   12.333   12.333   12.333   12.333
 17:  12.333   12.333   12.333   12.333   12.333   12.333   12.333   12.333
 18:  12.333   12.333   12.333   12.333   12.333   12.333   12.333   12.333
 19:  12.333   12.333   12.333   12.333   12.333   12.333   12.333   12.333
 20:  12.333   12.333   12.333   12.333   12.333   12.333   12.333   12.333
> B1          Form=12.333
Width:  9  Memory: 24 Last Col/Row:H20     ? for HELP
  1>■
```

A particular cell on the worksheet may have several formats defined for it. For instance, if you format row 4 as Integer (I), and format column C as Dollar ($), then cell C4 will have two conflicting formats defined for it. If you also define a Global format and an Entry level format for cell C4, this cell will have four different formats defined for it. To some degree human beings can tolerate conflicting instructions, but computers can't. So, the designers of

SuperCalc established a priority system for conflicting formats. Formats for which you select the Entry level have the highest priority; they override all others. Row level formats come next; they will override Column level formats and Global formats. Column level formats override Global formats, and Global formats control any cells not otherwise formatted.

Enter **/F** and press the letter **G** for "Global." A Global format will affect every cell on the worksheet that is not already formatted. You are now prompted to enter the format definitions you want. Enter **I** for Integer format and press **<RET>** to complete the command. Every entry on the worksheet will change to "12," the nearest whole number to 12.333.

	A	B	C	D	E	F	G	H
1	12	12	12	12	12	12	12	12
2	12	12	12	12	12	12	12	12
3	12	12	12	12	12	12	12	12
4	12	12	12	12	12	12	12	12
5	12	12	12	12	12	12	12	12
6	12	12	12	12	12	12	12	12
7	12	12	12	12	12	12	12	12
8	12	12	12	12	12	12	12	12
9	12	12	12	12	12	12	12	12
10	12	12	12	12	12	12	12	12
11	12	12	12	12	12	12	12	12
12	12	12	12	12	12	12	12	12
13	12	12	12	12	12	12	12	12
14	12	12	12	12	12	12	12	12
15	12	12	12	12	12	12	12	12
16	12	12	12	12	12	12	12	12
17	12	12	12	12	12	12	12	12
18	12	12	12	12	12	12	12	12
19	12	12	12	12	12	12	12	12
20	12	12	12	12	12	12	12	12

```
> B1          Form=12.333
Width:  9  Memory: 24 Last Col/Row:H20     ? for HELP
   1>
```

If you set the format level to Row or Column you must define what row or column you want the /Format command to affect. Enter **/F** and press the letter **C** for "Column." You are now prompted to enter a column letter. Enter **D <RET>** to specify column D. Now type **G <RET>** for General formatting. All the entries in column C will change to 12.333. This column level format has overridden the Global format previously entered.

```
     :    A    ::    B    ::    C    ::    D    ::    E    ::    F    ::    G    ::    H    :
   1:       12       12   12.333        12        12        12        12        12
   2:       12       12   12.333        12        12        12        12        12
   3:       12       12   12.333        12        12        12        12        12
   4:       12       12   12.333        12        12        12        12        12
   5:       12       12   12.333        12        12        12        12        12
   6:       12       12   12.333        12        12        12        12        12
   7:       12       12   12.333        12        12        12        12        12
   8:       12       12   12.333        12        12        12        12        12
   9:       12       12   12.333        12        12        12        12        12
  10:       12       12   12.333        12        12        12        12        12
  11:       12       12   12.333        12        12        12        12        12
  12:       12       12   12.333        12        12        12        12        12
  13:       12       12   12.333        12        12        12        12        12
  14:       12       12   12.333        12        12        12        12        12
  15:       12       12   12.333        12        12        12        12        12
  16:       12       12   12.333        12        12        12        12        12
  17:       12       12   12.333        12        12        12        12        12
  18:       12       12   12.333        12        12        12        12        12
  19:       12       12   12.333        12        12        12        12        12
  20:       12       12   12.333        12        12        12        12        12
> B1          Form=12.333
Width:   9  Memory: 24 Last Col/Row:H20     ? for HELP
  1>
```

To try the Row level format, first move the active cell to A10 (**=A10 <RET>**). Type /**F R** to select Row level and press **<RET>** to define row 10. Type **$ <RET>** to specify a Dollar format for this row. All the cells in this row, including the ones formatted at the Column level, have changed to Dollar format (12.33) with two decimal places.

```
     :    A    ::    B    ::    C    ::    D    ::    E    ::    F    ::    G    ::    H    :
   1:       12       12   12.333        12        12        12        12        12
   2:       12       12   12.333        12        12        12        12        12
   3:       12       12   12.333        12        12        12        12        12
   4:       12       12   12.333        12        12        12        12        12
   5:       12       12   12.333        12        12        12        12        12
   6:       12       12   12.333        12        12        12        12        12
   7:       12       12   12.333        12        12        12        12        12
   8:       12       12   12.333        12        12        12        12        12
   9:       12       12   12.333        12        12        12        12        12
  10:    12.33    12.33    12.33     12.33     12.33     12.33     12.33     12.33
  11:       12       12   12.333        12        12        12        12        12
  12:       12       12   12.333        12        12        12        12        12
  13:       12       12   12.333        12        12        12        12        12
  14:       12       12   12.333        12        12        12        12        12
  15:       12       12   12.333        12        12        12        12        12
  16:       12       12   12.333        12        12        12        12        12
  17:       12       12   12.333        12        12        12        12        12
  18:       12       12   12.333        12        12        12        12        12
  19:       12       12   12.333        12        12        12        12        12
  20:       12       12   12.333        12        12        12        12        12
> A10         Form=12.333
Width:   9  Memory: 24 Last Col/Row:H20     ? for HELP
  1>
```

Enter **/F E** for an Entry level format. An Entry format requires that you define a range of cells for the command to act on. This range can be from one cell to the entire worksheet. Enter the range as **F7:H14 <RET>** and the format as **E <RET>** for "Exponential." All the cells in this range will change to exponential format.

```
  :    A   ::    B   ::    C   ::    D   ::    E   ::    F   ::    G   ::    H   :
 1:       12        12   12.333        12        12        12        12        12
 2:       12        12   12.333        12        12        12        12        12
 3:       12        12   12.333        12        12        12        12        12
 4:       12        12   12.333        12        12        12        12        12
 5:       12        12   12.333        12        12        12        12        12
 6:       12        12   12.333        12        12        12        12        12
 7:       12        12   12.333        12        12 1.2333e1  1.2333e1  1.2333e1
 8:       12        12   12.333        12        12 1.2333e1  1.2333e1  1.2333e1
 9:       12        12   12.333        12        12 1.2333e1  1.2333e1  1.2333e1
10:    12.33     12.33    12.33     12.33     12.33 1.2333e1  1.2333e1  1.2333e1
11:       12        12   12.333        12        12 1.2333e1  1.2333e1  1.2333e1
12:       12        12   12.333        12        12 1.2333e1  1.2333e1  1.2333e1
13:       12        12   12.333        12        12 1.2333e1  1.2333e1  1.2333e1
14:       12        12   12.333        12        12 1.2333e1  1.2333e1  1.2333e1
15:       12        12   12.333        12        12        12        12        12
16:       12        12   12.333        12        12        12        12        12
17:       12        12   12.333        12        12        12        12        12
18:       12        12   12.333        12        12        12        12        12
19:       12        12   12.333        12        12        12        12        12
20:       12        12   12.333        12        12        12        12        12
> A10          Form=12.333
Width:  9  Memory: 24 Last Col/Row:H20      ? for HELP
  1>
```

To confirm that the format priorities described do in fact exist, and that it is not just the last format defined that has priority, make the following entries. Format row 13 with a Dollar format by typing **/F R 13 <RET> $ <RET>**. Note that this format will not override the Entry level format. Cells FB, G13, and H13 still display Exponential format. Format column G with a General format by typing **/F C G <RET> G <RET>**. Note that this format does not affect either the Entry level formats or the Row level formats. When you are finished, your worksheet should appear as shown.

```
   :    A    ::    B    ::    C    ::    D    ::    E    ::    F    ::    G    ::    H    :
  1:       12        12   12.333        12        12        12   12.333        12
  2:       12        12   12.333        12        12        12   12.333        12
  3:       12        12   12.333        12        12        12   12.333        12
  4:       12        12   12.333        12        12        12   12.333        12
  5:       12        12   12.333        12        12        12   12.333        12
  6:       12        12   12.333        12        12        12   12.333        12
  7:       12        12   12.333        12        12 1.2333e1 1.2333e1 1.2333e1
  8:       12        12   12.333        12        12 1.2333e1 1.2333e1 1.2333e1
  9:       12        12   12.333        12        12 1.2333e1 1.2333e1 1.2333e1
 10:    12.33     12.33    12.33     12.33     12.33 1.2333e1 1.2333e1 1.2333e1
 11:       12        12   12.333        12        12 1.2333e1 1.2333e1 1.2333e1
 12:       12        12   12.333        12        12 1.2333e1 1.2333e1 1.2333e1
 13:    12.33     12.33    12.33     12.33     12.33 1.2333e1 1.2333e1 1.2333e1
 14:       12        12   12.333        12        12 1.2333e1 1.2333e1 1.2333e1
 15:       12        12   12.333        12        12        12   12.333        12
 16:       12        12   12.333        12        12        12   12.333        12
 17:       12        12   12.333        12        12        12   12.333        12
 18:       12        12   12.333        12        12        12   12.333        12
 19:       12        12   12.333        12        12        12   12.333        12
 20:       12        12   12.333        12        12        12   12.333        12
> A10           Form=12.333
Width:  9  Memory: 24 Last Col/Row:H20     ? for HELP
 1>
```

Entering Several Formats Simultaneously

You can enter more than one format specification in a single command, but some format specifications are obviously mutually exclusive. The program will use whichever format you entered last, even if two are entered in the same command. In other words, if you enter /F C E, I, $, the display will be in Dollar format, not in Integer. This last entered, last used rule does not have any impact on the priority levels described previously. When you enter a Global level format, this format won't override a format defined at another level. A format specification of E,L,TR,20 is perfectly valid, and all of these entries will affect the worksheet. (Numbers will be flush left in exponential format, text will be flush right, and the column will be 20 characters wide.) To try this, enter **/F C A , E L TR 20 <RET>**.

```
   :         A          ::   B  ::   C  ::   D  ::   E  ::    F   ::    G    :
 1: 1.2333e1                 12      12      12      12        12   12.333
 2: 1.2333e1                 12      12      12      12        12   12.333
 3: 1.2333e1                 12      12      12      12        12   12.333
 4: 1.2333e1                 12      12      12      12        12   12.333
 5: 1.2333e1                 12      12      12      12        12   12.333
 6: 1.2333e1                 12      12      12      12        12   12.333
 7: 1.2333e1                 12      12      12      12 1.2333e1 1.2333e1
 8: 1.2333e1                 12      12      12      12 1.2333e1 1.2333e1
 9: 1.2333e1                 12      12      12      12 1.2333e1 1.2333e1
10: 12.33                 12.33   12.33   12.33   12.33 1.2333e1 1.2333e1
11: 1.2333e1                 12      12      12      12 1.2333e1 1.2333e1
12: 1.2333e1                 12      12      12      12 1.2333e1 1.2333e1
13: 12.33                 12.33   12.33   12.33   12.33 1.2333e1 1.2333e1
14: 1.2333e1                 12      12      12      12 1.2333e1 1.2333e1
15: 1.2333e1                 12      12      12      12        12   12.333
16: 1.2333e1                 12      12      12      12        12   12.333
17: 1.2333e1                 12      12      12      12        12   12.333
18: 1.2333e1                 12      12      12      12        12   12.333
19: 1.2333e1                 12      12      12      12        12   12.333
20: 1.2333e1                 12      12      12      12        12   12.333
> A10          Form=12.333
Width: 20  Memory: 24 Last Col/Row:H20     ? for HELP
  1>
```

Changing Text Formats

Now that you have learned to format numbers, it's time to see how to make text entries display the way you want them to. Text entries are displayed flush left under the default format settings.

Text can be displayed either flush left or flush right. Flush left means that the text starts at the left side of the cell and runs to the right. Flush right means that the text ends at the right edge of the cell. These two options allow you to align column heads with whatever is displayed below, but there is more to consider when selecting either flush left or flush right text entries.

The Text Left option aligns the first character of the text at the left edge of the cell, but it also allows the display of text entries that are longer than the width of the cell they are entered into. In this format, text entries are allowed to display across unoccupied cells to the right of the entry up to their full length, which can be up to 116 characters. This makes putting titles on a worksheet or adding notes and instructions quite easy. An occupied cell, however, will truncate a long text entry at the occupied cell's left edge.

As Chapter 2 demonstrated, the Text Right option aligns the last character of the text at the right edge of the cell. This is good for column headings with numbers. But when you use the Text Right option, entries longer than the cell width cannot extend over the cell boundaries. The cell still contains the entire text, but the text display is truncated at the left cell boundary and the beginning of a long entry is not visible. You can adjust column widths, change the format to Text Left, or edit your entries to correct the display.

To illustrate the effects of these formats, clear the worksheet with **/ZY** and make the following entries. In cell A1, enter "**This entry is over 65 characters long and crosses many cell boundaries.** This one entry will extend clear across the worksheet display. Enter **4.5** in cell D3. Next, in cell A3 enter "**This text is truncated because of an occupied cell.** This entry displays only as far as the left edge of cell D3 because of the number that is in D3.

Move to cell B5 and enter "**This is right**. Enter **/F E, B5, TR <RET>** to format this entry so that it is displayed in Text Right format. The text in B3 will move one character to the left so that it ends at the right edge of the cell, and the first characters are not displayed. To confirm that the entire text is still contained in the cell, move the active cell to cell B5 and look at the status line at the bottom of the display.

```
    |  A  ||  B  ||  C  ||  D  ||  E  ||  F  ||  G  ||  H  |
   1|This entry is over 65 characters long and crosses many cell boundaries
   2|
   3|this text is truncated beca      4.5
   4|
   5|         is right?
   6|
   7|
   .
   .
   .
  15|
  16|
  17|
  18|
  19|
  20|
< B5     TR     Text="this is right?
Width:  9  Memory: 26 Last Col/Row:D5     ? for HELP
   1>█
```

On the status line, you can see the complete entry in cell B5. Note that only the display is truncated; the actual content of the cell is what you originally entered. Across the top row of the display is the text that you entered into cell A1. It displays across the screen because there are no occupied cells in the first row. The text entry in row 3 is truncated at the left edge of cell D3, because of the entry in that cell.

Cell Protection (/Protect)

Cell protection is an important feature of SuperCalc. It allows you to protect certain portions of your worksheet from inadvertent changes. You will find this a very reassuring feature when you start building worksheets for other people to use. The thought of someone accidentally entering a "1" into the wrong cell and destroying a complicated formula is not very comforting. Cell protection prevents this kind of problem.

When cells are protected, neither the cells' contents nor their formats can be changed. If a protected cell contains a formula, the value that is calculated and displayed may change, but the formula itself cannot be changed. Cells are protected not only from new text and values, but also from other commands, like /Blank, /Edit, /Format, /Copy, /Replicate, /Delete, and /Load. Using any of these commands on a protected cell causes SuperCalc to display the message "Protected Entry". Protected cells within the range of any of these commands will not be affected, but unprotected cells will be changed.

Because of the way protected cells interact with these commands, you can selectively change data on your worksheet by protecting some entries and not protecting others. You can then load another file over the existing worksheet and have only the unprotected cells change. The techniques and applications of the /Load command will be covered in depth later.

WARNING: Cell protection does not stop either the /Zap or /Quit commands. They clear the entire worksheet of both protected and unprotected cells.

To use the /Protect command, you enter /P and the program completes the word "/Protect," and prompts you for a range. As usual, the range can be one cell, a partial row or column, a complete row or column, a block, the word "All," or just <RET>. If you enter <RET> the command acts on only the active cell.

The /Unprotect command works the same way. You enter /U and then a range.

Protected cells are displayed at half intensity on terminals that have this capability. With SuperCalc^2 on an IBM PC attached to a color monitor, protected cells will display characters in yellow.

The /Protect command invokes cell protection on the cells in the specified range. The /Unprotect command removes cell protection from the cells in the specified range. Note, however, that since the /Unprotect command is just as easy to use as the /Protect command, there is no way to protect a worksheet from someone else's deliberate changes. The best defense for this is to make a backup copy of the disk containing your models.

The Budget Worksheet can be easily protected against accidental changes. The simplest way to protect a worksheet of this type, where all but a block of cells in the center need to be protected, is to protect the entire worksheet, and then unprotect the cells that don't require protection. First clear your display (**/ZY**) and then load the Budget Worksheet (enter **/L B:FIRSTTRY <RET> A**).

Enter **/P ALL <RET>**. This protects the entire worksheet. Now enter **/U B6:G12 <RET>**.

The following illustration shows how your worksheet should look after these entries are made. If your terminal has the capability, the protected cells will display at half intensity.

```
  :   A   ::   B   ::   C   ::   D   ::   E   ::   F   ::   G   ::   H   :
 1:Simple Budget Worksheet
 2:
 3:              JAN      FEB      MAR      APR      MAY      JUN    Y.T.D
 4:========================================================================
 5:INCOME:
 6:SALARY        1000     1000     1000     1050     1050     1050     6150
 7:========================================================================
 8:EXPENSES:
 9:RENT           500      500      500      500      500      500     3000
10:FOOD           280      280      280      280      280      280     1680
11:UTIL            90       90       90       90       90       90      540
12:AUTO           120      120      120      120      120      120      720
13:------------------------------------------------------------------------
14:TOTAL          990      990      990      990      990      990     5940
15:========================================================================
16:SAVINGS:
17:MONTHLY         10       10       10       60       60       60      210
18:CUMM.           10       20       30       90      150      210
19:========================================================================
20:
< A15       P Rtxt='=
Width:  9  Memory: 25 Last Col/Row:H19     ? for HELP
  1>█
```

Try entering some data to prove to yourself that you can't modify protected cells. Then change the data in an unprotected cell. Notice that the values of the protected cells change, but that the formulas contained in them do not. Try to use the /Edit command on an entry in a protected cell—you must completely clear the entry line after attempting to make an entry into a protected cell.

CHAPTER FIVE

Finding the Answers

In creating the Budget Worksheet, we used the addition operator (+) and the built-in function SUM. This chapter will introduce you to the rest of the arithmetic capabilities of SuperCalc.

Basic Arithmetic

SuperCalc can do all the basic arithmetic operations, addition, subtraction, multiplication, and division, plus raise a number to a power. You use symbols, which are known as *arithmetic operators,* to build calculations for SuperCalc. The arithmetic operators that SuperCalc understands are

+	Addition
−	Subtraction
*	Multiplication
/	Division
^	Raising to a power (exponentiation)

These symbols can be combined with numbers and cell names into formulas. SuperCalc evaluates formulas in proper mathematical order, from left to right, with exponentials evaluated first, then multiplication and division, and then addition and subtraction.

Starting with a clear worksheet, move to cell A3. Enter the formula **4+3*2+5^2**. The result that appears on the screen will be 35.

Here is how SuperCalc evaluates this formula. First it looks for the exponential operator. In the formula that you entered there is an exponential operator between the 5 and the 2. The symbols 5^2 mean 5 to the second power (5×5). SuperCalc evaluates this to 25 and simplifies the rest of the formula to 4+3*2+25.

Then SuperCalc looks for multiplication and division operators. There is a multiplication operator between the 3 and the 2. SuperCalc multiplies 3×2 to get 6. This simplifies the formula again to 4+6+25.

Finally, SuperCalc does the addition and subtraction. Adding 4+6+25 results in 35, which is displayed in cell A3.

SuperCalc evaluates all formulas this way; however, you can use parentheses to change the order of calculation. Any part of a formula that is enclosed in parentheses is calculated before the rest of the formula. To see how the order of calculation and the result are changed by parentheses, move to cell A4 and enter **(4+3)*2+5^2**. The result of this formula is 39.

In this formula, SuperCalc first does the calculation between the parentheses. The 4 is added to the 3, resulting in 7. This simplifies the formula to 7*2+5^2. Try the following formulas to see other examples of how parentheses change formulas.

Cell	*Entry*	*Result*
A5	**4+3*(2+5^2)**	85
A6	**(4+3)*(2+5^2)**	189

Formulas can be made of numbers (as in the examples here) or they can include cell names, as you have seen. When the name of a cell is used in a formula, SuperCalc automatically enters the value contained in the cell into the formula. The cell referred to may contain a number or another formula. If it contains a formula, the current value of that formula is used.

The ability to use the value of one cell in a different formula is one of the features that gives SuperCalc its power. By creatively combining these elements, many different kinds of problems can be solved. As an example, we will calculate the amount of the payments required in order to repay a loan over a specified time period. The equation for this is shown in Figure 5-1.

The meanings of the elements in the formula in Figure 5-1 are as follows:

R	Regular payment
P	Principal amount of the loan
i	Annual simple interest rate
N	Number of payments per year
Y	Number of years of the loan

We start by assigning cell locations to the input values. The principal amount of the loan (P) will be in cell D6, the annual interest rate (i) in cell F9, the number of payments per year (N) in cell D12, and the years of the loan (Y) in cell D15. Cell D18 will be used for the results.

Enter the following initial values and labels on a clear worksheet into the locations given.

Cell	*Entry*
A1	**"Regular Payments on a Loan**
A4	**"Description**
C4	**"Variable**
A6	**"Principal amount:**
C6	**" (P)**
A9	**"Interest rate in %**
C9	**" (i)**
A12	**"Payments per year**
C12	**" (N)**
A15	**"Years of the loan**
C15	**" (Y)**
A17	**'=**
A18	**"Monthly payment**
C18	**" (R)**
A20	**'=**
E17	**"**
E20	**"**
D6	**10000**
F9	**.095**
D12	**12**
D15	**5**

When these values are entered your worksheet should appear as follows:

```
  :  A   ::  B   ::  C   ::  D   ::  E   ::  F   ::  G   ::  H  :
 1:Regular Payments on a Loan
 2:
 3:
 4:Description       Variable
 5:
 6:Principle amount:  (P)        10000
 7:
 8:
 9:Interest Rate in % (i)                          .095
10:
11:
12:Payments per year  (N)           12
13:
14:
15:Years of the loan  (Y)            5
16:
17:==============================================
18:Monthly Payment    (R)
19:
20:==============================================
< A1           Text="Regular Payments on a Loan
Width:  9  Memory: 26 Last Col/Row:F20    ? for HELP
 1>█
```

The equation in Figure 5-1 is in algebraic notation. This must be converted to a different notation to work with SuperCalc. All formulas must be written on one line using the SuperCalc arithmetic symbols.

The equation for the Regular Payments on a Loan Model using the symbols for SuperCalc is

R = (i*P/N)/(1−1/(i/N+1)^(N*Y))

But to use this formula in SuperCalc, each of the variables in the equation must be converted to the cell names that we have assigned to them. After

$$R = \frac{i * P/N}{\left(1 - \frac{1}{\left(\frac{i}{N} + 1\right)^{N*Y}}\right)}$$

Figure 5-1.

Loan repayment equation

doing this, the equation looks like this:

D18 = (F9*D6/D12)/(1−1/(F9/D12+1)^(D12*D15))

However, in SuperCalc you enter this formula into cell D18, which will automatically display the result. Thus you don't need the "D18 =". In cell D18, enter

(F9*D6/D12)/(1−1/(F9/D12+1)^(D12*D15))

Format this cell for dollar display by entering **/F E D18 , $<RET>**. Your screen should appear as follows, with the answer (210.02) displayed in cell D18:

```
   !  A   !!   B   !!   C   !!   D   !!   E   !!   F   !!   G   !!   H   !
  1!Regular Payments on a Loan
  2!
  3!
  4!Description        Variable
  5!
  6!Principle amount:  (P)          10000
  7!
  8!
  9!Interest Rate in % (i)                           .095
 10!
 11!
 12!Payments per year  (N)             12
 13!
 14!
 15!Years of the loan  (Y)              5
 16!
 17!====================================
 18!Monthly Payment    (R)         210.02
 19!
 20!====================================
< D18   $       Form=(F9*D6/D12)/(1-1/(F9/D12+1)^(D12*D15))
Width:  9  Memory: 26 Last Col/Row:F20     ? for HELP
  1>█
```

This all works fine, but it would be simpler to read if the interest rate were displayed as a percent instead of as a decimal fraction. We can let SuperCalc do the converting. We will make cell D9 be the annual simple interest rate in percent. In cell D9 enter **9.5**. Now we will make cell F9 convert this to a decimal fraction. In cell F9 enter **D9/100**. Now the formula in D18 is using a value determined by the formula in F9 to calculate the final answer.

The answer to the problem hasn't changed, but the information on the screen is easier to read and easier to use. You can now change any of the input values and watch the results change. This is just what SuperCalc is designed for. By trying different input values, it is easy to compare different loans to see which one is the best deal.

Besides being a useful worksheet for comparing loans, this worksheet will be used while exploring the capabilities of SuperCalc with this book. Use the /Save command to save this worksheet on disk in a file named **B:LOAN**.

SuperCalc Functions

The model you just created required several input values and one rather complex formula using arithmetic operators. However, in addition to the basic arithmetic operators, other complex models can be built with very simple formulas using SuperCalc's built-in functions. There are list evaluating functions like maximum, minimum, average, and sum, and there are functions for scientific and engineering problems like trigonometric and logarithmic functions.

To use one of these functions, you give it one or more input values. The function then performs a mathematical operation and returns a value that can be displayed or used in a formula just like any other value.

You already know how to use one of the built-in functions: the SUM function. We will analyze the SUM function to learn the terms that will be used in describing the other functions.

The SUM function looks like this:

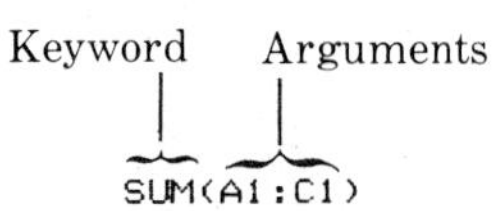

Like most of SuperCalc's built-in functions, the SUM function is formed by a *keyword* followed by one or more *arguments* (or input values) contained in parentheses. (A few built-in functions don't require any arguments.) The letters "SUM" form the keyword for the SUM function. The range of cells to be summed is contained in parentheses and forms the argument.

The next sections demonstrate how to use functions and introduce the mathematical, trigonometric, and list evaluation functions. Clear the worksheet before starting this section.

Function	Description
SQRT(*value*)	Square root of *value*
INT(*value*)	Integer part of *value*
ABS(*value*)	Absolute value of *value*
MOD(*value1,value2*)	Remainder of *value1* divided by *value2*
ROUND(*value1,value2*)	Rounds *value1* to *value2* places
EXP(*value*)	Raises *e* to the power of *value*
LN(*value*)	The natural log of *value*
LOG10 (*value*)	The common log of *value*

Table 5-1.

SuperCalc Mathematical Functions

Mathematical Functions

There are eight built-in mathematical functions in SuperCalc. They are shown in Table 5-1. The SQRT function gives you the square root of the argument. Move to cell B3 and enter **SQRT(2)**. The result (1.414214) will be displayed. In this case we specified the number 2 as the input value. But we can also take the square root of the value of a cell by specifying the name of the cell. For instance, enter **4** in cell A4 and **SQRT(A4)** in cell B4. Cell B4 will display 2, the square root of the value in cell A4 (4).

```
  :    A    ::   B    ::   C    ::   D    ::   E    ::   F    ::   G    ::   H    :
 1:
 2:
 3:          1.414214
 4:        4        2
 5:
 6:
 7:
 8:
 9:
10:
11:
12:
13:
14:
15:
16:
17:
18:
19:
20:
< B4          Form=SQRT(A4)
Width:  9  Memory: 26 Last Col/Row:B4      ? for HELP
 1>█
```

The INT function returns the integer part of the input value. Move to cell B6 and enter **INT(B3)**. This function will display 1. The number 1 is the integer part of the value of cell B3 (1.414214).

You can build a formula with the INT function to round off numbers. Make the following entries on your worksheet:

Cell	*Entry*
A7	**7.645**
B7	**INT(A7*100+.5)/100**

The answer (7.65) is the value in cell A7 rounded to two decimal places. This is shown in the following illustration:

```
   :  A   ::  B   ::  C   ::  D   ::  E   ::  F   ::  G   ::  H   :
  1:
  2:
  3:        1.414214
  4:     4         2
  5:
  6:               1
  7:  7.646     7.65
  8:
  9:
 10:
 11:
  .
  .
  .
 19:
 20:
< B7          Form=INT(A7*100+.5)/100
Width:  9  Memory: 26 Last Col/Row:C7     ? for HELP
  1>■
```

Notice two things about the formula you entered. The argument, or input value, of the INT function is itself a formula (A7*100+.5), and the whole INT function is part of a larger formula. The value returned by the INT function is in turn divided by 100.

Here is how SuperCalc evaluates this formula. First (A7*100+.5) is calculated. This results in 765.1. Then the INT function takes the integer part of 765.1 which is 765. Finally 765 is divided by 100.

If you are using SuperCalc^2 or SuperCalc^3 you can do the same thing with the ROUND function. The ROUND function will round a value to a specified number of places. The ROUND function requires two values for arguments. The first value is the number that is to be rounded, and the second value is the number of places that you want to round to. Move to cell B8 and enter **ROUND(A7,2)**. The result is the same as in cell B7.

```
   !  A  !!  B  !!  C  !!  D  !!  E  !!  F  !!  G  !!  H  !
  1!
  2!
  3!           1.414214
  4!        4         2
  5!
  6!                  1
  7!   7.646       7.65
  8!               7.65
  9!
 10!
 11!
  •
  •
  •
 18!
 19!
 20!
^ B8            Form=ROUND(A7,2)
Width:  9  Memory: 26 Last Col/Row:C8      ? for HELP
  1>■
```

The ABS function takes the *absolute* or positive value of the argument. The ABS function always returns a number that is greater than or equal to 0, even if the input value is less than 0. Enter **ABS(−5)** in cell B9. The result is 5.

Some functions require a positive input value. The SQRT function is one that does. The SQRT function displays "ERROR" if the argument is negative. The ABS function can be used to ensure that the argument of the SQRT function is positive. Move to cell B5 and enter **SQRT(ABS(A4))**. Now change the value in cell A4 to **−4**. Cell B5 still displays the result (2), but cell B4 now displays ERROR. The ABS function kept the argument of the SQRT function positive in cell B5. Your worksheet after these entries should look like this:

```
   !  A  !!  B  !!  C  !!  D  !!  E  !!  F  !!  G  !!  H  !
  1!
  2!
  3!           1.414214
  4!       -4     ERROR
  5!                  2
  6!                  1
  7!   7.646       7.65
  8!               7.65
  9!                  5
 10!
 11!
  •
  •
  •
 18!
 19!
 20!
^ A3
Width:  9  Memory: 26 Last Col/Row:D9      ? for HELP
  1>■
```

If you are using SuperCalc^2 then you can perform modular arithmetic using the MOD function. Like the ROUND function, the MOD function also requires two values as arguments. The MOD function calculates the remainder of the division of one value by a second value. Move to cell B10 and enter **MOD(25,4)**. The remainder of 25 divided by 4 is 1, which is the result displayed on the worksheet:

```
    :   A   ::   B   ::   C   ::   D   ::   E   ::   F   ::   G   ::   H   :
  1:
  2:
  3:            1.414214
  4:       -4      ERROR
  5:                   2
  6:                   1
  7:    7.646       7.65
  8:                7.65
  9:                   5
 10:                   1
 11:
 12:
 13:
 14:
 15:
 16:
 17:
 18:
 19:
 20:
 ^ B10           Form=MOD(25,4)
Width:   9  Memory: 26 Last Col/Row:D10     ? for HELP
   1>
```

With the MOD and the INT functions you have an easy way to convert from inches to feet and inches. Clear your worksheet (enter **/Z Y**) and make the following entries:

Cell	*Entry*
A3	**"Total Inches**
A5	**"Converts to**
B6	**"Feet**
B7	**"Inches**
C3	**89**
C6	**INT(C3/12)**
C7	**MOD(C3,12)**

Your worksheet should look like this after you complete these entries:

```
   :   A    ::   B    ::   C    ::   D    ::   E    ::   F    ::   G    ::   H    :
  1:
  2:
  3:Total Inches             89
  4:
  5:Converts to:
  6:          Feet            7
  7:          Inches          5
  8:
  9:
 10:
 11:
 12:
 13:
 14:
 15:
 16:
 17:
 18:
 19:
 20:
v C8
Width:  9  Memory: 26 Last Col/Row:F7      ? for HELP
  1>
```

The INT function in cell C6 calculates the number of feet by displaying the number of times that 12 divides itself into the value in cell C3. The MOD function calculates the remaining inches by returning the remainder of the division of the value in cell C3 by 12. Try different values in cell C3 to confirm that this works.

Exponential and Logarithmic Functions

The EXP function raises the number *e* to the power of the argument. The number *e* is a mathematical constant called Euler's constant with a value of approximately 2.718.

One of the uses of this function is compound interest calculations. The EXP function makes it easy to calculate continuously compounding interest. Continuous compounding is a very good approximation of daily compounding. The formula to compute the balance at the end of a year of an amount invested at a particular interest rate is

$$B = P * e^{i}$$

where B is the balance after one year, P is the principal invested, and i is the annual simple interest rate. In SuperCalc you specify e^i as EXP(i). Make the following entries to enter this formula on a blank worksheet:

Cell	*Entry*
A3	**"Principal**
A4	**"Interest**
A6	**"Balance**
B3	**1000**
B4	**.085**
B6	**B3*EXP(B4)**
	/F E B6 , $ <RET>

After you are finished, your screen will look like this:

```
   :  A  ::  B  ::  C  ::  D  ::  E  ::  F  ::  G  ::  H  :
 1:
 2:
 3:Principal      1000
 4:Interest       .085
 5:
 6:Balance     1088.72
 7:
 8:
 9:
10:
11:
12:
13:
14:
15:
16:
17:
18:
19:
20:
> B6      $        Form=B3*EXP(B4)
Width:  9  Memory: 26 Last Col/Row:B6      ? for HELP
  1>■
```

The result (1088.72) displayed in cell B6 approximates the final balance. The actual final balance with daily compounding is 1088.71, so you can see that this is a very good approximation.

The LN function is the reverse of the EXP function. The LN function gives the power to which e must be raised to equal the input value. This value is referred to as the *natural logarithm.*

One of the uses of the LN function is to calculate how long it will take for an investment to double in value. Move to cell A8 and enter **"Time to double in value**. Now in cell B9 enter **LN(2)/B4** and in C9 enter **"years**. The result is a model showing the number of years it will take for an investment to double in value given the interest rate in cell B4.

```
    :   A   ::   B   ::   C   ::   D   ::   E   ::   F   ::   G   ::   H   :
   1:
   2:
   3:Principal      1000
   4:Interest        .14
   5:
   6:Balance     1150.27
   7:
   8:Time to double in value
   9:           4.951051 years.
  10:
  11:
  12:
  13:
  14:
  15:
  16:
  17:
  18:
  19:
  20:
 < B9          Form=LN(2)/B4
Width:  9  Memory: 26 Last Col/Row:E15     ? for HELP
  1>■
```

The LOG10 function calculates the base 10 logarithm of a number. The base 10 logarithm of a number is the "power" to which 10 must be raised in order to equal the number. If you have forgotten what logarithms and powers are, here is a quick review.

The "power" of 10 is the number of times 10 occurs as a multiple. For instance, in cell A1 enter **LOG10(100)**. The result is 2. This results in 2 because 100 equals 10 × 10 and thus 10 occurs two times to get 100. In cell A2 enter **LOG10(1000)**. The result is 3 since 10 occurs three times to get 1000 (10 × 10 ×10 is 1000). Now in A4 enter **LOG10(10)**. The answer is 1. Ten only occurs one time to result in 10. To see this another way,

1000 = 10 × 10 × 10	10 occurs 3 times so LOG10(1000) is 3
100 = 10 × 10	10 occurs 2 times so LOG10(100) is 2
10 = 10	10 occurs 1 time so LOG10(10) is 1

Now in cell A3 enter **LOG10(1)**. The answer is 0. To get the number 1, the multiple 10 occurs 0 times. How do you make a multiple occur 0 times? You divide it by itself. Ten divided by 10 is 1. In fact any number divided by itself will equal 1, so any number raised to the power of 0 is also 1, and so the log of 1 in any base, including base 10, is always 0.

If the logarithm of 1 is 0, then what is the logarithm of 0, LOG10(0)? Unfortunately, the number of multiples of 10 you would have to use to equal 0 is a very small number called "minus infinity." This number is so small that it is not usable in SuperCalc; SuperCalc will only display ERROR.

As you can see from the examples you have entered into cells A1, A2, and A3, the logarithms of base 10 are very handy to express large numbers (and small numbers except 0) because they tell you the number of places in the number after the first digit. For this reason, the logarithms of base 10, also called *common logarithms*, are used quite frequently. Base 10 logarithms are used to compare or present numbers that vary widely by the order of their magnitudes. Such measurements as the force of earthquakes (the well-known Richter Scale), the brightness of stars, or the intensity of sound are more readable when expressed in base 10 logarithms. For example, the equation for calculating decibels (dB) from measurements of sound intensity (loudness) is

$$dB=10*\text{LOG10}(M/.0002)$$

where M is the measured intensity in dynes per cm^2. The number .0002 dynes per cm^2 is the threshold below which you cannot hear any sound at all.

The following illustration shows the approximate intensity of various noise levels:

```
  :  A   ::  B   ::  C   :: D ::     E     : :     G      : :  I  :
 1:                               Intensity
 2:                              measured in         Relative
 3:Sound                          Dynes/cm^2         Magnitude    Decibels
 4:----------------------------  -------------  ----------------  ---------
 5:Threshold of Hearing. . . . . .        .0002
 6:Empty Recording Studio. . . . .         .002
 7:Empty Living Room . . . . . . .          .02
 8:Quiet Conversation. . . . . . .            2
 9:Noon on 8th Ave & 47th St . . .         2000
10:5 PM on the B'Way Local (Subway)      200000
11:Jack Hammer on 8th Ave & 47th St   200000000
12:Rock Concert, 1st Row . . . . .   2000000000
13:Threshold of Pain . . . . . . .   6000000000
14:Jet Engine. . . . . . . . . . .  200000000000
15:
16:
17:
18:
19:
20:
> E14          Form=200000000000
Width: 13  Memory: 25 Last Col/Row:J14    ? for HELP
 1>
```

To enter this in SuperCalc, first clear the worksheet (/**ZY**) and format the columns as follows:

/F C D , 4
/F C E , TR 13
/F C F , 2
/F C G , TR I 17
/F C H , 2
/F C I , TR I

Then enter the text and numbers shown in the illustration. To calculate the relative magnitude of the measured intensities, first enter **E5/.0002** in cell G5. Then replicate this down column G. (Enter /**R G5 , G6:G14 <RET>**).

This will create the formula E6/.0002 in cell G6, E7/.0002 in cell G7, and so on, thus showing the magnitude of each sound relative to the threshold of hearing, 0.0002 dynes/cm^2. To calculate decibels from this, move to cell I5 and enter **10*LOG10(G5)** and replicate this down column I (enter /**R I5 , I6:I14 <RET>**). When you are finished, your screen should look like this:

```
   |  A  ||  B  ||  C  || D ||      E      ||        G        ||    I    |
  1|                              Intensity
  2|                             measured in           Relative
  3|Sound                         Dynes/cm^2          Magnitude   Decibels
  4|---------------------------  -------------  ----------------  ---------
  5|Threshold of Hearing. . . . .        .0002                 1          0
  6|Empty Recording Studio. . . .         .002                10         10
  7|Empty Living Room . . . . . .          .02               100         20
  8|Quiet Conversation. . . . . .            2             10000         40
  9|Noon on 8th Ave & 47th St . .         2000          10000000         70
 10|5 PM on the B'Way Local (Subway)    200000        1000000000         90
 11|Jack Hammer on 8th Ave & 47th St 200000000     1000000000000        120
 12|Rock Concert, 1st Row . . . .   2000000000    10000000000000        130
 13|Threshold of Pain . . . . . .   6000000000    30000000000000        135
 14|Jet Engine. . . . . . . . . . 200000000000  1000000000000000        150
 15|
 16|
 17|
 18|
 19|
 20|
> I5     I        Form=10*LOG10(G5)
Width:  9  Memory: 25 Last Col/Row:J14     ? for HELP
 1>
```

Notice that the numbers in column I are much easier to read and understand than the numbers in the other columns, E and G.

Trigonometric Functions

SuperCalc has six built-in trigonometric functions. These functions are summarized in Table 5-2. SIN(*value*), COS(*value*), and TAN(*value*) return the common trigonometric functions of sine, cosine, and tangent of *value* respectively. ASIN(*value*), ACOS(*value*), and ATAN(*value*) return the arcsine, arccosine, and arctangent of *value* respectively. The arcsine of a value is that angle whose sine is equal to the value. The same idea holds for arccosine and arctangent.

SuperCalc also has the PI function, which returns the constant *pi* (approximately 3.141593). You can use the PI function to convert degrees to radians. Normally when we use angles we express them in degrees (45°, 30°, or 90°, for example). However, computer programs usually express angles in radians instead of degrees. This means that if you want to find the sine, cosine, or tangent of an angle, you must first convert the degrees to radians. To do this, multiply the angle by *pi* and divide by 180. For example, in order to calculate the sine of 45 degrees you would enter SIN(45*PI/180).

NOTE: The tangent of *pi*/2 and 3**pi*/2 radians (90 degrees and 270 degrees) is infinity. Since that is beyond SuperCalc's range, it displays "ERROR" instead.

Figure 5-2 demonstrates the trigonometric built-in functions and also gives you an idea of the accuracy of SuperCalc. The trigonometric functions are shown to 14 digits in cells E9 through E15. Cell A6 contains an angle in

Function	Description
SIN(*value*)	Sine of *value*
COS(*value*)	Cosine of *value*
TAN(*value*)	Tangent of *value*
ASIN(*value*)	Arcsine of *value*
ACOS(*value*)	Arccosine of *value*
ATAN(*value*)	Arctangent of *value*
PI	*Pi*, which is always 3.14159

Table 5-2.

SuperCalc Trigonometric Functions

```
  |  A  ||  B  ||  C  ||  D  ||        E        || F ||        G          |
 1|Trigonometric Functions
 2|
 3|Angle in
 4|Degrees              In Radians
 5|---------            ---------
 6|      25              .4363323
 7|
 8|
 9|                               SIN (C6)  .42261826174070     .4226182617406995
10|                               COS (C6)  .90630778703665     .9063077870366506
11|                               TAN (C6)  .46630765815500     .4663076581549983
12|
13|                     180/PI*ASIN(E9)     25.000000000000     25.00000000000003
14|                     180/PI*ACOS(E10)    25.000000000000     24.99999999999994
15|                     180/PI*ATAN(E11)    25.000000000000     25.00000000000001
16|
17|                                        <-- width 16 -->    <--  width 18  -->
18|                                        (14 digits of       (16 digits of
19|                                         precsision)         precision)
20|
v G15           Form=180/PI*ATAN(E11)
Width: 18  Memory: 26 Last Col/Row:G19    ? for HELP
  1>█
```

Figure 5-2.

Trigonometric functions

degrees, which is converted to radians in cell C6. The sine, cosine, and tangent are displayed in cells E9, E10, and E11. Cells E13, E14, and E15 display the arc functions. These formulas convert trigonometric ratios back to the angle degrees. Notice that when the trigonometric ratios are converted back, there is a round-off error after the 15th digit.

List Evaluation Functions

Table 5-3 shows the SuperCalc functions that evaluate lists. These functions help reduce the work required to build worksheets. Although we have looked at the SUM function several times, it has capabilities that we have

Function	Description
SUM(*list*)	Sum of cells in *list*
AVERAGE(*list*)	Average of cells in *list*
COUNT(*list*)	Count of cells in *list*
MIN(*list*)	Minimum value of cells in *list*
MAX(*list*)	Maximum value of cells in *list*

Table 5-3.

SuperCalc List Evaluation Functions

not explored yet. Begin by clearing your worksheet and making the entries shown in the following illustration:

```
  :  A  ::  B  ::  C  ::  D  ::  E  ::  F  ::  G  ::  H  :
 1:Rental Income Analysis
 2:                         Monthly Rents
 3:
 4:Location                     Unit 1    Unit 2    Unit 3
 5:==========================================================
 6:101 First Street . . . . .   200.00    220.00    200.00
 7:202 Second Ave . . . . . .   200.00    240.00    190.00
 8:303 Third Way. . . . . . .   300.00
 9:404 Fourth Boulevard . . .   400.00    410.00
10:505 Fifth Alley. . . . . .   200.00
11:808 Eighth Highway . . . .   500.00
12:==========================================================
13:
14:         Total Rents
15:         Average Rent
16:         Count:                        Units
17:         Minimum Rent
18:         Maximum Rent
19:
20:
> E16          Text=" Units
Width:  9  Memory: 26 Last Col/Row:H18    ? for HELP
  1>
```

This model gives a breakdown of the monthly rental income from a group of rental properties and will be used to explore the list evaluation functions.

You need two format commands for this model. Enter **/F G $ <RET>** and **/F E D4:F4 , TR <RET>**. After you move to cell D14, enter the function **SUM(D6:D11,E6:E11,F6:F11)**. This SUM function is taking the sum of three groups of cells. The result is the sum of all the monthly rents. The SUM function and the other list evaluation functions can use a *list* as an argument. A *list* can be made up of as many groups of cells as you like. Here are some other examples of lists:

SUM(A3,B4,C5)	A list of individual cells
SUM(A3:A12,C3:C12)	A list of cell ranges
SUM(A3,B3:B12,C4,C8:C12)	A list including cells and cell ranges

The AVERAGE function takes the average of a group of cells. Move to cell D15 and enter **AVERAGE(D6:F11)**. The average of the rents is displayed in cell D15. Notice that the same group of cells that is defined by a list in the SUM function is defined as a block in the AVERAGE function.

Move to cell D16 and enter **COUNT(D5:F12)**. The COUNT function gives a count of *non-blank* cells. A non-blank cell is a cell that contains any value.

The COUNT function treats text entries as blank cells. A cell with a 0 in it, however, is considered non-blank and is counted.

The range in the formula in cell D16 is different from that in cell D15. We have included an extra row at the top and bottom. The rows that we included do not have any values in them and therefore do not affect any of the calculations. However, including these rows in the range makes our worksheet more flexible. You can now delete the top row that contains values without creating an error, or you can add a row above the top row of values and it will still be within the range. Including extra rows works with all the functions that take a list as an argument.

Move to cell D17 and enter **MIN(D5:F12)**; next move to cell D18 and enter **MAX(D5:F12)**. The MIN and MAX functions give you the minimum and maximum values of a group of cells. In SuperCalc[2] the MIN function does not look at blank cells or cells with text entries, but it does look at cells with a value of 0. However, if you are using an earlier version of SuperCalc the MIN function *does* look at blank cells and cells that contain text. Thus cell D17 will display (.00) if you are using an older version of SuperCalc.

The following illustration shows the completed model:

```
   :  A  ::  B  ::  C  ::  D  ::  E  ::  F  ::  G  ::  H  :
  1:Rental Income Analysis
  2:                      Monthly Rents
  3:
  4:Location                  Unit 1    Unit 2    Unit 3
  5:=========================================================
  6:101 First Street . . . . .   200.00    220.00    200.00
  7:202 Second Ave . . . . . .   200.00    240.00    190.00
  8:303 Third Way. . . . . . .   300.00
  9:404 Fourth Boulevard . . .   400.00    410.00
 10:505 Fifth Alley. . . . . .   200.00
 11:808 Eighth Highway . . . .   500.00
 12:=========================================================
 13:
 14:         Total Rents        3060.00
 15:         Average Rent        278.18
 16:         Count:               11.00 Units
 17:         Minimum Rent        190.00
 18:         Maximum Rent        500.00
 19:
 20:
^ D15         Form=AVERAGE(D6:F11)
Width:  9  Memory: 26 Last Col/Row:H18    ? for HELP
  1>█
```

CHAPTER SIX

Expanding the Worksheet

The ability to copy one section of a worksheet to another makes building large and complicated worksheets a manageable project. The /Copy command and the /Replicate command are tools for doing this.

Copying a Block of Cells (/Copy)

/Copy is similar to /Replicate in many ways. They both copy cells from one part of the worksheet to another and they both share the same options. There are differences, however, that make both commands useful. /Replicate can make multiple copies of the source range, while /Copy can make only one. However, /Copy can copy a whole block in one operation, while /Replicate can copy a column or a row at most.

Normally the /Copy command will automatically adjust formulas as /Replicate does; however, both have options to control the adjustment of formulas.

Load the Loan model (/L **B:LOAN <RET> A**) in order to experiment with the /Copy command. You will copy the functional area of this worksheet so that you can compare two different loans side by side. To start the /Copy command, type **/C**. SuperCalc will prompt you to enter a range to copy from.

```
  :  A  ::  B  ::  C  ::  D  ::  E  ::  F  ::  G  ::  H  :
 1:Regular Payments on a Loan
 2:
 3:
 4:Description        Variable
 5:
 6: Principal amount:  (P)        10000
 7:
 8:
 9:Interest Rate in % (i)          9.5              .095
10:
11:
12:Payments per year  (N)           12
13:
14:
15:Years of the loan  (Y)            5
16:
17:====================================
18:Monthly Payment     (R)       210.02
19:
20:====================================
< F9          Form=D9/100
From? (Enter Range)
 7>/Copy,
```

The source range can be a single cell, a partial row or column, a complete row or column, or a block. For this example, enter the range **D6:F20** and press **<RET>**. This defines the upper-left and lower-right corners of the block of cells that you want to copy.

You are now prompted to enter a cell to define where you want to copy to.

```
   :  A   ::  B   ::  C   ::  D   ::  E   ::  F   ::  G   ::  H   :
  1:Regular Payments on a Loan
  2:
  3:
  4:Description        Variable
  5:
  6:Principal amount:  (P)         10000
  7:
  8:
  9:Interest Rate in % (i)           9.5               .095
 10:
 11:
 12:Payments per year  (N)            12
 13:
 14:
 15:Years of the loan  (Y)             5
 16:
 17:=====================================
 18:Monthly Payment     (R)        210.02
 19:
 20:=====================================
v F9           Form=D9/100
To? (Enter Cell), then Return; or "," for Options
 14>/Copy,d6:f20,█
```

The cell you enter must be the upper-left cell of the block that you want to copy to.

Type **G6** to define a destination with cell G6 in the upper-left corner, and press **<RET>** to execute the command. (The options will be explained later in this chapter.) You will now have a screen like the following one, with a duplicate set of cells in the block with G6 in the upper left.

```
   :  A   ::  B   ::  C   ::  D   ::  E   ::  F   ::  G   ::  H   :
  1:Regular Payments on a Loan
  2:
  3:
  4:Description        Variable
  5:
  6:Principal amount:  (P)         10000                     10000
  7:
  8:
  9:Interest Rate in % (i)           9.5               .095    9.5
 10:
 11:
 12:Payments per year  (N)            12                        12
 13:
 14:
 15:Years of the loan  (Y)             5                         5
 16:
 17:=====================================
 18:Monthly Payment     (R)        210.02                    210.02
 19:
 20:=====================================
> F9           Form=D9/100
Width:  9  Memory: 26 Last Col/Row:I20    ? for HELP
  1>█
```

Although you cannot see it, the block you created also includes cell I9. If all of the cells in column F had been used, the new block would extend to I20 in the lower right. Now it is possible to make changes to one loan and compare the results with the other. Move the active cell to G9 and enter **10.5**. This changes the interest rate and calculates a new payment value in cell G8. Your display screen should now appear as follows:

```
   :  A  ::  B  ::  C  ::  D  ::  E  ::  F  ::  G  ::  H  :
  1:Regular Payments on a Loan
  2:
  3:
  4:Description      Variable
  5:
  6:Principal amount:  (P)       10000                 10000
  7:
  8:
  9:Interest Rate in % (i)         9.5         .095     10.5
 10:
 11:
 12:Payments per year  (N)          12                    12
 13:
 14:
 15:Years of the loan  (Y)           5                     5
 16:
 17:====================================
 18:Monthly Payment    (R)      210.02                214.94
 19:
 20:====================================
> H9
Width:  9  Memory: 26 Last Col/Row:I20    ? for HELP
  1>█
```

With the /Replicate command, you can copy a row or a column of cells but not a block. The ability to copy a block of cells is what makes the /Copy command unique.

The /Copy command enables you to construct complicated worksheets with a minimum of effort. With this command and the /Replicate command, it becomes easy to build large and powerful models with SuperCalc.

WARNING: Don't try to copy a group of cells over itself. The results are unpredictable. Be sure that the source and destination ranges do not overlap.

It is possible to copy a formula and adjust its references so that the cells it refers to are not anywhere on the worksheet. Save your model and clear the screen. Enter the formula **A4+C4** into cell B4. Now copy this formula into cell A5 by entering

/C B4 <RET> A5 <RET>

Now position the active cell to cell A5 and look at the formula that appears on the status line. It should look like this:

```
ERROR+B5
```

The original formula in cell B4 referred to cell A4, the cell to its left. Since there can be no cell to the left of column A, SuperCalc substituted the ERROR function for this cell reference. The ERROR function causes the word "ERROR" to be displayed in the cell.

Copying With /Replicate

With the /Replicate command, a cell can be replicated into several cells along a row or a column. A row or column of cells can also be replicated into a block. If the source is a row, you specify the destination as a column to generate a block of rows down this column. Conversely, if the source is a column, the destination must be a row.

To review, when you enter /R, SuperCalc completes the word "/Replicate," and prompts for a source range. You specify a cell, a part of a row, or a part of a column and press <RET>. (If by mistake you specify a block, SuperCalc will display the message "Range Error". You now need to correct the source range and press <RET> again.)

After you have entered a valid source range, you are prompted to enter a destination range. You may enter a single cell address to make a single copy of the source range. As demonstrated in Chapter 2, you may make multiple copies of one cell by specifying a row or column range for the destination. /Replicate is different from the /Copy command, which will only make a single copy.

Here is a short demonstration of how to create a column, a row, and a block using /Replicate. Clear the worksheet with **/Z Y** and make the following entries. These are all text entries showing the name of the cells they are in.

Cell	*Entry*
A1	**"A1**
B6	**"B6**
B7	**"B7**
B8	**"B8**
B9	**"B9**
B10	**"B10**

Type /**R** to start the /Replicate command and then define the source range as **A1 <RET>**. Enter **C2:H2** as the destination range. Press **<RET>**. You have replicated a single cell, A1, into a row of cells all displaying "A1".

```
   :  A  ::  B  ::  C  ::  D  ::  E  ::  F  ::  G  ::  H  :
  1:A1
  2:              A1       A1       A1       A1       A1       A1
  3:
  4:
  5:
  6:         B6
  7:         B7
  8:         B8
  9:         B9
 10:         B10
 •
 •
 •
< A1          Text="A1
Width:  9  Memory: 26 Last Col/Row:H10     ? for HELP
  1>■
```

To make a column, enter **/R A1 <RET> A6:A16 <RET>**. You should now have a column of cells displaying "A1" down column A.

```
   :  A  ::  B  ::  C  ::  D  ::  E  ::  F  ::  G  ::  H  :
  1:A1
  2:              A1       A1       A1       A1       A1       A1
  3:
  4:
  5:
  6:A1       B6
  7:A1       B7
  8:A1       B8
  9:A1       B9
 10:A1       B10
 11:A1
 12:A1
 13:A1
 14:A1
 15:A1
 16:A1
 17:
 •
 •
 •
< A1          Text="A1
Width:  9  Memory: 26 Last Col/Row:H16     ? for HELP
  1>■
```

/Replicate can form a block of cells by replicating a row across a column, or vice versa. Type **/R B6:B10 <RET>**. This defines the source range as a portion of column B from row 6 through row 10. Now enter **D4:F4 <RET>**. The column has been reproduced three times to form a block of cells from D4 to F8.

Your display screen should now appear as shown in the following:

```
   :  A  ::  B  ::  C  ::  D  ::  E  ::  F  ::  G  ::  H  :
  1:A1
  2:                 A1     A1     A1     A1     A1     A1
  3:
  4:                        B6     B6     B6
  5:                        B7     B7     B7
  6:A1        B6            B8     B8     B8
  7:A1        B7            B9     B9     B9
  8:A1        B8            B10    B10    B10
  9:A1        B9
 10:A1        B10
 11:A1
 12:A1
 13:A1
 14:A1
 15:A1
 16:A1
 17:
 18:
 19:
 20:
< A1          Text="A1
Width:  9  Memory: 26 Last Col/Row:H16    ? for HELP
  1>█
```

Using Adjustment Options With /Copy and /Replicate

You may have noticed by now that the prompt for a "To?" range in both the /Copy and /Replicate commands includes the phrase

then Return; or "," for Options

If you want to use the options, you must enter a comma instead of <RET>. Usually, a comma and a <RET> are interchangeable in commands. But here, pressing <RET> tells SuperCalc to automatically adjust cell references, while pressing the comma allows you to select adjustment options. The same is true with the /Copy and /Load commands.

If you press a comma, you are presented with four options for cell reference adjustment. The first option is "N(o Adjust)". Selecting this option will copy the exact contents of the source cells to the destination cells. In other words, if a cell that you are copying contains the formula B4 + B3, the formula in the destination cell will also be B4 + B3.

The second option is "A(sk for Adjust)". If you select this option, SuperCalc asks you whether you want to adjust each cell that appears in all the formulas to be copied in turn. The source location and the cell reference in question are displayed on the prompt line, and you are prompted to answer "Adjust Y(es) or N(o)". The entire formula is displayed on the entry line with the cell in question highlighted. You must tell the program "Y"(es) to adjust each cell or "N"(o) to not adjust the cell. This sounds harder than it is; it actually goes very quickly.

A word of warning about the "Ask for Adjust" option: the command cannot be aborted after you have selected this option. CTRL-Z has no effect and you must complete the command. Make sure that you are doing the right thing before you select the A option.

The next option is "V(alues only)". This option moves only the actual numeric values from the source cells to the destination cells. No matter what kind of formula is in the source cell, only the numeric value is copied. Cell format information and text entries are also copied with this option.

SuperCalc^2 and later versions have four options: +, −, *, and /. The + takes the value in the source cells and adds it to the value in the destination cells. The −, *, and / options subtract from, multiply, and divide the destination cells using the source cells.

Figure 6-1 shows examples of these first three options. Cells C6 through C9 are the source cells. The figure is displaying the formulas in the cells so you can see what was actually copied.

To try these examples, first clear the worksheet and then enter the following:

Cell	*Entry*
A1	**"Adjustment Options**
C6	**15**
C7	**C6 + 5**
C8	**C7 − C6**
C9	**"George**
	/G F
	/C C6:C9 , F6 , V
	/C C6:C9 , C14 , N
	/C C6:C9 , F14 <RET>

```
  :   A   ::   B   ::   C   ::   D   ::   E   ::   F   ::   G   ::   H   :
 1:Adjustment Options
 2:
 3:
 4:
 5:                  Source                    Values Only          + Option
 6:                   15                        15                   30
 7:                   C6+5                      20                   40
 8:                   C7-C6                     5                    10
 9:                  George                    George               George
10:
11:
12:
13:                  No Adjust                 With Adjust (RETURN)
14:                   15                        15
15:                   C6+5                      F14+5
16:                   C7-C6                     F15-F14
17:                  George                    George
18:
19:
20:
v C6          Form=15
Width:  9  Memory: 26 Last Col/Row:H17     ? for HELP
  1>
```

Figure 6-1.

Adjustment examples

If you are using SuperCalc², also enter the following:

> **/C C6:C9, H6, N**
> **/C C6:C9, H6, +**

Finally, label each section as follows:

C5	**"Source**
F5	**"Values Only**
H5	**"+ Option**
C13	**"No Adjust**
F13	**"With Adjust (RETURN)**
H13	**"Ask**

Cells F6:F9 were copied using the "Values Only" option. Cells C14:C17 were copied with the "No Adjust" option. These formulas are identical to the formulas in the source cells. Cells F14:F17 were copied using automatic adjustment. These formulas refer to cells in the same relative position as the formulas in the source cells.

Using the "Ask for Adjust" Option

You will occasionally find it necessary to use the "Ask for Adjust" option. Figure 6-2 shows an example. This is a simple cost analysis model. Figure 6-2 also shows the formulas used in the model.

On a clear worksheet, enter the text and formulas shown in Figure 6-2. Then enter /**G F** so that the formulas are visible. Finally, set the column widths for column F to **17**, G to **15**, and B to **5** so that you can see all of the formulas. Now enter the following /Replicate command with the final comma after the destination range (do not press <RET>):

/R, D9:G9 , D10:D20 ,

This /Replicate command duplicates the formulas in row 10 to create formulas for additional products in rows 11 and 12. Figure 6-3 shows the /Replicate command as it is being entered. Cells C10 through F10 will be replicated.

The reason the "Ask for Adjust" option is necessary with this procedure is because some of these formulas refer to cells C3 and C4, which contain the

```
  ;  A   ;;   B   ;;   C   ;;   D   ;;   E   ;;        F        ;;      G      ;
 1;Costing Model for "Ask to Adjust" example
 2;
 3;Labor rate . . . . 12.50
 4;Mark-up %. . . . . 25
 5;
 6;Description of     Labor    Labor     Mat'l    Mark-up           Selling
 7;Product            Hours    Cost      Cost     Amount            Price
 8;===========================================================================
 9;Toaster Oven        2.6     C9*C3     14.35    (D9+E9)*C4/100 SUM(D9:F9)
10;
11;
12;
13;
14;
15;
16;
17;
18;
19;
20;
^ F7     TL      Text="Amount
Width: 15  Memory: 26 Last Col/Row:G11     ? for HELP
 1>
```

Figure 6-2.

Costing Model formulas

```
  :    A   ::    B   ::    C   ::    D   ::    E   ::       F       ::      G   :
 1:Costing Model for "Ask to Adjust" example
 2:
 3:Labor rate . . . . 12.50
 4:Mark-up %. . . . . 25
 5:
 6:Description of     Labor     Labor     Mat'l     Mark-up          Selling
 7:Product            Hours     Cost      Cost      Amount           Price
 8:==========================================================================
 9:Toaster Oven        2.6      C9*C3     14.35     (D9+E9)*C4/100 SUM(D9:F9)
10:
11:
12:
13:
14:
15:
16:
17:
18:
19:
20:
v D9    $          Form=C9*C3
N(o Adjust), A(sk for Adjust), V(alues), +, -, *, /
 26>/Replicate,D9:G9,d10:d20,
```

Figure 6-3.

Replicating row 9

labor rate and mark-up percentage. Consider the formula in cell D9, which calculates labor costs by multiplying rate by hours. The labor rate will always be in cell C3, but the labor hours for row 10 will be in cell C10 and the hours for row 11 will be in cell C11. Thus, the formula in cell D10, which calculates labor cost, needs to contain C10 * C3, while cell D11 should contain C11 * C3, and D12 should contain C12 * C3.

In rows 10, 11, and 12, the first cell reference must be adjusted, but the reference to labor rate must always be to cell C3. Thus, to replicate cell D9 correctly, you need to adjust the reference to cell C9, but not adjust the reference to cell C3.

The same is true for replicating cell F9. This cell refers to cell C4 and two other cells on row 9 (D9 and E9). The references to these last two cells must be adjusted, but C4 should not be adjusted as shown in the following:

```
   :  A  ::  B  ::  C  ::  D  ::  E  ::    F    ::   G   :
  1:Costing Model for "Ask to Adjust" example
  2:
  3:Labor rate . . . . 12.50
  4:Mark-up %. . . . . 25
  5:
  6:Description of    Labor    Labor    Mat'l    Mark-up         Selling
  7:Product           Hours    Cost     Cost     Amount          Price
  8:====================================================================
  9:Toaster Oven        2.6    C9*C3    14.35    (D9+E9)*C4/100  SUM(D9:F9)
 10:                           C10*C3
 11:                           C11*C3
 12:                           C12*C3
 13:                             ...
 14:
 15:                             ...
 16:
 17:
 18:                             ...
 19:
 20:                           C20*C3
^ D9    $     Form=C9*C3
Width:  9  Memory: 26 Last Col/Row:G20    ? for HELP
  1>
```

Notice that in the formulas in cells D10 through D20, the reference for labor hours has been adjusted, but cell C3 is still referred to for the labor rate.

To make SuperCalc do this, you must select the "Ask for Adjust" option by pressing the letter **A**. You will then see the following prompt:

```
   :  A  ::  B  ::  C  ::  D  ::  E  ::    F    ::   G   :
  1:Costing Model for "Ask for Adjust" Example
  2:
  3:Labor rate   . . .  12.50
  4:Mark-up%. . . . .   25
  5:
  6:Description of    Labor    Labor    Mat'l    Mark-up          Selling
  7:Product           Hours    Cost     Cost     Amount           Price
  8:=====================================================================
  9:Toaster Oven        2.6    C9*C3    14.35    (D9+E9)*C4/100   SUM(D9:F9)
 10:
 11:
 12:
 13:
 14:
 15:
 16:
 17:
 18:
 19:
 20:
Source cell D9. Adjust C9 (Y or N)?y
Replicating...D
 27>C9*C3
```

SuperCalc is asking you if you want to adjust the reference to cell C9 in the formula C9 * C3. You do, so say yes by pressing the letter **Y**. Another prompt will appear:

```
   |  A  ||  B  ||  C  ||  D  ||  E  ||    F     ||   G   |
  1|Costing Model for "Ask to Adjust" example
  2|
  3|Labor rate . . . . 12.50
  4|Mark-up %. . . . . 25
  5|
  6|Description of     Labor    Labor    Mat'l    Mark-up          Selling
  7|Product            Hours    Cost     Cost     Amount           Price
  8|=========================================================================
  9|Toaster Oven        2.6      C9*C3    14.35    (D9+E9)*C4/100 SUM(D9:F9)
 10|
 11|
 12|
 13|
 14|
 15|
 16|
 17|
 18|
 19|
 20|
Source cell D9. Adjust C3 (Y or N)?n
Replicating...D
 27>C9*C3
```

This prompt is for the reference to cell C3. You do not want to adjust this, so press the letter **N**.

The adjustment instructions for replicating cell D9 are complete. However, the /Replicate command you entered also includes cells F9 and G9 in the source range. Additional prompts now appear for these cells. Answer these as follows:

Source Cell	*Formula*	*Reference to Adjust*	*Entry*
F9	(D9+E9)*C4/100	D9	**Y**
		E9	**Y**
		C4	**N**
G9	SUM(D9:F9)	D9	**Y**
		F9	**N**

When you have finished these entries, your worksheet should appear as follows:

```
  :  A  ::  B  ::  C  ::  D  ::  E  ::        F        ::    G    :
 1:Costing Model for "Ask for Adjust" Example
 2:
 3:Labor rate   . . .  12.50
 4:Mark-up%. . . . .   25
 5:
 6:Description of      Labor    Labor    Mat'l    Mark-up           Selling
 7:Product             Hours    Cost     Cost     Amount            Price
 8:========================================================================
 9:Toaster Oven         2.6      C9*C3    14.35    (D9+E9)*C4/100    SUM(D9:F9)
10:                             C10*C3   14.35    (D10+E10)*C4/100  SUM(D10:F10)
11:                             C11*C3   14.35    (D11+E11)*C4/100  SUM(D11:F11)
12:                             C12*C3   14.35    (D12+E12)*C4/100  SUM(D12:F12)
13:                             C13*C3   14.35    (D13+E13)*C4/100  SUM(D13:F13)
14:                             C14*C3   14.35    (D14+E14)*C4/100  SUM(D14:F14)
15:                             C15*C3   14.35    (D15+E15)*C4/100  SUM(D15:F15)
16:                             C16*C3   14.35    (D16+E16)*C4/100  SUM(D16:F16)
17:                             C17*C3   14.35    (D17+E17)*C4/100  SUM(D17:F17)
18:                             C18*C3   14.35    (D18+E18)*C4/100  SUM(D18:F18)
19:                             C19*C3   14.35    (D19+E19)*C4/100  SUM(D19:F19)
20:                             C20*C3   14.35    (D20+E20)*C4/100  SUM(D20:F20)
< D9          Form=C9*C3
Width:  9  Memory: 25 Last Col/Row:G20     ? for HELP
 1>█
```

There are several factors to take into account when you are deciding whether or not to adjust a particular cell reference. In general, if several rows or columns of formulas all refer to the same cell (such as the labor rate in the example), then you want to select "N" for no adjustment when SuperCalc prompts you for the adjustment of that cell. Also, as a rule of thumb, when a formula refers to a cell that is in the same row or column as the source range, you should usually adjust it (answer "Y").

CHAPTER SEVEN

Rearranging the Worksheet

As you develop applications you will probably need to reorganize or rearrange the information in your models. The SuperCalc program allows you to do this in a number of ways. You can insert or delete complete columns or rows, move columns or rows to different positions, and change the way that SuperCalc displays the worksheet. In this chapter we will explore the commands that provide these capabilities.

/Blank Revisited

Lesson 4 in Chapter 1 demonstrated how to use the /Blank command to clear individual cells. You can also use this command to clear several cells at once. The /Blank command not only clears the information out of a cell or a group of cells, but it also clears entry level formats (entered with /FE). The /Blank command does not, however, clear formats that you declared at the column, row, or global level; you can clear these only with the /Format command.

When you enter "/B" the program will complete the word "/Blank" and request a range. As you saw in Chapter 1, just pressing <RET> instead of entering a range will blank the active cell. To remove the information from a block of cells, you enter a range, such as C5:F10. This will clear all the data from rows 5 through 10 in columns C through F.

The /Blank command clears only unprotected cells. If you specify a range containing both protected and unprotected cells, the unprotected cells will be cleared but the protected cells will remain unchanged. If you use /Blank to clear cells that are protected, SuperCalc will advise you by displaying the message "Protected Entry".

Note that blanking unprotected cells is irreversible; there is no way to recover information lost by blanking the wrong cell or cells.

Inserting and Deleting Rows and Columns

When you develop a new worksheet or modify an existing worksheet, it may become necessary to add or remove a row or a column. The /Insert and /Delete commands are used to do this.

The /Insert command inserts complete rows or columns. New rows are always inserted just above the row specified. New columns are always inserted just to the left of the column specified. All formulas on the worksheet are adjusted automatically. In most cases, inserting columns or rows will not change how the worksheet operates.

To illustrate the use of the /Insert command, we will use the example shown in Figure 7-1.

```
   :   A    ::    B    ::    C    ::    D    ::    E    ::    F    ::    G    ::    H    :
  1:National League West               Standings of the Clubs
  2:
  3:
  4:                                            Games     Games     Games  Won-Loss
  5:City              Team               Rank      Won      Lost      Back         %
  6:Atlanta           Braves                1       62        43         0       590
  7:San Diego         Padres                2       63        44         0       589
  8:Los Angeles       Dodgers               3       65        47        .5       580
  9:San Francisco     Giants                4       57        49       5.5       538
 10:Mudville          Nine                  5        0         1        10         0
 11:Cincinnati        Reds                  6       40        67        23       374
 12:Houston           Astros                7       35        72        28       327
 13:
 14:Total                                          322       323
  •
  •
  •
v G12          Form=(E6-E12+F12-F6)/2
Width:  9  Memory: 25 Last Col/Row:J14     ? for HELP
  1>█
```

Figure 7-1.

Baseball standings

To create this example, enter the city, team, rank, games won, games lost, and the headings for columns A through H. Format cells D4:H5 to TextRight (enter **/F E D4:H5 , TR <RET>**). Then you may enter the numbers in columns G and H directly, or you may have them calculated using the following formulas:

Cell	*Entry*
H12	**E12/(E12 + F12) * 1000**
H12	**/R, H12 , H6:H11 <RET>**
G12	**(E7 − E12 + F12 − F7)/2**
G12	**/R, G12 , G6:G11 , A N Y Y N**

The formula in cell G12 calculates the number of games that the Houston Astros are behind the division leader (Atlanta). The second /Replicate command uses the "Ask for Adjust" option (which was discussed in Chapter 6) to create a similar formula for the other teams in cells G11, G10, G9, and so on. Each of these new formulas must refer to cells E7 and F7, so references to these cells are not adjusted.

Now enter **/I R**. This begins the /Insert command and specifies that a row is to be inserted. Press the number **6** to specify that the row is to be inserted where the existing row 6 is. Press **<RET>**, and your screen should look like this:

```
    :  A   ::   B   ::   C   ::   D   ::   E   ::   F   ::   G   ::   H   :
   1:National League West             Standings of the Clubs
   2:
   3:
   4:                                         Games      Games      Games Won-Loss
   5:City             Team           Rank       Won       Lost       Back        %
   6:
   7:Atlanta          Braves            1        62         43          0      590
   8:San Diego        Padres            2        63         44          0      589
   9:Los Angeles      Dodgers           3        65         47         .5      580
  10:San Francisco    Giants            4        57         49        5.5      538
  11:Mudville         Nine              5         0          1         10        0
  12:Cincinnati       Reds              6        40         67         23      374
  13:Houston          Astros            7        35         72         28      327
  14:
  15:Total                                      322        323
  16:
   .
   .
   .
  20:
v A6
Width:  9  Memory: 25 Last Col/Row:J15     ? for HELP
  1>█
```

The command separates the old rows 5 and 6 and inserts a new row 6 between them. Notice that all the information cells below the new row 6 have been moved down one row.

Using the /Insert command can cause a problem only if you have data in row 254 or column BK of the worksheet. Some versions of SuperCalc do not check for this condition. With these versions, if you have information in row 254 or column BK and you insert a row or column, the old row 254 or column BK will be pushed off the worksheet and the information contained in it will be lost. Protecting cells in the last column or row does not help because /Insert does not check for cell protection. You may want to find out if your version of SuperCalc checks the last row and column before it inserts new rows or columns in order to avoid this problem.

The /Delete command removes entire columns or rows. The action of this command is permanent. If you delete the wrong row or column, the only way to get it back is to insert a blank row or column and reenter the information in each cell. /Delete can cause other problems on the worksheet as well. If other cells on the worksheet contain references to cells in a row or column that is deleted, these references are changed to "ERROR". SuperCalc has no way of knowing how to adjust a formula that refers to a deleted cell. Also, you cannot delete a row or column that contains a protected cell. If you attempt to, the message "Protected Entry" is displayed and the command is canceled. None of the cells in the column or row is affected.

As Figure 7-1 shows, this year the Mudville Nine lost their first game of the season. They were so upset because of this that they failed to show up for the rest of the season. So as Commissioner of Baseball, it is your job to suspend them from the Western Division of the National League. Move the active cell to A10. Type **/D R** to start the /Delete command for a row. Now instead of specifying a row by letter, just press **<RET>**. The row containing the active cell (row 10) is deleted. All rows below row 10 are moved up to fill the vacant row. Now your worksheet will look like the following:

```
   :  A  ::  B  ::  C  ::  D  ::  E  ::  F  ::  G  ::  H  :
  1:National League West            Standings of the Clubs
  2:
  3:
  4:                                    Games    Games    Games Won-Loss
  5:City            Team        Rank      Won     Lost     Back        %
  6:
  7:Atlanta         Braves         1       62       43        0      590
  8:San Diego       Padres         2       63       44        0      589
  9:Los Angeles     Dodgers        3       65       47       .5      580
 10:San Francisco   Giants         4       57       49      5.5      538
 11:Cincinnati      Reds           6       40       67       23      374
 12:Houston         Astros         7       35       72       28      327
 13:
 14:Total                                 322      322
  •
  •
  •
< A11          Text="Cincinnati
Width:  9  Memory: 25 Last Col/Row:J14    ? for HELP
 1>■
```

The /Insert and /Delete commands give you the ability to add or remove entire rows and columns. These commands make major restructuring of worksheets possible. It's hard to destroy anything with the /Insert command, but the /Delete command should be used with caution. It is irreversible, and it can cause surprising effects on formulas.

The /Delete command has one more option than the /Insert command, the File option. After SuperCalc spells out the word "/Delete," it asks you to enter R, C, or F, for row, column, or file. If you enter "F", the /Delete command prompts you to enter a file name. You can also press <RET> to see the disk directory. When you enter a file name, the file specified is deleted from the disk. Once you have deleted a file it is irrevocably removed from the disk and is no longer available.

Moving Rows and Columns

The /Move command allows you to move complete rows or columns from one location to another on the worksheet. Like /Replicate, the /Move command will adjust formulas. To try the /Move command, enter **/M**. SuperCalc completes the word "Move," and prompts "Row or Column?" Press the letter **C** for "Column". The program then asks "From?" and requests you to enter a "column range". As usual, if you enter a comma or press <RET> without entering a row number or column letter, the row or column containing the active cell will be entered. For this example, press the letter **D** to define column D as the column that is to be moved and then press **<RET>**.

SuperCalc now asks where you want to move this column by prompting "To?". It again requests you to enter a column letter. Press the letter **G** to define column G as the destination and press **<RET>**.

Figure 7-2 shows the worksheet after this move has been completed. The numbers that were in column D are now in column G, while all the entries that were in columns E, F, and G have moved one column to the left.

Save (**/S**) this example on disk B in a file called **NLWEST**. The list of teams is currently arranged so that the team with the highest win-lose percentage is listed first. Using the /Move command, can you sort the rows so that the teams are ordered by most games won? Check your results against Figure 7-3. Then clear the worksheet (**/Z Y**) and reload the model (enter **/L B:NLWEST , A**)

```
    :  A   ::  B   ::  C   ::  D   ::  E   ::  F   ::  G   ::  H   :
  1:National League West      Standings of the Clubs
  2:
  3:
  4:                            Games    Games    Games       Won-Loss
  5:City             Team        Won     Lost     Back    Rank      %
  6:
  7:Atlanta          Braves       62       43        0      1      590
  8:San Diego        Padres       63       44        0      2      589
  9:Los Angeles      Dodgers      65       47       .5      3      580
 10:San Francisco    Giants       57       49      5.5      4      538
 11:Cincinnati       Reds         40       67       23      6      374
 12:Houston          Astros       35       72       28      7      327
 13:
 14:Total                        322      322
 15:
  •
  •
  •
 20:
< A11          Text="Cincinnati
Width:  9  Memory: 25 Last Col/Row:J14     ? for HELP
  1>█
```

Figure 7-2.

Teams' standing listed in column G

```
    :  A   ::  B   ::  C   ::  D   ::  E   ::  F   ::  G   ::  H   :
  1:National League West      Standings of the Clubs
  2:
  3:
  4:                            Games    Games    Games       Won-Loss
  5:City             Team        Won     Lost     Back    Rank      %
  6:
  7:Los Angeles      Dodgers      65       47       .5      3      580
  8:San Diego        Padres       63       44        0      2      589
  9:Atlanta          Braves       62       43        0      1      590
 10:San Francisco    Giants       57       49      5.5      4      538
 11:Cincinnati       Reds         40       67       23      6      374
 12:Houston          Astros       35       72       28      7      327
 13:
 14:Total                        322      322
 15:
 16:
 17:
 18:
 19:
 20:
< A11          Text="Cincinnati
Width:  9  Memory: 25 Last Col/Row:J14     ? for HELP
  1>█
```

Figure 7-3.

Teams ranked by games won

Sorting the Worksheet (/Arrange)

The /Move command provides a fast way to move a row or a column around on the worksheet. But suppose that you want to alphabetize a list of entries. If you have SuperCalc², you can do this easily with the /Arrange command.

The /Arrange command can sort rows or columns into alphabetical or numerical order. It is fairly fast, and it can sort large amounts of data. However, if you are not careful, it can also scramble your worksheet so that you won't recognize it. Using the Baseball Standings model, we will look at several examples of how to use the /Arrange command and one example of how not to use it!

Figure 7-2 shows this worksheet as it now stands. First, to prevent catastrophes before using /Arrange, it is a good idea to create a series of numbers that can be used to return the worksheet to its original order. For this example, the "rank" in column G will serve this purpose.

Now we will sort the team in order by games won. Enter **/A**. SuperCalc asks you whether you wish to arrange a row or a column. You wish to order the rows, so you must sort them in a column. Enter **C**. Now SuperCalc asks you which column you wish to sort. We will use column D, which contains the number of games won.

Press the letter **D** to sort on column D and press the comma (,) to request options for the /Arrange command. You will almost always use the options with the /Arrange command, and to do this, always enter a comma. The first option that you have is to define a range of rows to be sorted. We want to sort rows 7 through 12, so enter **7:12 <RET>**.

You now have the choice of an ascending or descending sort. Ascending means the smallest value is at the top. Descending means the largest value is at the top. Since you want the largest value at the top, enter **D** for descending.

Finally, you are asked if you want to adjust the formulas. Generally, sorting destroys the relationships between formulas that are moved. Therefore there is no meaningful adjustment possible. As a rule of thumb, you should not adjust formulas with the /Arrange command. Press **N** for no adjust. The /Arrange command is now executed. The teams should be ordered by games won, as shown in Figure 7-3.

We can also order the rows alphabetically by team name (column C). To do this we will sort on column C. Type **/A** to start the /Arrange command.

Enter **C C** to specify column C. Press the comma (,) so that you can use the options, and enter a row range of **7:12**. Press **A** for an ascending sort and **N** for no adjust. When the /Arrange command has finished, your worksheet should look like this:

```
  |  A  ||  B  ||  C  ||  D  ||  E  ||  F  ||  G  ||  H  |
 1|National League West      Standings of the Clubs
 2|
 3|
 4|                              Games     Games     Games            Won-Loss
 5|City              Team          Won      Lost      Back      Rank         %
 6|
 7|Houston           Astros         35        72        28         7       327
 8|Atlanta           Braves         62        43         0         1       590
 9|Los Angeles       Dodgers        65        47        .5         3       580
10|San Francisco     Giants         57        49       5.5         4       538
11|San Diego         Padres         63        44         0         2       589
12|Cincinnati        Reds           40        67        23         6       374
13|
14|Total                           322       322
15|
 .
 .
 .
20|
< A11          Text="San Diego
Width:  9  Memory: 25 Last Col/Row:J14    ? for HELP
 1>■
```

Now enter **/A C G , 7:12, A N**. The list is now back to its original order as shown in Figure 7-2. We are going to use the /Arrange command on this worksheet one more time to illustrate how easy it is to jumble a worksheet. First save the worksheet on the disk in drive B in a file called NLWEST (if you have not already done so). Now enter **/A C A <RET>**. You have just sorted the entire worksheet on column A. Your worksheet should look like the following:

```
  |  A  ||  B  ||  C  ||  D  ||  E  ||  F  ||  G  ||  H  |
 1|Atlanta           Braves         62        43         0         1       590
 2|Cincinnati        Reds           40        67        23         6       374
 3|City              Team          Won      Lost      Back      Rank         %
 4|Houston           Astros         35        72        28         7       327
 5|Los Angeles       Dodgers        65        47        .5         3       580
 6|National League West      Standings of the Clubs
 7|San Diego         Padres         63        44         0         2       589
 8|San Francisco     Giants         57        49       5.5         4       538
 9|Total                           322       322
10|
11|
12|                              Games     Games     Games            Won-Loss
 .
 .
 .
20|
< A11
Width:  9  Memory: 25 Last Col/Row:J12    ? for HELP
 1>■
```

The rows are completely reorganized. There is no way to reverse what has been done except by using the /Move command to rearrange the rows. You would also have to reenter the formulas in column F.

How /Arrange Sorts

In order to sort a group of entries, the /Arrange command divides the entries into four groups: text entries, text values, dates, and numeric values. The items within each group are sorted in either ascending or descending order, as you choose. The text entries always appear first, and numeric values are always sorted last. Generally, all the items that you sort should be of the same type.

The /Arrange command sorts text entries in a way that is much more useful than most computer sorts. In many sort programs, uppercase and lowercase letters are treated as two separate groups of characters. Most programs would place a word beginning with a lowercase "a" after a word beginning with an uppercase "Z". But SuperCalc sorts upper- and lowercase letters together. In this way a word beginning with a lowercase "a" winds up where it belongs, grouped with the words starting with "A".

To see how this works, enter the following on a blank worksheet:

Cell	*Entry*
B3	**"French bread**
B4	**"garlic**
B5	**"cheese**
B6	**"Fritos**
B7	**"applesauce**
B8	**"lettuce**
B9	**"Twinkies**
B10	**"tea**

Now use the /Arrange command to alphabetize column B. Your worksheet should look like the example shown when you are done:

```
     :  A  ::  B  ::  C  ::  D  ::  E  ::  F  ::  G  ::  H  :
   1:        applesauce
   2:        cheese
   3:        French bread
   4:        Fritos
   5:        garlic
   6:        lettuce
   7:        tea
   8:        Twinkies
   9:
  10:
  11:
  12:
  13:
  14:
  15:
   •
   •
   •
  20:
 > B12
Width:  9  Memory: 26 Last Col/Row:B8      ? for HELP
   1>
```

Title Locks and Windows

Many times you will use up more rows or columns than will fit on the display screen. In these cases you may need to see two parts of the worksheet at the same time. The /Title and /Window commands give you the ability to view two (or more) sections of the worksheet at the same time.

Keeping Titles in Place

With the /Title command you can lock a portion of the worksheet to prevent it from scrolling. In this way you keep titles on the screen while moving the active cell to other parts of the worksheet.

A title lock can lock one or more columns at the left of the display, one or more rows at the top of the display, or both columns and rows. A title lock forms a new "edge" of the display. The area of cells below or to the right of the title lock will scroll normally, but the locked cells remain stationary.

The locked cells will, however, move along the lock border to maintain proper alignment with the cells beyond the lock. For example, if column A is locked, it will scroll vertically as required to maintain proper alignment of the rows, but it will not scroll horizontally.

Load the Budget model (/**L B:FIRSTTRY , A**) to use in studying the /Title and /Window commands. As it exists, this worksheet fits on the screen. Let's add columns for the remaining six months of the year to make it larger. To do this, make the following entries:

Cell	*Entry*
	/I C H
	/I C I
	/I C J
	/I C K
	/I C L
	/I C M
H3	**"JUL**
I3	**"AUG**
J3	**"SEP**
K3	**"OCT**
L3	**"NOV**
M3	**"DEC**
	/R G14 , H14:M14
	/R G17 , H17:M17
	/R G18 , H18:M18

```
   :    G    ::   H    ::   I    ::   J    ::   K    ::   L    ::   M    ::   N   :
 1:
 2:
 3:       JUN       JUL       AUG       SEP       OCT       NOV       DEC     Y.T.D
 4:========================================================================
 5:
 6:     1050                                                                6150
 7:========================================================================
 8:
 9:      500                                                                3000
10:      280                                                                1680
11:       90                                                                 540
12:      120                                                                 720
13:------------------------------------------------------------------------
14:      990         0         0         0         0         0         0    5940
15:========================================================================
16:
17:       60         0         0         0         0         0         0     210
18:      210       210       210       210       210       210       210
19:========================================================================
20:
v G18         Form=F18+G17
Width:  9  Memory: 24 Last Col/Row:N19    ? for HELP
  1>█
```

Now the need to lock titles becomes apparent. When you scroll to look at the year to date (Y.T.D.) column you can no longer see the expense descriptions in column A. Move to cell A1 and enter **/T V**. This creates a vertical title lock. Now scroll to cell N1. As you move, notice that column A stays on the screen while columns B, C, and D disappear. In this way you can look at the Y.T.D. column and still have the descriptions on the screen, as follows:

```
  :    A    ::    H    ::    I    ::    J    ::    K    ::    L    ::    M    ::    N    :
 1:Simple Bu
 2:
 3:                   JUL       AUG       SEP       OCT       NOV       DEC     Y.T.D
 4:=================================================================================
 5:INCOME:
 6:SALARY                                                                      6150
 7:=================================================================================
 8:EXPENSES:
 9:RENT                                                                        3000
10:FOOD                                                                        1680
11:UTIL                                                                         540
12:AUTO                                                                         720
13:---------------------------------------------------------------------------------
14:TOTAL                0         0         0         0         0         0     5940
15:=================================================================================
16:SAVINGS:
17:MONTHLY              0         0         0         0         0         0      210
18:CUMM.              210       210       210       210       210       210
19:=================================================================================
20:
> N1
Width:  9  Memory: 24 Last Col/Row:N19     ? for HELP
 1>█
```

Scroll down to row 25. There is nothing in row 25, but look at column A. It has moved with the rest of the worksheet so that the descriptions always stay in their proper rows.

The other options available with the /Title command are "H" for Horizontal title lock, "B" for Both horizontal and vertical title lock, and "C" for Clear title lock. The position of the active cell determines the location of the title lock. The row or column containing the active cell is the last one locked.

While this command is called /Title, its use is not restricted to titles. It is useful for locking one column of figures to compare it to several other columns of figures. It is not limited in the number of rows or columns that can be locked. It is possible to lock all but the right-hand column or all but the bottom row.

However, the active cell cannot be scrolled into a locked region. The effect is the same as trying to scroll left of column A. Instead you must use the Goto (=) command to move the active cell into the locked region. Once the active cell is in the locked region it can be scrolled, but if it moves out of the region it cannot scroll back in. Using the Goto command without an address moves the active cell to the upper-left cell of the unlocked region.

Dividing the Display Into Two Windows

The /Window command splits the screen into two separate display windows. With a large model, you can view results while using different assumptions in the input areas.

Using the Budget model with column A locked, scroll the worksheet so that column O is the far right column on the screen and the active cell is in cell N1. Now enter **/W V**. Your screen should look like the following, with a second set of row numbers dividing the screen into two windows:

```
   :    A   ::    I    ::    J    ::    K    ::    L    ::    M    :     :    N    :
  1:Simple Bu                                                         1:
  2:                                                                  2:
  3:              AUG       SEP       OCT       NOV       DEC         3:    Y.T.D
  4:===================================================================4:=========
  5:INCOME:                                                           5:
  6:SALARY                                                            6:     6150
  7:===================================================================7:=========
  8:EXPENSES:                                                         8:
  9:RENT                                                              9:     3000
 10:FOOD                                                             10:     1680
 11:UTIL                                                             11:      540
 12:AUTO                                                             12:      720
 13:-------------------------------------------------------------------13:---------
 14:TOTAL            0         0         0         0         0       14:     5940
 15:===================================================================15:=========
 16:SAVINGS:                                                         16:
 17:MONTHLY          0         0         0         0         0       17:      210
 18:CUMM.          210       210       210       210       210       18:
 19:===================================================================19:=========
 20:                                                                 20:
< M3              Text="DEC
Width:   9  Memory: 24 Last Col/Row:N19     ? for HELP
  1>█
```

The active cell is now in the right window of this model. To move to the other window, press the semicolon (;). Now you can move to any column in the left window and still see the Y.T.D. column in the right window. SuperCalc remembers your position in each window. As you move back and forth you will return to the cell from which you left.

The position of the active cell at the time the /Window command is executed determines the position of the division on the screen. The column or row that the active cell is in will be replaced by a second border display to indicate the division between the windows. If the borders are not displayed, a space is left between the windows.

If you try to execute the /Window command while the active cell is against the edge of the worksheet, SuperCalc will display an error message reporting that there is not enough room to form a window. If you move the active cell away from the edge of the display and try again, you should then be able to create a window with no further problems.

The /Window command has the following options: "H" for Horizontal windows, "V" for Vertical windows, "S" for Synchronized scrolling, "U" for Unsynchronized scrolling, and "C" for Clearing the windows. A horizontal window splits the screen into top and bottom windows. A vertical window splits the screen into left and right windows.

Synchronized scrolling moves the cells in both windows the same way when scrolled parallel to the division. This allows you to view the same cells in two different formats at the same time.

Unsynchronized scrolling allows you to move about in one window without changing the position of the other window. This allows you to keep an important cell in view in one window while you are moving the active cell around in the other window. A window can be as small as one column or one row, so you can use almost all of the display for input variables and still keep the results visible.

You must also clear any existing window before creating a new one. When a window is cleared, the formats and global options assigned to the upper or left window predominate. The whole screen takes on the attributes of the upper or left window.

Global format or option commands entered while you are in a window affect only that window. You can even view the values and the formulas on your worksheet at the same time.

Hiding Cells (/Format Hide)

One of the /Format options that we haven't investigated yet is the /Format Hide option. The Hide option makes cells disappear. They are still on the worksheet, and they still contain whatever information you put in them, but they do not show up on the display or on printed reports.

The /Format Hide option is useful for hiding intermediate calculations so they cannot confuse the casual user. For instance, on the Loan model, cell F9 contains an intermediate calculation. Load this model (**/L B:LOAN, A**), and take a look at cell F9. It calculates and displays the decimal fraction that represents the interest rate. We need the value for the formula in cell D19, but we do not need to see it.

Move to cell F9 and enter **/F E ,** (for an entry level format of the current cell). Then enter **H <RET>**. The value will no longer be displayed, but if you look at the status line you will see that the formula is still in the cell. The (.095) in cell F9 should disappear, as shown in the screen display.

Through the use of title locks, windows, and /Format Hide, especially with the border display off, sophisticated worksheets can be made to appear attractive and easy to use. This is a real plus when other people must use your worksheets, especially when their knowledge of SuperCalc is limited.

CHAPTER EIGHT

Special Report Formatting

The flexibility of formatting that SuperCalc provides allows you to create reports in a number of different formats. With SuperCalc^2 you can define special numeric formats that give a polished look to your reports. You can also produce technical documentation of your worksheets.

User-Defined Formats: Financial Reports

If you are using SuperCalc^2, you can use the eight user-defined options, U1 through U8, of the /Format command. A user-defined format lets you create formats from a menu of options. Figure 8-1 is a very simple financial statement. It illustrates several of the abilities of the user-defined formats.

The figures in the middle column are in thousands of dollars, as noted at the top of the column. They have commas where required, and some have

```
   :  A  ::      B      ::  C  ::  D  ::  E  ::  F  ::  G  :
  1:                     AJAX DISTRIBUTING, INC.
  2:                       Financial Statement
  3:                     For the period ending
  4:                            6/30/83
  5:
  6:                               (In 1000's)     Per Cent
  7:
  8:       Sales                    $31,200           100.0%
  9:       Cost of Goods Sold        21,900            70.2%
 10:       ------------------------------------------------------------
 11:       Gross Profit              $9,300            29.8%
 12:
 13:       Marketing                   $245               .8%
 14:       Research & Development       332              1.1%
 15:       Administrative             1,254              4.0%
 16:       Other Expenses (Income)  (   234)             -.8%
 17:       ------------------------------------------------------------
 18:       Total Operating Expenses  $1,597              5.1%
 19:
 20:       Income Before Taxes       $7,703             24.7%
^ D9    2    Form=21900000
Width:  9  Memory: 25 Last Col/Row:F21    ? for HELP
  1>■
```

Figure 8-1.

A financial statement

```
   :  A  ::      B      ::  C  ::  D  ::  E  ::  F  ::  G  :
  1:                     AJAX DISTRIBUTING, INC.
  2:                       Financial Statement
  3:                     For the period ending
  4:                            6/30/83
  5:
  6:                               (In 1000's)     Per Cent
  7:
  8:       Sales                   31200000         D8/D8
  9:       Cost of Goods Sold      21900000         D9/D8
 10:       ------------------------------------------------------------
 11:       Gross Profit            D8-D9            D11/D8
 12:
 13:       Marketing               245000           D13/D8
 14:       Research & Development  332000           D14/D8
 15:       Administrative          1254000          D15/D8
 16:       Other Expenses (Income) -234000          D16/D8
 17:       ------------------------------------------------------------
 18:       Total Operating Expenses SUM(D13:D16)    D18/D8
 19:
 20:       Income Before Taxes     D11-D18          D20/D8
> B6
Width: 15  Memory: 25 Last Col/Row:F21    ? for HELP
  1>■
```

Figure 8-2.

Numbers and formulas

dollar signs. The right-hand column shows percent with one decimal place of the sales figures. All of these features were specified with user-defined formats.

To create this model, enter the text, numbers, and formulas shown in Figure 8-2. Set the width of column B to 15. To center the top headings, place blanks in front of the entries (for example, in cell C4 enter "   **6/30/83**). When you have finished, your display screen will appear as follows:

```
     :  A  ::      B      ::  C  ::  D  ::  E  ::  F  ::  G  :
   1:                   AJAX DISTRIBUTING, INC.
   2:                    Financial Statement
   3:                   For the period ending
   4:                          6/30/83
   5:
   6:                        (In 1000's)        Per Cent
   7:
   8:       Sales                   31200000                 1
   9:       Cost of Goods Sold      21900000          .7019231
  10:       ---------------------------------------------------
  11:       Gross Profit             9300000          .2980769
  12:
  13:       Marketing                 245000          .0078526
  14:       Research & Development    332000          .0106410
  15:       Administrative           1254000          .0401923
  16:       Other Expenses (Income)  -234000            -.0075
  17:       ---------------------------------------------------
  18:       Total Operating Expenses 1597000          .0511859
  19:
  20:       Income Before Taxes      7703000          .2468910
v F20      Form=D20/D8
Width:  9  Memory: 25 Last Col/Row:F21     ? for HELP
  1>█
```

Now we will define the special formats needed for this report. Enter **/F D**.

The display screen will change. The worksheet will disappear, and your screen will appear as follows:

```
                    User-defined formats
                    1  2  3  4  5  6  7  8

Floating $          Y  Y  Y  Y  Y  Y  Y  Y

Embedded Commas     Y  Y  Y  Y  Y  Y  Y  Y

Minus in ( )        N  N  N  N  N  N  N  N

Zero as Blank       N  N  N  N  N  N  N  N

%                   N  N  N  N  N  N  N  N

Decimal Places      2  2  2  2  2  2  2  2

Scaling factor      0  0  0  0  0  0  0  0


CTRL-Z to return to worksheet.


v F20         Form=D20/D8
Y(es) or N(o) ?
 15>/Format,Define
```

To create the finished model, you need to set up three user-defined formats. You will make changes to the first three columns of this matrix. The first format is for the dollar amounts with dollar signs. The second will be for dollar amounts without dollar signs, and the third will be for the percentage figures.

To set up a user-defined format you simply select which of the options you want. To do this, you move the curser to the proper location by pressing the arrow keys, much the way you move around the worksheet. Each column represents a different format. On the first five rows of each column you enter a "Y" or an "N", depending on whether you want the option or not.

Here is what these options mean. "Floating $" puts a dollar sign to the left of the first digit of the value that is displayed. It is called a *floating* dollar sign because as the value gets larger or smaller the dollar sign will move so that it is always adjacent to the first digit.

"Embedded commas" means commas will be placed every three digits to make it easy to read large numbers. The number 50000 would appear as "50,000".

"Minus in ( )" means that negative numbers will be enclosed in parentheses instead of having a minus sign. Thus −535 would appear as "(535)".

"Zero as Blank" means that cells that have a value of zero which would normally appear as 0 will instead appear to be empty.

"%" means that values will have the decimal shifted two places to the left, and a percent sign displayed after the value. Thus the value .05 would appear as "5%".

The last two options require a number instead of only a Y or an N. "Decimal places" sets the number of decimal places that you want displayed. For instance, if you set this number to 3 the number 6.5 will appear as "6.500".

"Scaling Factor" specifies a power of 10 by which the values are scaled down when they are displayed. Format U3 for percentages requires scaling by 1000. One thousand (1000) is 10 to the third power, so enter **3** for the scaling factor in the third column.

The first user-defined format will have a floating dollar sign, embedded commas, and negative numbers in parentheses. The second format (column 2) will be just like the first except that "Floating $" will be set to N. The third format is for percentages. It will have the top four rows set to N and the fifth row (%) set to Y. Change the first three columns so that your screen looks like Figure 8-3. Change the top five rows of these columns by typing

```
                    User-defined formats
                    1  2  3  4  5  6  7  8

Floating $          Y  N  N  Y  Y  Y  Y  Y

Embedded Commas     Y  Y  N  Y  Y  Y  Y  Y

Minus in ( )        Y  Y  N  N  N  N  N  N

Zero as Blank       N  N  N  N  N  N  N  N

%                   N  N  Y  N  N  N  N  N

Decimal Places      0  0  1  2  2  2  2  2

Scaling factor      3  3  0  0  0  0  0  0

CTRL-Z to return to worksheet.

^ D9     2       Form=21900000
Y(es) or N(o) ?
 15>/Format,Define
```

Figure 8-3.

User format settings

"Y" or "N", and enter the required numbers in the bottom two rows. To move around, press the arrow keys. When all the changes have been made, press CTRL-Z. This returns you to the worksheet.

You have defined three formats called U1, U2, and U3, and you can now use them as format options. Start with column D. This column should be formatted with User-defined format 1. Enter **/F C D , U 1 <RET>**. Next, format column F with User-defined format 3 by entering **/F C F , U3**. Finally, format cells D9 and D14 through D16 with User-defined format 2. Enter **/F E D14:D16 , U2** and **/F E D 9 , U2**. When you are done, your worksheet should look like Figure 8-1.

Now this is nearly a formal financial report. The only remaining thing to do is remove the borders around the worksheet. You can do this by using one of the options of the /Global command.

Global Formatting Options (/Global)

The /Global command has eight options that affect the entire worksheet. These options are listed in Table 8-1.

The /Global command begins like all the other commands. Enter **/G** and SuperCalc completes the word "Global", and prompts you with the list of options. But here the similarity ends. The /Global command allows you to enter only one letter specifying a single option. As soon as you have entered

Table 8-1.

/Global Options

Option	Description
F(orm.)	Display the formulas in each cell instead of the calculated result (on/off).
N(ext)	Turn off/on automatic advance of the active cell.
T(ab)	Inhibit moving the active cell so that it can only be positioned to unprotected cells that contain data (on/off).
R(ow)	Calculate row by row.
C(ol.)	Calculate column by column.
M(an.)	Only calculate when exclamation mark (!) is pressed.
A(uto)	Calculate automatically each time data is entered or changed.
G(raphics)	SuperCalc[3] only. See Chapter 12.

the letter the command is executed; you do not end the command with <RET> or a comma.

Turning Off the Borders

To complete our financial statement we will have to remove the borders of the worksheet. The borders are the letters and numbers along the top and left of the worksheet and the adjoining lines. The Border option switches the display of the worksheet borders on and off. By turning off the borders you can print your worksheet without borders.

Turn off the borders on your worksheet by entering **/G B**. The display should now appear as follows:

```
                         AJAX DISTRIBUTING, INC.
                          Financial Statement
                         For the period ending
                                6/30/83

                              (In 1000's)        Per Cent

          Sales                $31,200            100.0%
          Cost of Goods Sold    21,900             70.2%
          ----------------------------------------------------------
          Gross Profit          $9,300             29.8%

          Marketing               $245               .8%
          Research & Development   332              1.1%
          Administrative         1,254              4.0%
          Other Expenses (Income)  (   234)         -.8%
          ----------------------------------------------------------
          Total Operating Expenses  $1,597          5.1%

          Income Before Taxes   $7,703             24.7%
^ D9     2      Form=21900000
Width:   9  Memory: 25 Last Col/Row:F21     ? for HELP
  1>■
```

This command works like a switch. If the borders are on, this command turns them off. If the borders are off, this command will turn them back on. To turn the borders back on just enter **/G B** again.

Displaying Formulas on the Worksheet

The formulas on the worksheet can be displayed by using the /Global Formula option. When you enter /G F, the formulas you have entered in each cell are displayed instead of the calculated values in the cells. If the cell contains a number, it is displayed as you originally entered it. If the global format is

Text Left, both numerical and formula entries are displayed starting at the left edge of the cell and will display over adjacent empty cells.

The /Global Formula option alternates between formulas and normal display. Turn the borders back on by typing /**G B** and then type /**G F** to see your financial statement worksheet in Formula display mode. This will appear as was shown in Figure 8-2.

Printing Formatted Reports (/Output)

Turn the border off again (/**G B**) and return the values to the cells (/**G F**). Now the financial report is ready for printing. To print the report use the /Output command. Type /**O D A1:F20 , P**. The printed report should look just like Figure 8-4.

The Importance of Documentation

To create useful worksheets it is important to document them so that you and others using the worksheets understand them. Good documentation should also allow you to reconstruct the worksheet if it is accidentally erased

```
                    AJAX DISTRIBUTING, INC.
                     Financial Statement
                    For the period ending
                           6/30/83

                           (In 1000's)        Per Cent

Sales                        $31,200            100.0%
Cost of Goods Sold            21,900             70.2%
------------------------------------------------------
Gross Profit                  $9,300             29.8%

Marketing                       $245               .8%
Research & Development           332              1.1%
Administrative                 1,254              4.0%
Other Expenses (Income)     (    234)             -.8%
------------------------------------------------------
Total Operating Expenses      $1,597              5.1%

Income Before Taxes           $7,703             24.7%
```

Figure 8-4.

Printout without borders

from disk. Printing your worksheet after formatting it with the /Global Formula option will provide you with the documentation for you or another user to reconstruct your model.

Printing Models With Formulas Displayed

You can print a worksheet with the formulas displayed just as you print the worksheet with the values displayed. Often formulas are too long to be completely displayed in the width of the columns used to display the cell values. So before printing, remember to change the width of your columns by using the /Format command. Now enter **/O D A1:F20 , P** again. This printed worksheet will look like Figure 8-5. Note that this report was produced using the Display option of the /Output command. There is one other method for listing formulas, the Contents option of the /Output command.

Listing Cell Contents

The /Output Contents report provides a list of the contents of each cell on the worksheet. The report is formatted with the SuperCalc version and worksheet title at the top, followed by the name and contents of each cell. This report uses a lot of paper; there is only one cell listed per line, but it provides

```
  !  A  !!      B        !!  C  !!  D  !!  E  !!  F  !
 1!                   AJAX DISTRIBUTING, INC.
 2!                     Financial Statement
 3!                    For the period ending
 4!                          6/30/83
 5!
 6!                              (In 1000's)       Per Cent
 7!
 8!        Sales                 31200000           D8/D8
 9!        Cost of Goods Sold    21900000           D9/D8
10!        ------------------------------------------------
11!        Gross Profit          D8-D9              D11/D8
12!
13!        Marketing             245000             D13/D8
14!        Research & Development 332000            D14/D8
15!        Administrative        1254000            D15/D8
16!        Other Expenses (Income) -234000          D16/D8
17!        ------------------------------------------------
18!        Total Operating Expenses SUM(D13:D16)    D18/D8
19!
20!        Income Before Taxes   D11-D18            D20/D8
```

Figure 8-5.

Printout with formula display on

complete information for reconstructing the worksheet. To produce a contents report for thé financial statement enter **/O C All , P**. Take a look at Figure 8-6, which shows the worksheet listed in the Contents report format. The contents of each cell, just as it was entered, is listed at the right (following the =). The "2"is formatted with user-defined format 2. A "P" (as on cell C1) indicates that the cell is protected. The row, column, and global formats, the global options, and the user-defined formats that have been defined are not given by this report. Note that even though we used three user-defined formats on this worksheet, only the "2" format shows on this report in cells D9, D14, D15, and D16. This is because the other two formats, U1 and U3, were applied at the column level.

```
SuperCalc ver.  1.00

C1         = "AJAX DISTRIBUTING, INC.
C2         = " Financial Statement
C3         = "For the period ending
C4         = "         6/30/83
D6         = "(In 1000's)
F6         = "Per Cent
B8         = "Sales
D8         = 31200000
F8         = D8/D8
B9         = "Cost of Goods Sold
D9 2       = 21900000
F9         = D9/D8
B10        = '-
B11        = "Gross Profit
D11        = D8-D9
F11        = D11/D8
B13        = "Marketing
D13        = 245000
F13        = D13/D8
B14        = "Research & Development
D14 2      = 332000
F14        = D14/D8
B15        = "Adiministrative
D15 2      = 1254000
F15        = D15/D8
B16        = "Other Expenses (Income)
D16 2      = -234000
F16        = D16/D8
B17        = '-
B18        = "Total Operating Expenses
D18        = SUM(D13:D16)
F18        = D18/D8
B20        = "Income Before Taxes
D20        = D11-D18
F20        = D20/D8
```

Figure 8-6.

Printout of cell contents

Sending Reports to a Word Processor

The SuperCalc /Output command has the ability to produce a file on disk. If you write a file to disk with /Output, the file can be read by most word-processing programs. The "D" (Disk) option will direct the output to a disk file. A file that you produce this way is not a SuperCalc file. The file will contain the same characters that SuperCalc would normally send to the printer. To write the financial statement to disk as a report file, enter **/O D All , D**.

You are asked for a file name where the report will be stored. As with the /Load and /Save commands, you can review the disk directory. In this case enter the name **B: REPORT** and press **<RET>**. If no extension is entered, SuperCalc adds the extension ".PRN" to the file name.

Controlling the Printer

The /Output Setup option provides a method for changing the page width and page length and for sending special command codes to the printer. To select the Setup option enter **/O D All , S**. The screen display changes to look like Figure 8-7.

Two of the the options presented in this menu allow you to change the page length (L), and the page width (W). When you first see this menu there are already values for the page length and page width. These are the default values stored in the SuperCalc program. If you change the page length or width on the Setup menu, these changes will be remembered only until you exit from SuperCalc. After setting them you press **P** to print the report.

```
          Setup PRINTER:

L = Change page length
    (Length = 0 for continuous form.)
    (now  66 lines)
W = Change page width
    (now 132 chars)
A = Change Auto Form Feed Setting
    (now OFF)
D = Change Double Space Report Setting
    (now OFF)
S = Manual setup codes
P = Print report
CTRL-Z to cancel /O command
```

Figure 8-7.

Printer setup menu

You can also change these defaults permanently by using the INSTALL program that is furnished with SuperCalc. Refer to your SuperCalc installation instructions to be sure this program is available with your version.

Single and Double Spacing

If you are using SuperCalc², the next two options are A and D. These are toggle switches that you can set for single or double spacing. If you want to produce a double-spaced report, select the D option. If your printer is already producing double-spaced reports from SuperCalc, you need to select the A option if you want single-spaced reports. The A option tells SuperCalc that the printer is using an automatic line-feed feature, and accordingly SuperCalc removes line feeds from the output.

Setup String

From the Setup menu you can also select the S or Manual setup option. This allows you to control the special functions of your printer by sending it a *setup string.* A setup string is a series of characters that the printer understands as special control codes. The most common reason to use setup strings on a dot matrix printer is to print condensed characters in order to print more columns. These control codes are specific to each brand of printer. The following example will show how to use condensed print with the Epson MX, FX, or RX, Novell, Star (Gemini), and C. Itoh ProWriter printers. To send control codes to the printer, press the letter **S**. You will be prompted to "Enter codes (CR when done)". On Epson, Star, or Novell printers, the code for condensed print is ASCII code 15. This code is produced by holding down the CTRL key and pressing the letter O. Hold the **CTRL** key down and press **O**.

On C. Itoh (ProWriter) printers the code for condensed print is ESC Q. To enter this you first press the **ESCAPE** key. Then press **SHIFT** and **Q** together. Then press **<RET>**. You can now press **P** for Print, and the report will be printed in condensed type. The printer will remain in condensed type mode until you reset it to normal mode by entering CTRL R or until the printer is turned off and on again. Figure 8-8 shows the FIRSTTRY worksheet printed in condensed type.

```
  ¦    A    ¦¦    B    ¦¦    C    ¦¦    D    ¦¦    E    ¦¦    F    ¦¦    G    ¦¦    H    ¦
 1¦Simple Budget Worksheet
 2¦
 3¦                 JAN       FEB       MAR       APR       MAY       JUN     Y.T.D
 4¦==========================================================================
 5¦INCOME:
 6¦SALARY          1000      1000      1000      1050      1050      1050      6150
 7¦==========================================================================
 8¦EXPENSES:
 9¦RENT             500       500       500       500       500       500      3000
10¦FOOD             280       280       280       280       280       280      1680
11¦UTIL              90        90        90        90        90        90       540
12¦AUTO             120       120       120       120       120       120       720
13¦--------------------------------------------------------------------------
14¦TOTAL            990       990       990       990       990       990      5940
15¦==========================================================================
16¦SAVINGS:
17¦MONTHLY           10        10        10        60        60        60       210
18¦CUMM.             10        20        30        90       150       210
19¦==========================================================================
```

Figure 8-8.

Condensed printout of FIRSTTRY

CHAPTER NINE

Transferring Files and Automatic Operation

Situations often arise in which you need to transfer data from one SuperCalc model to another. For instance, suppose you are tracking inventory cash flow for several departments on a monthly basis. Each month new purchases are made and existing inventory is sold.

You may want to view this information in several different ways. To look at the cash flow for a single month, you need to obtain the starting balance for each department from the previous month. You may also wish to look at a consolidated cash flow for several months or for a whole year. You can do both if you store the inventory cash flow for each month separately and then use SuperCalc commands to collect the information together as explained in this chapter.

Chapter 3 explained how to save a SuperCalc model on disk and load it back into the worksheet. Now we are going to delve deeper into the /Save and /Load commands and learn some special file-handling capabilities of the SDI

(Super Data Interchange) program. We are also going to look at ways to make SuperCalc work automatically.

/Save Command Options

In addition to storing the entire contents of a model on disk, the /Save command can also store just a portion of a model. Or, it can store only a model's values without the formulas.

Some of the earlier versions of SuperCalc do not have the ability to save a portion of a model. This option was added because some computers have enough memory to create a model that is too big to fit on a single diskette.

Saving Values Only

As we saw earlier, the /Save command, after completing the word "/Save", prompts you for a file name. After you enter a file name, SuperCalc displays the prompt "(A)ll, (V)alues, or (P)art?" You already know that saving "All" means saving the entire model, including the formats and the global options.

Saving *values* will preserve only the current calculated values of the model. Saving a model this way does *not* save any of its formulas. Therefore if you save values only, you cannot modify and recalculate the model. Before you save a model using the Values option, you should save the same model using the All option in another file. This will allow you to modify the model in the future.

Saving in Sections

SuperCalc versions 1.10 and later give you an additional option. The Part option allows you to save a portion of a model. In addition to giving you the ability to save, in portions, a model that is too large to fit on one disk, this option can be used to combine sections of several models into a new, longer model.

Here is an application for the /Save Part option. The example that we will use is an inventory model. The /Save Part option will be used to save only the information that changes from period to period. The main model will be saved separately. One reason for saving a model in this manner is to save disk space. In an especially large application, this can make a significant difference in the amount of disk storage used.

Clear your worksheet with /**ZY** and make the following entries to create the master inventory model:

Cell	*Entry*
A3	**"Inventory record for the period of:**
B6	**"Dept A**
C6	**"Dept B**
D6	**"Dept C**
E6	**"Total**
A8	**"Beginning Inv.**
A9	**"Purchases**
A10	**"Usage**
A12	**"Ending Inv.**
B11	**'=**
F11	**'**
E8	**SUM(B8:D8)**
	/R E8 , E9:E10 <RET>
B12	**B8+B9−B10**
	/R B12 , C12:E12 <RET>
	/F G $ 12
	/F C A , 15
	/F R 6 , TR
	/F E A8:A12 , TR
	/P ALL

When these entries are made, your display screen should appear as follows:

```
   :       A       ::   B   ::   C   ::   D   ::   E   ::   F   ::   G   :
  1:
  2:
  3:Inventory record for the period of:
  4:
  5:
  6:                   Dept A   Dept B   Dept C    Total
  7:
  8: Beginning Inv.                                  .00
  9:      Purchases                                  .00
 10:          Usage                                  .00
 11:               ====================================
 12:    Ending Inv.       .00      .00      .00      .00
 13:
 14:
 15:
 16:
 17:
 18:
 19:
 20:
^ B12          Form=B8+B9-B10
Width:  9  Memory: 26 Last Col/Row:F12     ? for HELP
  1>
```

```
      :       A       ::   B   ::   C   ::   D   ::   E   ::   F   ::   G   :
    1:
    2:
    3:Inventory record for the period of:          August
    4:
    5:
    6:                    Dept A   Dept B   Dept C     Total
    7:
    8: Beginning Inv.    450.00   600.00   850.00  1900.00
    9:      Purchases    150.00   300.00   550.00  1000.00
   10:          Usage    250.00   500.00   900.00  1650.00
   11:               ====================================
   12:    Ending Inv.    350.00   400.00   500.00  1250.00
   13:
    •
    •
    •
   20:
   > E3           Text="August
  Width:  9  Memory: 26 Last Col/Row:F12    ? for HELP
    1>
```

Figure 9-1.

August inventory

Save this model as B:MASTER (/**S B:MASTER , A**).

Now enter the inventory figures as shown in Figure 9-1. All these numbers are in the range B8:D10. Also enter "**August** in cell D3. Save this as B:AUGUST.

One section of the inventory model changes from month to month, the block B9:D10. This part of the model we will save as "values only." Enter /**S B:AUG-DATA** , to start the /Save command and give it a file name. Type **P** for Part and **V** for Values. Now enter the range to be saved, **B9:D10**, and press <**RET**>. The range we specified will be saved on disk B.

To see what was actually saved, clear your worksheet with /**ZY** and load the file B:AUG-DATA (/**L B:AUG-DATA** , **A**). Your screen should appear as follows:

```
      :       A       ::   B   ::   C   ::   D   ::   E   ::   F   ::   G   :
    1:
    •
    •
    •
    8:
    9:                    150.00   300.00   550.00
   10:                    250.00   500.00   900.00
   11:
    •
    •
    •
   20:
  ^ B9           Form=150
Width:  9  Memory: 26 Last Col/Row:D10    ? for HELP
  1>
```

With the Part option you can save formulas by using the All option, or you can save the values only. The /Save command saves the formats and the global options even if you just save a part of the model.

To save a model that won't fit on a single disk, you must carefully analyze it and decide how to break it into several sections. Each section must fit on a single disk without leaving out any cells of the model. This can become somewhat tedious if the model needs to be saved often. (Chapter 11 will show how you can do this automatically, so that with a given model you only need to figure this out once.)

/Load Command Options

As well as saving part of a worksheet, you can also load part of a worksheet, and you can load it anywhere you want. This feature gives you a lot of flexibility. You can update figures on one model by loading values from others.

Using the monthly inventory sheets that we created earlier, we will take the inventory balance at the end of one month and use it as the beginning inventory for the next month. First clear the worksheet (**/ZY**) and load the model (**/L B:MASTER , A**). Enter the word **"September** in cell D3. Now we will use the /Load Part option to load the ending inventory figures from B:AUGUST. Enter **/L B:AUGUST <RET>** to begin the /Load command.

Press the letter **P** to select the Part option. When you select the Part option, you are asked to enter a "From?" range. This range defines which part of the model you will load; however, this is not necessarily the range that will be displayed on the screen.

Enter **B12:D12 <RET>** to define the source range. Once the "From?" range is entered, the program asks you where you want it to load "To?". Like the /Copy command, you must enter the name of a single cell which will be the upper left-hand corner of the range to be loaded into. Also, you make your next choice of options by entering either a comma or <RET>. Entering <RET> executes the command with automatic readjustment of the cell references. Entering a comma allows you to choose among the "No Adjust", "Ask for Adjust", and "Values" options. These options function exactly as they do with the /Copy and /Replicate commands. To picture this process more clearly, imagine that you are making a copy from the worksheet on disk to the worksheet on the screen.

For this example enter **B8** , **V**. The upper-left cell of the area to load to will be B8, and this will load the values only.

```
  :      A      ::   B   ::   C   ::   D   ::   E   ::   F   ::   G   :
 1:
 2:
 3:Inventory record for the period of:        September
 4:
 5:
 6:                  Dept A   Dept B   Dept C    Total
 7:
 8: Beginning Inv.   350.00   400.00   500.00  1250.00
 9:      Purchases                                  .00
10:          Usage                                  .00
11:               ===================================
12:    Ending Inv.   350.00   400.00   500.00  1250.00
13:
14:
15:
16:
17:
18:
19:
20:
< B9
Width:  9  Memory: 26 Last Col/Row:F12    ? for HELP
 1>
```

The totals from August are now entered as the beginning inventory for September.

You cannot load information into cells that are protected. If you attempt to load data into a protected cell, SuperCalc will display the message "Protected Entry". The /Load command will continue to load the unprotected cells. You can use this feature to your advantage by protecting certain cells and loading over other ones.

The normal range definitions are valid. The range for a partial load can be a single cell, a partial row or column, a block, or "All".

WARNING: The "All" specification is unreliable. On several versions of SuperCalc the "All" specification loads only cell A1. Test your version of SuperCalc before you try to use "All" as a range with the Part option.

At first glance it may seem unlikely that you would want to load an entire worksheet with the Part option. It is simpler just to specify the All option, but there is actually a good reason to load an entire worksheet with the Part option. Using the Part option, you can relocate the worksheet as it is loaded, and you can choose to load just the current values or the formulas from the model file on disk.

Consolidating Worksheets

With the /Load Consolidate option you can add the results of several SuperCalc files together. We will use the monthly inventory model again to see how this works. Enter the inventory figures for September that are shown in Figure 9-2. Enter only the values that are in rows 9 and 10. Now we will make a file called B:SEP-DATA as we did for August by entering **/S B:SEP-DATA <RET> P V B9:D10 <RET>**. We will use the /Load Consolidate option to create a worksheet that combines the figures for August and September.

First clear your worksheet and load the B:AUGUST worksheet. Enter **"August-September** in cell D3. Now to consolidate, start the /Load command by typing **/L B:SEP-DATA <RET>**.

Select the Consolidate option by typing **C**. When you do, the values in the B:SEP-DATA file are added to the corresponding values in the worksheet that is on the screen.

```
   |      A      ||    B    ||    C    ||    D    ||    E    ||    F    ||    G    |
  1|
  2|
  3|Inventory record for the period of:       August-September
  4|
  5|
  6|                 Dept A    Dept B    Dept C     Total
  7|
  8| Beginning Inv.    450.00    600.00    850.00   1900.00
  9|      Purchases    350.00    550.00   1150.00   2050.00
 10|          Usage    450.00   1050.00   1600.00   3100.00
 11|               ========================================
 12|    Ending Inv.    350.00    100.00    400.00    850.00
 13|
 14|
 15|
 16|
 17|
 18|
 19|
 20|
< E3          Text="August-September
Width:   9  Memory: 26 Last Col/Row:F12     ? for HELP
  1>
```

The new values are the inventory adjustment figures for the combined two-month period. Notice that we do not need to change the beginning balance figures because the beginning balance for the two-month period is the same as the beginning balance was for August.

```
    |     A      ||    B    ||    C    ||    D    ||    E    ||    F    ||    G    |
  1|
  2|
  3|Inventory record for the period of:          September
  4|
  5|
  6|                    Dept A    Dept B    Dept C      Total
  7|
  8| Beginning Inv.     350.00    400.00    500.00   1250.00
  9|      Purchases     200.00    250.00    600.00   1050.00
 10|          Usage     200.00    550.00    700.00   1450.00
 11|                  ====================================
 12|    Ending Inv.     350.00    100.00    400.00    850.00
 13|
 14|
 15|
 16|
 17|
 18|
 19|
 20|
< D10           Form=700
Width:  9  Memory: 26 Last Col/Row:F12      ? for HELP
  1>
```

Figure 9-2.

September inventory

There are some rules that govern the Consolidate option. The Consolidate option will *only* update cells where you already have numbers or formulas in *both* the model on disk and the model on your display screen. Empty cells and cells that contain text will remain unchanged. Also, protected cells will not be changed.

In addition to the Consolidate option, which adds two complete models, the /Load command gives you the opportunity to add, subtract, multiply, or divide (+, −, *, /) any range of cells as you combine two models. These options work just as they do in the /Copy command. If you want to try one of the arithmetic options of the /Load command, first select the Part option, then press the comma (,).

Exchanging Data With a BASIC Program

The newer versions of SuperCalc come with a program called the SuperData Interchange (SDI) utility. SDI can change a SuperCalc file into a file that can be read by other programs, such as a BASIC program. Such a file is called a

```
                 Sorcim File Conversion Utility
                        Version :  1.12
              ----------------------------
              These are the File Conversions Available :
        A. SuperCalc file to Comma Separated Value file
        B. Comma Separated Value file to SuperCalc file
        C. SuperCalc file to SuperData Format file
        D. SuperData Format file to SuperCalc file
        X. Exit program

                Enter Your choice (A, B, C, D, or X) ?
```

Figure 9-3.

Running the SDI program

Comma Separated Values file. The SDI program can also change a file written by a BASIC program into a SuperCalc model file so that you can load it into SuperCalc.

To run the SuperData Interchange program, exit from SuperCalc (/**Q Y**) and type **SDI <RET>**. SDI will start up and present you with a menu that looks like Figure 9-3.

We will investigate only the first two items on this menu. The SuperData Format files that the second two items work with are used to move information between SuperCalc and other Sorcim programs. They do not have the general applications that the Comma Separated Values files have.

Select the first option, "SuperCalc file to Comma Separated Values file", by pressing the letter **A**. The prompt "Enter Source File Name:" will appear below the menu. Enter **B:AUGUST <RET>**. This selects the file B:AUGUST.CAL. Just like SuperCalc, SDI will automatically assume the file name extension .CAL if you do not enter one.

The line "Opening file: B:AUGUST.CAL" will appear on the display, and you will then see "Enter Destination File Name:". Enter **B:AUGUST** again. The SDI program will add the extension .CSV to the name of this file so it will not conflict with the SuperCalc file. It will tell you "Opening File : B:AUGUST.CSV"; then it will report that it is doing the conversion and finally that it is finished. The menu will reappear.

Now exit the program by typing **X**. At the A> prompt, enter the following line to display the contents of the Comma Separated Values file so that you can see what you have created:

A>**TYPE B:AUGUST.CSV**

Figure 9-4 shows what you should see on the screen.

Each row of the worksheet produced one line in this file. Each cell in the row is separated from its neighbors by a comma. The first two lines have only commas on them since there were no entries on the worksheet in these rows. The third line has a text entry, which is contained in double quotes. The eighth line has a text entry in quotes, followed by four numeric values. Each line ends with a carriage return and a line feed.

The format of this file is what a BASIC program expects to see in a data file. The following BASIC program will read this file:

```
LIST
5 J=0
7 WIDTH 255
10 OPEN "I",#1,"B:AUGUST.CSV"
20 IF EOF(1) THEN GOTO 100
25 J=J+1
30 INPUT #1,A$
35 PRINT TAB((J-1)*15);
40 PRINT A$;
45 IF J>5 THEN J=0
50 GOTO 20
100 END
Ok
```

You can also write a file with a BASIC program that you can load into SuperCalc. To do this you convert the BASIC file to a SuperCalc file using SDI.

```
A>TYPE B:AUGUST.CSV
,,,,,
,,,,,
"Inventory record for the period of:",,,,"August",
,,,,,
,,,,,
,"Dept A","Dept B","Dept C","Total",
,,,,,
"Beginning Inv.",450,600,850,1900.0,
"Purchases",150,300,550,1000.0,
"Usage",250,500,900,1650.0,
,"'=",,,,"'"
"Ending Inv.",350.0,400.0,500.0,1250.0,
```

Figure 9-4.

A Comma Separated Values file

Making SuperCalc Work Automatically (/eXecute)

The /eXecute command executes commands you write on a disk file. With this command you can perform repetitive operations on a worksheet with a minimum of effort. It can be used to perform complex tasks automatically without the operator understanding how the SuperCalc program works.

The /eXecute command is available in SuperCalc versions 1.10 and later.

To use this command, simply enter /X, and SuperCalc completes the word "/eXecute". Then enter a file name. The file is read, and the commands contained in it are executed. As with the /Load command, the /eXecute command allows you to view the file directory if you wish.

However, before using /X you need to create a file of commands for the /eXecute command to read. This file must contain the exact characters as if you were going to enter these characters from the keyboard to use the commands that you want.

Execute files have a default extension of .XQT. This means that if you enter a file name to the /eXecute command with no extension, SuperCalc will look for a file name with the extension .XQT. If the file you want to use has a different extension, you must enter it as part of the file name.

You can create execute files using SuperCalc, or you can create an execute file using your system text editor or word processor if it creates regular files and does not leave extra characters in the file. Either way, you have to do everything just right or it will not work.

To create an execute file using SuperCalc, you enter each line of commands in a separate cell. Start in cell A1 and work down column A. Do not put a title on the worksheet and do not skip any cells. You must store all the required characters in the file, and no more. <RET> counts as a character. An extra <RET> acts exactly as it would when you press <RET> directly from the keyboard. It moves the active cell in the direction of the arrow on the entry line, so you must be careful not to insert extra <RET> characters.

When you have entered all the commands you want, there are two things to do before saving the file. First, make sure that column A is wide enough to contain the full length of all the command lines you have entered. Second, turn off the display of the borders. SuperCalc cannot execute a file with borders.

Now you need to save the file in two ways. First use the /Save command to save it as a normal SuperCalc file, so you can reload it and edit it (because you will probably need to). Next, you use the /Output command to write the commands to another disk file. Use the Display option and enter the range as "All". Give the file an .XQT file name extension so the /eXecute command can find it. This second file will be the actual execute file. Now you are ready to execute your file and see how it works. You will be able to see the execute file as it works because all the commands are displayed just as if you had entered them from the keyboard. You will also find this feature helpful if you need to find an error in your execute file.

We will create an execute file that will automatically combine the two inventory worksheets we combined manually. The execute file will automatically move the ending inventory values from one month's worksheet to the beginning inventory values of the next month's worksheet.

The tasks the execute file will do can be broken down as follows:

1. Save the values from the previous month's inventory in a disk file called B:WORK.
2. Zap the worksheet.
3. Load the master inventory file.
4. Consolidate the previous month's ending values into the current month's beginning inventory values.
5. Delete the work file so it will not cause a problem the next time this execute file is used.

To build the execute file, first set the width of column A to 20 (/**F C A , 20**) and turn off the borders with /**G B**. Then make the following entries on a clear worksheet:

Cell	*Entry*
A1	**"/SB:WORK**
A2	**"V/ZY/LB:MASTER**
A3	**"A/LB:WORK**
A4	**"PB12:D12,B8**
A5	**"/DFB:WORK**

Notice that the line breaks occur when a <RET> is needed, but they do not necessarily occur between commands. The first command saves the file B:WORK. It takes the first cell, A1, and the first character of the second cell.

This is because a <RET> is needed to define the end of the file name, but no <RET> is required after the "V" for values. The /Zap command (/ZY) in cell A2 requires no <RET> so it is sandwiched between two other commands. The /Load commands for the file MASTER and the file WORK both include parts of two lines. The /Delete command that removes the file WORK and the Go to (=B9) are the only commands that are entirely on their own lines.

Save this as B:UPDATE using the /Save command. Using the /Output command, write a disk file named UPDATE.XQT. (Enter **/O D ALL , D B:UPDATE.XQT <RET>**.) This will be the execute file.

Now to try it, clear the worksheet (**/ZY**), and load the file named B:AUGUST. Now enter **/XB:UPDATE**. Watch what happens. If everything is correct, the actions described will take place as you watch, and you will be left with a worksheet looking like Figure 9-5.

/Global Command Options

Several /Global options control the automatic functions of SuperCalc. They give you control over the automatic cell advance, the order in which calculations are performed, and automatic recalculation.

Automatic Cell Advance

The automatic advance of the active cell can be turned off and on with the /Global Next option. The auto-advance feature is handy when entering data into a worksheet. It saves you from having to advance the active cell with the arrow keys between each entry. But when you wish to try several different values in one cell to see what effect they have on a model you have developed, the automatic cell advance feature is not required. In fact it gets in the way in this situation. By using the /Global Next option (/G N) you can turn this feature on and off. This option works like a switch. If the auto-advance function is on, the /G N command turns it off; if the auto-advance function is off, /G N turns it back on again. You can tell if the auto-advance feature is on by looking for the direction arrow at the left of the entry line. When the auto-advance function is on, the direction arrow is displayed; when the auto-advance function is off, the arrow is not displayed. Try this by entering **/G N**. Then enter some data into a cell, press **<RET>**, and watch what happens. The active cell

```
   :      A       ::   B   ::   C   ::   D   ::   E   ::   F   ::   G   :
  1:
  2:
  3:Inventory record for the period of:
  4:
  5:
  6:                    Dept A   Dept B   Dept C    Total
  7:
  8: Beginning Inv.     350.00   400.00   500.00  1250.00
  9:       Purchases                                  .00
 10:           Usage                                  .00
 11:                ====================================
 12:     Ending Inv.    350.00   400.00   500.00  1250.00
 13:
 14:
 15:
 16:
 17:
 18:
 19:
 20:
^ B9
Width:  9  Memory: 26 Last Col/Row:F12    ? for HELP
  1>
```

Figure 9-5.

Automatic loading of beginning inventory

stays in the same place. Load the B:LOAN file and try testing different interest rates in cell D9.

Locating Input Cells Automatically

The /Global Tab option provides a useful function when setting up a SuperCalc model for someone else to use. When the Tab option is on, the active cell will only move to unprotected cells with entries in them. Protected cells and blank cells are skipped. This makes it hard for a person using the model to destroy any of the formulas or headings you have set up. It also makes it easy for a user to enter the required input data; the active cell automatically moves to the cells that need input values. You must remember to put some initial value into cells that you want the user to access; with the Tab option on, the active cell will skip over empty cells.

To see better how this option works, load the file B:MASTER. First you must set up this model to use the Tab option. Enter **"Enter month here** in cell E3. Enter **0** into each of the nine cells in the block B8:D10. Earlier you protected the cells containing labels and the cells with the formulas that give the results, leaving only the cells for input data unprotected.

Make sure that the auto-advance arrow is pointing to the right (>) by pressing the **RIGHT ARROW** key once. Move the active cell to B8 by entering **=B8 <RET>**. Now activate the Tab option by entering **/G T**. When you have completed these steps, your worksheet should appear as follows:

```
  :      A      ::    B    ::    C    ::    D    ::    E    ::    F    ::    G    :
 1:
 2:
 3:Inventory record for the period of:          Enter month here
 4:
 5:
 6:                      Dept A    Dept B    Dept C     Total
 7:
 8: Beginning Inv.          .00       .00       .00       .00
 9:       Purchases         .00       .00       .00       .00
10:           Usage         .00       .00       .00       .00
11:                ========================================
12:     Ending Inv.         .00       .00       .00       .00
13:
14:
15:
16:
17:
18:
19:
20:
> B8            Form=0
Width:   9  Memory: 26 Last Col/Row:F12     ? for HELP
  1>
```

Now save the model into a file called B:TABTEST. Any time you reload this file, the Tab function will be on.

Enter some new input values into cells B8 through D10. What happened when you pressed <RET> after entering the value into D8? The active cell jumped to B9, ready for you to enter the next set of values.

This action is called *rollover*. As you reach the end of a row or column, SuperCalc automatically moves you to the start of the next row or column.

When you reach the end of the last row or column, however, you must manually move back to the beginning. You can move back to the first entry cell either by using the arrow keys or by using the Go to (=) command. Finish entering the values in cells B8 through D10. When you press <RET> in D10, the active cell will not move because this is the last data entry cell.

Move up to cell E3 (enter **=E3 <RET>**). The Goto command works well because it does not affect the direction of the auto-advance arrow. Enter **"October**. When you press <RET> you will advance to cell B8.

If you do not want to change the value of a cell as it becomes the active cell, just press <RET>. This will move the active cell to the next location without changing the cell value.

Like the other /Global options discussed so far, the Tab option operates like a switch. Entering /G T again will turn the Tab option off.

Changing How SuperCalc Calculates

The rest of the /Global options (Row, Column, Manual, and Automatic) all affect the way SuperCalc performs calculations.

Manual and Automatic Recalculation

When you first turn the program on, SuperCalc automatically recalculates the entire worksheet each time an entry is made. However, if you have a large or complicated model, it can take several seconds or more to recalculate. If you must enter data into many differentials before an answer can be obtained, you can save much time by turning off the automatic recalculation feature of the program. To turn off the automatic recalculation feature you enter /G M. This sets the worksheet in the manual recalculation mode, and it will only recalculate when you press the exclamation point (!). This key recalculates all entries on the worksheet whether it is in manual or automatic mode, but it is the only way to get the worksheet to recalculate in the manual mode.

The worksheet can be put back into the automatic recalculation mode with the /Global Auto. option (/G A).

The B:LOAN worksheet that we have been working with is a good candidate for using the manual recalculation mode. You must input four values before you can get any meaningful results. If you use the manual recalculation mode with this worksheet, entering the input values will be quicker because you will not have to wait for the worksheet to recalculate between the entry of each value. When all the values are entered, use the exclamation point (!) to calculate the model.

Changing the Order of Calculation

The Row option instructs the program to perform calculations row by row. In this mode the program calculates all the cells in row 1, from left to right, and then all the cells in row 2. This process continues down the entire worksheet.

The Column option instructs the program to perform calculations column by column. The columns are calculated from top to bottom, in turn from left to right. Each column is completely calculated before the next is processed.

The importance of being able to calculate by rows or columns can be shown by a few quick examples. Starting with a clear worksheet, make the following entries:

Cell	*Entry*
A1	**4**
A2	**6**
A3	**SUM(A1:A2)**
B1	**A3**

Your worksheet should appear as follows:

```
     !   A   !!   B   !!   C   !!   D   !!   E   !!   F   !!   G   !!   H   !
   1!        4        10
   2!        6
   3!       10
   4!
   •
   •
   •
  20!
 < A1           Form=4
 Width:   9  Memory: 26 Last Col/Row:B3      ? for HELP
   1>
```

Everything looks fine; both A3 and B1 display (10), which is the sum of 6 and 4. Change the value in cell A1 to **3**. Now there is a problem. Cell B1 is trying to convince us that 6 + 3 equals 10. This is because the value of B1 was determined before cell A3 had been recalculated. This is called a *forward reference;* cell B1 is referencing forward to a cell, A3, which has not been recalculated yet.

```
     !   A   !!   B   !!   C   !!   D   !!   E   !!   F   !!   G   !!   H   !
   1!        3        10
   2!        6
   3!        9
   4!
   •
   •
   •
  20!
 < A1           Form=3
 Width:   9  Memory: 26 Last Col/Row:B3      ? for HELP
   1>
```

Recalculate the model by pressing **!**. Now cell B1 displays the correct value (9). Recalculating is a quick test for forward references. If anything on the worksheet changes during the second recalculation, a forward reference exists.

The default calculation option is by rows, so all of row 1 was calculated before rows 2 and 3 were calculated. To correct this problem, change the order of calculation to columns by entering **/G C**. Now try different values in cells A1 and A2. Everything works fine as long as the order of calculation is set the proper way.

This example was easily corrected, but it is possible to build a worksheet that cannot be recalculated correctly. You can have a forward reference that exists when the worksheet is calculated by rows and another one that exists when the worksheet is calculated by columns. To fix this condition you will have to move something on the worksheet, or else you will have to recalculate an extra time each time you want to see the results.

Another case where a worksheet cannot be recalculated correctly is when there are two cells that refer to each other, either directly or indirectly. This condition is called a *circular reference*. The easiest way to understand this is through an example.

Change the entry in cell A1 to **A3** and observe the results. Press the exclamation point (**!**) to recalculate the model, and notice that the results change. Try changing the order of calculation and press the exclamation point again. Either way it is still in error. The numbers keep increasing.

This is an example of a circular reference. Cell A1 is referred to by cell A3 which is referred to by cell A1.

A circular reference will never result in a correct answer. Recalculate as many times as you like, and the answer will always change. A circular reference is always the result of an incorrect formula and can be tested for by doing multiple recalculations.

CHAPTER TEN

Advanced Functions

SuperCalc has advanced functions that enable you to do scheduling and financial analysis and to retrieve information from tables. The logical functions and operators allow you to "make decisions" on the worksheet.

SuperCalc's Calendar

SuperCalc^2 provides a built-in calendar. This calendar can be used to put dates on the worksheet and to solve scheduling problems. If you are not using SuperCalc^2, skip this section and continue with the next section, which discusses the LOOKUP function.

Displaying Dates (DATE, TODAY)

Dates are displayed in a conventional "Month/Day/Year" format. Move to cell B6 and enter **DATE(8,21,83)**.

```
    :  A  ::  B  ::  C  ::  D  ::  E  ::  F  ::  G  ::  H  :
  1:
  2:
  3:
  4:
  5:
  6:          8/21/83
  7:
  8:
  9:
 10:
 11:
 12:
 13:
 14:

 19:
 20:
< B6           Form=DATE(8,21,83)
Width:  9  Memory: 26 Last Col/Row:C7     ? for HELP
  1>
```

The DATE function uses the numbers that you entered as the month, day, and year to create the date that is displayed. If the column width is greater than 10, all four digits of the year will be displayed.

The TODAY function can be used to put the current date on your worksheet. It is updated automatically each time the worksheet is recalculated.

In cell A8 enter **"Today's date is:**. Now move to cell C8 and type the word **TODAY** (with no double quote). The current date should be displayed like this:

```
    :  A  ::  B  ::  C  ::  D  ::  E  ::  F  ::  G  ::  H  :
  1:
  2:
  3:
  4:
  5:
  6:          8/21/83
  7:
  8:Today's date is:    9/19/83
  9:
 10:
 11:
 12:
 13:
 14:

 19:
 20:
< C8           Form=TODAY
Width:  9  Memory: 26 Last Col/Row:C8     ? for HELP
  1>
```

NOTE: For the TODAY function to work on a CP/M-80 computer you may need to run a program called DATTIM to enter the correct date. To do this, exit from SuperCalc (/**QY**). The DATTIM program will be on the SuperCalc^2 installation disk. To run it, you enter **DATTIM <RET>**. Enter the date as month, day, and year, separated by slashes, and the time as hour, minutes separated by a colon. Then reenter SuperCalc^2 (enter **SC2<RET>**).

Now clear the worksheet and make the following entries. These labels will be used to investigate the other SuperCalc date functions.

Cell	*Entry*
	/ F C A, 20, TR
A6	**"The date:**
A8	**"Month:**
A9	**"Day of month:**
A10	**"Year:**
A11	**"Day of the week:**
A13	**"Mod. Julian Date:**
A14	**"And back to a date:**
A16	**"Days old:**
A17	**"B-day, day of year:**
A19	**"10th Birthday:**
D4	**"Month**
E4	**"Day**
F4	**"Year**
	/F R 4 , TR <RET>

Enter the month, day, and year that you were born in cells D6, E6, and F6, respectively. Those of you that were born before March 1, 1900 will have to use another date for this example—SuperCalc's calendar only covers the 200 years from March 1, 1900 to February 28, 2100. In this example we will use February 12, 1940. With these entries, your worksheet should look like Figure 10-1.

Move to cell B6 and enter **DATE(D6,E6,F6)**. The date that you were born will be displayed. Since you can create a date from three separate cell references (the month, day, and year) you have additional flexibility to do calculations. Now that we have created a date from the three parts, we will look at the functions that display parts of a date.

```
   :         A         ::  B  ::  C  ::  D  ::  E  ::  F  ::  G  :
  1:
  2:
  3:
  4:                                   Month      Day      Year
  5:
  6:       My birthday:                    2       12        40
  7:
  8:             Month:
  9:      Day of month:
 10:              Year:
 11:   Day of the week:
 12:
 13:    Mod. Julian Date
 14: And back to a date:
 15:
 16:          Days old:
 17: B-day, day of year:
 18:
 19:      10th Birthday:
 20:
> G6
Width:  9  Memory: 26 Last Col/Row:F19    ? for HELP
  1>
```

Figure 10-1.

Birthday worksheet

The MONTH, DAY, YEAR, and WDAY Functions

Make the following entries on the worksheet:

Cell	*Entry*
B8	**MONTH(B6)**
B9	**DAY(B6)**
B10	**YEAR(B6)**
B11	**WDAY(B6)**

```
   :         A         ::  B  ::  C  ::  D  ::  E  ::  F  ::  G  :
  •
  •
  •
  4:                                   Month      Day      Year
  5:
  6:       My birthday:  2/12/40           2       12        40
  7:
  8:             Month:        2
  9:      Day of month:       12
 10:              Year:     1940
 11:   Day of the week:        2
 12:
 13:    Mod. Julian Date
 14: And back to a date:
 15:
 16:          Days old:
 17: B-day, day of year:
 18:
 19:      10th Birthday:
 20:
^ B11       Form=WDAY(B6)
Width:  9  Memory: 26 Last Col/Row:F19    ? for HELP
  1>
```

From the results, it is fairly obvious what the first three of these functions do. MONTH returns a number from 1 to 12 that represents the month of the year; DAY returns the day of the month; and YEAR returns the year. The fourth function, WDAY, returns a number from 1 to 7 that represents the day of the week that the date falls on. The week starts with Sunday as 1.

Doing Calculations With Dates

To solve scheduling problems, we need to be able to do calculations with dates. SuperCalc allows you to do all reasonable calculations with dates.

You can add numbers to dates and subtract numbers from dates. In cell B19 we will calculate the date of your 10th birthday. Enter **B6+3652**. This is the date you were born, plus 10 years (365*10) plus allowance for two leap years. It may be off by a day. If there were three leap years before your 10th birthday, then you need to enter **B6+3653**. When these entries are done, your worksheet will appear as follows:

```
   :        A        ::   B   ::   C   ::   D   ::   E   ::   F   ::   G   :
  1:
  2:
  3:
  4:                                       Month       Day       Year
  5:
  6:         My birthday:  2/12/40             2         12         40
  7:
  8:              Month:         2
  9:       Day of month:        12
 10:               Year:      1940
 11:    Day of the week:         2
 12:
 13:    Mod. Julian Date
 14: And back to a date:
 15:
 16:           Days old:     15925
 17: B-day, day of year:        43
 18:
 19:      10th Birthday:   2/12/50
 20:
v B19         Form=B6+3653
Width:  9  Memory: 26 Last Col/Row:F19     ? for HELP
  1>■
```


You can calculate the elapsed time between two dates by subtracting them. In cell B16 enter **TODAY−B6**. TODAY is today's date and B6 contains the date that you were born, so cell B16 shows the number of days that you have lived.

In cell B17 we will use a slightly more complicated calculation to see what day of the year your birthday falls on. Enter **B6−DATE(1,0,YEAR(B6))**. B6 is your birth date. DATE (1,0,YEAR(B6)) is the last day of the year before you were born. But what we have entered is "January 0." This demonstrates an important feature of the SuperCalc calendar. The dates that you enter do not have to be "real" dates. SuperCalc will automatically convert

"January 0" to "December 31". This can make it easier to solve scheduling problems using formulas and the /Replicate command.

You cannot multiply or divide dates (or *by* dates), and although you can add a number to a date, you cannot add a date to a number.

The Modified Julian Calendar

SuperCalc's calendar is a *Modified Julian Calendar.* Internally, it represents each date with a Julian date number. These Julian dates range from 1 for March 1, 1900 to 73049 for February 28, 2100. The calendar is not a true Julian Calendar because it begins on an arbitrary date.

Julian dates are often useful in calculations. They are available through the DVAL and JDATE functions. Move to cell B13 and enter **JDATE(B6)**. This is the *Modified Julian Date* of your birth. Now, in cell B14, enter **DVAL(B13)**. This function converts the Modified Julian Date back to a conventional date. It should look the same as cell B6.

When these entries are complete, your worksheet should look like the following illustration, although the actual values will be different because the date you are using is different.

```
   :        A        ::    B    ::    C    ::    D    ::    E    ::    F    ::    G    :
 1:
 2:
 3:
 4:                                              Month       Day       Year
 5:
 6:        My birthday:  2/12/40                     2        12         40
 7:
 8:             Month:         2
 9:      Day of month:        12
10:              Year:      1940
11:   Day of the week:         2
12:
13:    Mod. Julian Date    14593
14: And back to a date:  2/12/40
15:
16:          Days old:     15925
17: B-day, day of year:       43
18:
19:      10th Birthday:  2/12/50
20:
^ B14          Form=DVAL(B13)
Width:  9  Memory: 26 Last Col/Row:F19     ? for HELP
  1>█
```

Finding Values in Tables (LOOKUP)

SuperCalc has another built-in function that selects values from a table. The LOOKUP function looks for a value in a range of cells and returns the value that appears in an adjacent cell. This is a highly useful function for many applications.

The syntax of the LOOKUP function is

LOOKUP(*value, range*)

The LOOKUP function searches the cells in the given range until it finds the last *value* less than or equal to the input *value*. The function then returns the value of the cell adjacent to the cell that it found. If the range is a partial row, the value returned is from the cell in the row below the matched cell. If the range is a partial column, LOOKUP returns the value from the cell in the column to the right of the matched cell. Values in the LOOKUP table range must be arranged in ascending order.

The example in Figure 10-2 finds freight rates based on weight. The

```
  |      A      ||   B   ||   C   ||   D   ||   E   ||   F   ||   G   |
 1|
 2|                                       1     1.35
 3|                                       2     1.55
 4|                                       3     1.75
 5|Package Weight         3               4     1.95
 6|Freight Charge      1.75               5     2.15
 7|                                       6     2.35
 8|                                       7     2.55
 9|                                       8     2.75
10|                                       9     2.95
11|                                      10     3.15
 .
 .
 .
20|
< B6          Form=LOOKUP(B5,D2:D11)
Width:  9  Memory: 26 Last Col/Row:E11     ? for HELP
 1>
```

Figure 10-2.

Freight rates with LOOKUP

LOOKUP function uses a table in columns D and E. Make the following entries on a blank worksheet to create this model:

Cell	*Entry*
	/F C A , 20
A5	**"Package Weight:**
A6	**"Freight Charge:**
D2	**1**
D3	**D2+1**
	/R D3 , D4:D11 <RET>
E2	**1.35**
E3	**E2+.20**
	/R E3 , E4:E11 <RET>

In cell B5 enter **3**. In cell B6 enter **LOOKUP(B5,D2:D11)**. This says "Find the value of B5 in the range D2:D11 and return the adjacent value from column E." The value displayed in cell B6 should be (1.75). Try some other values in cell B5 and confirm that the LOOKUP function is returning the correct values from column E.

The range you specify for the LOOKUP function must be in ascending order, but the adjacent values do not need to be in any particular order. For example, the values in the search range might be the identification numbers of the machines in a machine shop, while the values to be returned are the hourly rates charged for each machine. It would be quite a coincidence if the hourly rates varied in any mathematical relationship to the machine identification numbers.

Reporting Errors in LOOKUP Tables

Now let's try some incorrect values. In cell B5 enter **0**. The LOOKUP function has returned "N/A". This means not available. In this case, this is probably all right, but in many LOOKUP tables the first entry should be 0 so you can control the value returned. In cell B5 enter **11**. The value returned (3.15) is the same as for a 10-pound package. This is not right, and we should correct this. To do this enter **11** in cell D12 and **ERROR** (with no double quote mark) in cell E12. Change the LOOKUP function in cell B6 to incorporate D12 in its range. It should look like this: LOOKUP(B5,D2:D12). Now a weight of 11 will result in the word "ERROR" being displayed in cell B6.

The ERROR and NA functions are display functions that are used to report an error or an invalid result. The ERROR function displays the word "ERROR" in the cell in which it is a result and in any other cells that have references to it. The NA function works exactly the same, except it displays

"N/A" for not available. While useful in some situations, these functions are somewhat difficult to apply. While it might sometimes be useful to report that an intermediate value did not apply to the particular values being used, using the NA function will give a "N/A" result not only where it is wanted, but in any other cells with direct or indirect reference to the cell displaying "N/A". This includes references to a group of cells including the offending cell, as in SUM or AVERAGE.

The ERROR function is also automatically inserted into formulas whenever the cell references become invalid. This can happen if a row or column that contains a referred-to cell is deleted. The cell reference is changed to "ERROR". The same problem will occur during copying or replicating when normal cell reference adjustment would cause reference to a cell that does not exist.

Using LOOKUP With Text Values

If you are using SuperCalc^2, you can have the LOOKUP function return words instead of numbers. To do this you put *text values* in the LOOKUP table. A *text value* is a word that is enclosed in both parentheses and double quotes, like ("word"). The word may have as many as 9 characters in it (you are not limited to just letters). Text values are treated much like other values since they can be referenced by their cell location. This makes them very useful in LOOKUP tables. For instance, in the previous example change cell E12 to read **("Try again")**.

```
   |        A         ||    B    ||    C    ||    D    ||    E    ||    F    ||    G    |
  1|
  2|                                               1      1.35
  3|                                               2      1.55
  4|                                               3      1.75
  5|Package Weight            11                   4      1.95
  6|Freight Charge      Try again                  5      2.15
  7|                                               6      2.35
  8|                                               7      2.55
  9|                                               8      2.75
 10|                                               9      2.95
 11|                                              10      3.15
 12|                                              11Try again
 13|
 14|
 15|
 16|
  •
  •
  •
 20|
^ E12         Form=("Try again")
Width:  9  Memory: 26 Last Col/Row:E12    ? for HELP
  1>■
```

```
   :   A  ::   B  ::   C  ::   D  ::   E  ::   F  ::   G  ::   H  :
 1:
 2:                                                1   January
 3:                                                2  February
 4:                                                3     March
 5:Date       2/12/40                              4     April
 6:Day:        Monday                              5       May
 7:Month:    February                              6      June
 8:                                                7      July
 9:                                                8    August
10:                                                9September
11:                                               10   October
12:                                               11  November
13:                                               12  December
14:
15:        1        2        3        4        5        6        7
16:   Sunday   Monday  TuesdayWednesday Thursday   Friday Saturday
17:
18:
19:
20:
^ B7          Form=LOOKUP(MONTH(B5),F2:F13)
Width:  9  Memory: 25 Last Col/Row:G16     ? for HELP
  1>█
```

Figure 10-3.

LOOKUP with dates

One use of text values is to convert dates into words for months and days. Figure 10-3 is a worksheet that uses LOOKUP to do just that. Make the following entries to create the worksheet:

Cell	*Entry*
A5	**"Date**
A6	**"Day:**
A7	**"Month:**
B5	**TODAY**
F2	**1**
F3	**F2+1**
	/R F3 , F4:F13 <RET>
G2	**("January")**
G3	**("February")**
G4	**("March")**
G5	**("April")**
G6	**("May")**
G7	**("June")**
G8	**("July")**
G9	**("August")**

G10	**("September")**
G11	**("October")**
G12	**("November")**
G13	**("December")**
A15	**1**
B15	**A15+1**
	/R B15 , C15:G15 <RET>
A16	**("Sunday")**
B16	**("Monday")**
C16	**("Tuesday")**
D16	**("Wednesday")**
E16	**("Thursday")**
F16	**("Friday")**
G16	**("Saturday")**

Now we are ready to add the two LOOKUP functions that will give us the day and the month. Enter your birthday (or some other date) in cell B5 using the DATE function: **DATE(2,12,40)**. The LOOKUP function in cell B6 will take the WDAY function of the date in cell B5 and use the LOOKUP table to find the corresponding day in the text values. The formula for cell B6 is **LOOKUP(WDAY(B5),A15:G15)**. Notice that this LOOKUP table is in a row instead of a column; either form works just as well. To do the same for the month enter **LOOKUP(MONTH(B5),F2:F13)** in cell B7.

Finding the Value of an Investment (NPV)

SuperCalc provides the NPV (*Net Present Value*) function to calculate the *present value* of money you will receive in the future.

Money that you will receive in the future is not worth as much as money that you receive now. The NPV function discounts the value of future earnings to express them in today's money. NPV sums future earnings and discounts them according to how far in the future they will be received.

To use the NPV function, you forecast the amount of earnings that you expect to realize in the future. You then judge these expected earnings against what you would normally expect to earn in a very "safe" investment, like a savings account. The rate you would earn in this safe investment is called the *discount rate*. The NPV function uses this rate to discount the value of future earnings. The formula that the NPV function uses is

$$\text{NPV} = \frac{e1}{(1+d)^1} + \frac{e2}{(1+d)^2} + \frac{e3}{(1+d)^3} + \frac{e4}{(1+d)^4} + \ldots$$

where *e1*, *e2*, ... are the projected future earnings, and *d* is the discount rate. The earnings at the end of the first period are discounted once, the earnings at the end of the second period are discounted twice, and so on.

If you wish to compare an investment to keeping your money in the bank, you might select a discount rate equal to the interest rate that the bank will pay you.

The NPV function works like this:

NPV(*discount rate, range*)

where the *range* includes the earnings that will be received. It is assumed that the earnings are received at equal time periods and that the *discount rate* is the interest rate for each of those periods of time. The discount rate must be entered as a decimal number, not as a percent (a 5% discount is entered as .05). The *range* for this function can only be a partial row or column. The first cell in the range contains the earnings for the first period, the second cell the earnings for the second period, and so on. A block range will not work since the order of the cells is important.

Here is how you could use the NPV function. Suppose your brother-in-law has offered you a chance to invest $10,000 in a limited partnership. This limited partnership will pay you $1500 each year for ten years but have no remaining value at the end of that time. Figure 10-4 shows how you would set this up.

At first glance it looks like a good investment. You invest $10,000 and you receive $15,000 back. But how does it compare with putting that $10,000 in a bank at 8.5% annual interest? By using the NPV function you can answer this question.

Looking at Figure 10-4, the initial investment is shown in cell C2 (for reference only). Cell C3 contains the discount rate. This is the amount that dollars are devalued each year in the future. We are using 8.5% to compare with the interest rate available through a bank. The first year's "income" is −10,000, which is the amount invested. The rest of the income amounts are in cells D7 through D16. Cell D18 contains the total of the income payments.

The formula in cell D20 is

NPV(C3,D6:D17)

```
  :  A  ::  B  ::  C  ::  D  ::  E  ::  F  ::  G  ::  H  :
 1:                                      Investment Analysis
 2:Amount Invested:      10000
 3:Discount Rate:         .085
 4:
 5:                       Year    Amount
 6:Annual Earnings        1984    -10000
 7:                       1985      1500
 8:                       1986      1500
 9:                       1987      1500
10:                       1988      1500
11:                       1989      1500
12:                       1990      1500
13:                       1991      1500
14:                       1992      1500
15:                       1993      1500
16:                       1994      1500
17:                    ==================
18:Total Earnings                   5000
19:
20:Net Present Value:            -145.60
> D20   $      Form=NPV(C3,D6:D17)
Width:  9  Memory: 26 Last Col/Row:F20    ? for HELP
  1>■
```

Figure 10-4.

Net Present Value

The result is $-145.60. This means that the present value of your brother-in-law's investment is $145.60 less than leaving the money in the bank.

However, suppose you could only make 5.5% interest in your savings account. How would the investment look then? To find out, change the value of cell C3 to **.055**.

```
  :  A  ::  B  ::  C  ::  D  ::  E  ::  F  ::  G  ::  H  :
 1:                                      Investment Analysis
 2:Amount Invested:      10000
 3:Discount                .055
 4:
 5:                       Year    Amount
 6:Annual Earnings        1984    -10000
 7:                       1985      1500
 8:                       1986      1500
 9:                       1987      1500
10:                       1988      1500
11:                       1989      1500
12:                       1990      1500
13:                       1991      1500
14:                       1992      1500
15:                       1993      1500
16:                       1994      1500
17:                    ==================
18:Total Earnings                   5000
19:
20:Net Present Value:             1238.33
< B3
Width:  9  Memory: 26 Last Col/Row:F20    ? for HELP
  1>■
```

The net present value of the investment is now $1238.33. This means that you would be $1238.33 ahead (in today's dollars) by making the investment instead of leaving your money in the bank at 5.5% interest. Now save this in a file called B:NPV so that you can use it later in Chapter 12.

Making Decisions (IF, AND, OR, NOT)

SuperCalc has four built-in functions that allow you to make decisions in a model. These functions, which are the IF, AND, OR, and NOT functions, are often referred to as the logical functions because of this capability. Used with the relational operators, these functions provide you with powerful tools for building useful and efficient models.

The IF Function

SuperCalc's major decision-making device is the IF function. Suppose you want to test whether the values in cells A3 and B3 are equal. If they are equal, you want cell A8 to display the value (555) and if they are not equal you want cell A8 to display the value (10). In SuperCalc an IF function to do this looks like this:

IF(A3=B3,555,10)

This means "If A3 is equal to B3 take the value 555; otherwise, take the value 10." Now make the following entries:

Cell	*Entry*
A3	**3**
B3	**5**
C3	**7**
A4	**555**
B4	**10**
D1	**/WV**
A8	**IF(A3=B3,A4,B4)**

Now press the semicolon (;) to move back to the left window and set Formula display mode (enter **/G F**).

Your worksheet should look like Figure 10-5.

In the IF function there are three arguments separated by commas inside the parentheses. The first argument is called a *logical expression.* It is the

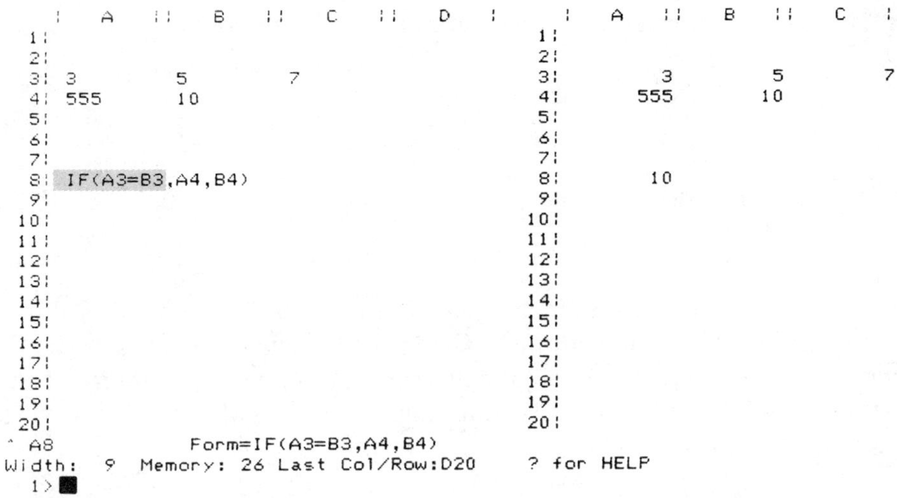

Figure 10-5.

The IF function

argument that the IF function bases its decision on. If this logical expression is *True*, the value of the second argument is used as the value for this cell. If the first expression is *False*, the value of the third argument is used.

But what do *True* and *False* mean to SuperCalc? *True* and *False* mean just what you are used to. The logical expression is *True* only when A is equal to B. Otherwise A=B is *False*.

Relational Operators and the IF Function

The equal sign between the A and B that we have just seen is used to compare the value of A in relation to B. It is not *saying* that A is equal to B, but rather it is *asking* if A is equal to B. There are several symbols like the equal sign that can be used to compare two numbers. These are called the *relational operators*.

The relational operators are somewhat like arithmetic operators. They are placed between two values, they act on those two values, and they produce a result. However, the results they produce are restricted to two values: 1 (for *True*) and 0 (for *False*).

Here is a list of the relational operators and their functions:

Operator	*Function*
=	is equal to
<>	is not equal to
<	is less than
<=	is less than or equal to
>	is greater than
>=	is greater than or equal to

Figure 10-5 shows these relational operators used in IF functions. Column A shows what is entered in column B. Column B shows the results of the IF functions with the various relational operators. To see how the values of the IF functions change with different values for the relational operators to work on, make the following entries:

Cell	*Entry*
A7	**"Relational Operators**
A8	**IF(A3=B3,A4,B4)**
A9	**IF(A3>B3,A4,B4)**
A10	**IF(A3<B3,A4,B4)**
A11	**IF(A3<>B3,A4,B4)**
A12	**IF(A3<=B3,A4,B4)**

Column A should look like the following:

```
    :   A    ::   B    ::   C    ::   D    :
 1:
 2:
 3: 3          5          7
 4: 555        10
 5:
 6:
 7:Relational Operators
 8: IF(A3=B3,A4,B4)
 9: IF(A3>B3,A4,B4)
10: IF(A3<B3,A4,B4)
11: IF(A3<>B3,A4,B4)
12: IF(A3<=B3,A4,B4)
13:
14:
15:
16:
17:
18:
19:
20:
^ A12          Form=IF(A3<=B3,A4,B4)
Width:  9  Memory: 26 Last Col/Row:D20    ? for HELP
 1>
```

```
    :   A    ::   B    ::   C    :
 1:
 2:
 3:         3         5         7
 4:       555        10
 5:
 6:
 7:Relational Operators
 8:        10
 9:        10
10:       555
11:       555
12:       555
13:
14:
15:
16:
17:
18:
19:
20:
```

If this is not the case, check your entries. Now try different values in A3 and B3. Be sure to try values where A3 is equal to B3 and A3 is larger than B3.

No matter how large or small the values in A3 and B3 are, the values produced by the IF functions are always either 555 or 10. The output of the relational operators is affected only by the relationship of the input values, not by their magnitude. This should give you a good idea of how the relational operators work in IF functions.

Arithmetic Operators and the IF Function

SuperCalc does not restrict you to just relational operators in IF functions. The first argument in the IF function can also be an arithmetic calculation. SuperCalc will regard any non-zero result as *True* and a zero result as *False.* Thus you can use mathematical operators in logical expressions, but you can also use relational operators in mathematical expressions. To illustrate this, make the following entry:

Cell	*Entry*
A13	**IF(A3–B3,A4,B4)**

```
   :    A    ::    B    ::    C    ::    D    :
  1:
  2:
  3: 3         5         7
  4: 555       10
  5:
  6:
  7:Relational Operators
  8: IF(A3=B3,A4,B4)
  9: IF(A3>B3,A4,B4)
 10: IF(A3<B3,A4,B4)
 11: IF(A3<>B3,A4,B4)
 12: IF(A3<=B3,A4,B4)
 13:
 14: IF(A3-B3,A4,B4)
 15:
 16:
 17:
 18:
 19:
 20:
^ A15
Width:  9  Memory: 26 Last Col/Row:C20     ? for HELP
  1>
```

```
   :    A    ::    B    ::    C    :
  1:
  2:
  3:        3         5         7
  4:      555        10
  5:
  6:
  7:Relational Operators
  8:       10
  9:       10
 10:      555
 11:      555
 12:      555
 13:
 14:      555
 15:
 16:
 17:
 18:
 19:
 20:
```

Enter some more arbitrary numbers in cells A3 and B3. Study the results of these expressions when A3 is equal to B3 and when they are not equal. Notice that any time they are not equal, even when B3 is larger than A3, the

IF function in cell A13 sees a *True*, and gives a result of (555). This is consistent with the definition of True being any non-zero number. A3—B3 is True any time it is not equal to zero. Now save this in a file called B:LOGIC.

Figure 10-6 shows the calculation of one company's sales commissions. Under this plan a 20-percent commission is paid to people with $2200 or less in sales, and a 22-percent commission is paid to people with more than $2200 in sales. The IF function is used to determine which of these two rates should be used in a calculation. The IF function in cell D8 gives a value of (22) if the value of cell D7 is greater than 2200, and a value of (20) if D7 is less than or equal to 2200. Cell D9 multiplies the rate determined in cell D8 by the sales in cell D7 to calculate the commission earned (D7*D8/100). Columns C and E work the same way.

Nested IF Functions

Sometimes you might want to have more than one condition in an IF function. You can do this by using the other logical functions inside the IF function. The other logical functions are AND, OR, and NOT. These logical functions are used to add conditions to an IF function. The meaning of such an IF

```
   |  A  ||        B        ||   C   ||   D   ||   E   ||   F   ||   G   |
  1|
  2|
  3|
  4|
  5|              Sales person:      Bill      Mary      John
  6|                            ==============================
  7|                     Sales:   2000.00   4000.00   2500.00
  8|            Comission rate:     20.00     22.00     22.00
  9|                Commission:    400.00    880.00    550.00
 10|
 11|
 12|
 13|
 14|
 15|                        Add 2% if sales are over:       2200.00
 16|
 17|
 18|
 19|
 20|
 ^ D8          Form=IF(D7>F15,22,20)
Width:   9  Memory: 26 Last Col/Row:F15     ? for HELP
  1>█
```

Figure 10-6.

Sales commissions

function in English is "If A is equal to B AND B is equal to C, take this; otherwise, take that."

Logical expressions, however, can quickly become complicated. Since SuperCalc functions must have the key word first, these logical functions must be written in a way that you are not used to reading. For instance, the AND function is constructed as follows:

AND(*expression1, expression2*)

The AND function results in *True* (a value of 1) if both logical *expression1* and *expression2* are *True* (non-zero). If either *expression1* or *expression2* is *False* (zero), the AND function results in *False* (a zero value). For example, clear the worksheet and in cell A4 enter **AND(A3=3,B3=5).**

This formula means "If A3 is equal to 3 and B3 is equal to 5, this function will have a value of 1; otherwise this function will have a value of 0."

Now here is how to use AND in an IF function. Clear your worksheet and reload the file B:LOGIC.

An IF function to solve the English sentence "If A is less than B and B is less than C, take this; otherwise, take that" looks like this:

IF(AND(A3<B3,B3<C3),A4,B4)

Enter this formula in cell A17, and in cell A16 enter **"And, Or**.

```
   :  A    ::   B    ::   C    ::   D   :
 1:
 2:
 3: 3        5        7
 4: 555      10
 5:
 6:
 7:Relational Operators
 8: IF(A3=B3,A4,B4)
 9: IF(A3>B3,A4,B4)
10: IF(A3<B3,A4,B4)
11: IF(A3<>B3,A4,B4)
12: IF(A3<=B3,A4,B4)
13:
14: IF(A3-B3,A4,B4)
15:
16:And, Or
17: IF(AND(A3<B3,B3<C3),A4,B4)
18:
19:
20:
^ A17          Form=IF(AND(A3<B3,B3<C3),A4,B4)
Width:  9  Memory: 26 Last Col/Row:C20    ? for HELP
 1>
```

```
   :  A    ::   B    ::   C    :
 1:
 2:
 3:        3        5        7
 4:      555       10
 5:
 6:
 7:Relational Operators
 8:       10
 9:       10
10:      555
11:      555
12:      555
13:
14:      555
15:
16:And, Or
17:      555
18:
19:
20:
```

Since both A3<B3 and B3<C3 are True, the IF function chooses the first value (A4), and 555 is displayed.

The syntax of the OR function is similar to the AND function:

OR(*expression1, expression2*)

The OR function results in *True* (a value of 1) if either *expression1* or *expression2* is *True* (non-zero). If neither expression is *True*, the result is *False* (a zero value). In cell A18 enter **IF(OR(A3=3,B3=7),A4,B4).**

```
     :   A   ::   B   ::   C   ::   D   :     :   A   ::   B   ::   C   :
   1:                                       1:
   2:                                       2:
   3: 3        5        7                   3:        3        5        7
   4: 555      10                           4:      555       10
   5:                                       5:
   6:                                       6:
   7:Relational Operators                   7:Relational Operators
   8: IF(A3=B3,A4,B4)                       8:       10
   9: IF(A3>B3,A4,B4)                       9:       10
  10: IF(A3<B3,A4,B4)                      10:      555
  11: IF(A3<>B3,A4,B4)                     11:      555
  12: IF(A3<=B3,A4,B4)                     12:      555
  13:                                      13:
  14: IF(A3-B3,A4,B4)                      14:      555
  15:                                      15:
  16:And, Or                               16:And, Or
  17: IF(AND(A3<B3,B3<C3),A4,B4)           17:      555
  18: IF(OR(A3=3,B3=9),A4,B4)              18:      555
  19:                                      19:
  20:                                      20:
v A18          Form=IF(OR(A3=3,B3=9),A4,B4)
Width:  9 · Memory: 26 Last Col/Row:C20     ? for HELP
 1>
```

The OR function results in *True* since A3 is equal to 3. If B3 were equal to 7, it would also result in 1. Otherwise, the result of this function is *False.*

The NOT function uses only one expression, as follows:

NOT(*expression*)

The NOT function results in *True* (a value of 1) if the *expression* is *False* (zero). The NOT function results in a value of zero if the *expression* is non-zero. In cell A19 enter **IF(NOT(A3=B3),A4,B4).**

```
   :   A    ::   B    ::   C    ::   D   :      :   A    ::   B    ::   C    :
  1:                                          1:
  2:                                          2:
  3: 3        5        7                      3:       3        5        7
  4: 555      10                              4:     555       10
  5:                                          5:
  6:                                          6:
  7:Relational Operators                      7:Relational Operators
  8: IF(A3=B3,A4,B4)                          8:      10
  9: IF(A3>B3,A4,B4)                          9:      10
 10: IF(A3<B3,A4,B4)                         10:     555
 11: IF(A3<>B3,A4,B4)                        11:     555
 12: IF(A3<=B3,A4,B4)                        12:     555
 13:                                         13:
 14: IF(A3-B3,A4,B4)                         14:     555
 15:                                         15:
 16:And, Or                                  16:And, Or
 17: IF(AND(A3<B3,B3<C3),A4,B4)              17:     555
 18: IF(OR(A3=3,B3=9),A4,B4)                 18:     555
 19: IF(NOT(A3=B3),A4,B4)                    19:     555
 20:                                         20:
^ A19          Form=IF(NOT(A3=B3),A4,B4)
Width:  9  Memory: 26 Last Col/Row:C20     ? for HELP
  1>
```

The NOT function shown results in *True* because A3 and B3 are not equal.

You may want to have IF be able to return more than two different alternatives. To do this you can use an IF function as one of the values to return within another IF function. For instance, in cell C4 enter **999**. Then enter the following formula in cell A1:

IF(A3<B3,IF(A3<C3,C4,B4),A4)

```
   :   A    ::   B    ::   C    ::   D   :      :   A    ::   B    ::   C    :
  1: IF(A3<B3,IF(A3<C3,C4,B4),A4)             1:     999
  2:                                          2:
  3: 3        5        7                      3:       3        5        7
  4: 555      10       999                    4:     555       10      999
  5:                                          5:
  6:                                          6:
  7:Relational Operators                      7:Relational Operators
  8: IF(A3=B3,A4,B4)                          8:      10
  9: IF(A3>B3,A4,B4)                          9:      10
 10: IF(A3<B3,A4,B4)                         10:     555
 11: IF(A3<>B3,A4,B4)                        11:     555
 12: IF(A3<=B3,A4,B4)                        12:     555
 13:                                         13:
 14: IF(A3-B3,A4,B4)                         14:     555
 15:                                         15:
 16:And, Or                                  16:And, Or
 17: IF(AND(A3<B3,B3<C3),A4,B4)              17:     555
 18: IF(OR(A3=3,B3=9),A4,B4)                 18:     555
 19: IF(NOT(A3=B3),A4,B4)                    19:     555
 20:                                         20:
^ A1           Form=IF(A3<B3,IF(A3<C3,C4,B4),A4)
Width:  9  Memory: 26 Last Col/Row:C20     ? for HELP
  1>
```

Now change the values in cells A3 through D3, and watch the values of the cells in column A change.

As with the LOOKUP function, you can also see text variables in the IF function. If you are using SuperCalc², you may also want to try the following:

Cell	*Entry*
A4	**("True")**
B4	**("False")**
C4	**("Humbug")**

```
  !    A    !!    B    !!    C    !!    D    !
 1! IF(A3<B3,IF(A3<C3,C4,B4),A4)
 2!
 3! 3         5         7
 4! ("True") ("False" ("Humbug")
 5!
 6!
 7!Relational Operators
 8! IF(A3=B3,A4,B4)
 9! IF(A3>B3,A4,B4)
10! IF(A3<B3,A4,B4)
11! IF(A3<>B3,A4,B4)
12! IF(A3<=B3,A4,B4)
13!
14! IF(A3-B3,A4,B4)
15!
16!And, Ur
17! IF(AND(A3<B3,B3<C3),A4,B4)
18! IF(OR(A3=3,B3=9),A4,B4)
19! IF(NOT(A3=B3),A4,B4)
20!
< C4            Form=("Humbug")
Width:  9  Memory: 26 Last Col/Row:C20     ? for HELP
 1>
```

```
  !    A    !!    B    !!    C    !
 1!   Humbug
 2!
 3!         3         5         7
 4!      True     False    Humbug
 5!
 6!
 7!Relational Operators
 8!     False
 9!     False
10!      True
11!      True
12!      True
13!
14!      True
15!
16!And, Or
17!      True
18!      True
19!      True
20!
```

CHAPTER ELEVEN

Applying SuperCalc

The SuperCalc program can be used for a wide variety of applications, but many of the program's capabilities may not be obvious when you begin to use it. This chapter discusses approaches to developing models for different kinds of applications and points out how to apply some special techniques to this process.

Developing a Model

Often the idea for a new application model is just that, an idea. Details of the required results, format, and input are not known at all. For example, you might say to yourself "I think I will make a model to balance my checkbook." When you have only thought this far, you may know little about how to set up this application. You may not know what the actual report will look like or what information you will need to include. In addition to keeping a current balance, will you also want to have a summary of expenditures and deposits by month or a record of outstanding checks and month-end reconciliations?

Development of a model for an application like this can be done right on the screen. You begin with what you know and build from there. In a check register, you will need to have an entry for each check, including the check number, who it was written to, and the amount. To begin, lay out a column on the display screen for each of these items. As you develop the model, you will probably think of other information you would like to include. When something useful comes to mind, use the /Insert command to add a new column or row wherever you want it.

Figure 11-1 shows the check register model "under construction" with some data already entered. Rows 3 and 4 describe the information that will be stored in the columns below: check number in column A, to whom it was written in column B, the date in column C, the amount in column D, and a running balance in column E. Note that using two rows for column headings makes them easier to read. To create the check register, first format the columns as follows:

/F C A , 5 , L
/F C B , 25
/F C D , $, TR
/F C E , $, TR

Now enter the headings across rows 3 and 4. Next, in cell A6 enter **101**, the first check number. To make SuperCalc display the second check number, enter **A6+1** in cell A7. Finally, replicate cell A8 down column A (**/R A7, A8:A15**) to create the other check numbers.

```
  | A ||            B             ||   C   ||    D    ||    E    ||    F    ||    G    |
 1|Check Register
 2|
 3|Check                           Date        Amount      Acct
 4|Numb Description (Paid to)      Written   of Check   Balance
 5|==========================================================================================
 6|  101 A. B. Landlord Realty     8/1/83      500.00
 7|  102 Wild Fling Travel Agency  8/2/83      375.00
 8|  103 Specific Gas & Electric   8/5/83       40.00
 9|  104 T. P. C.                  8/15/83      32.30
10|  105 Joe Turkey                8/15/83      25.98
11|  106 Roger Snyder
12|  107
13|  108
14|  109
15|  110
16|
17|
18|
19|
20|
> B11          Text="Roger Snyder
Width: 25  Memory: 26 Last Col/Row:G16    ? for HELP
  1> ■
```

Figure 11-1.

Building a check register

You will probably want to add a starting balance to this model. To do this you need to insert a new row. Suppose you want to show the starting balance just above the row for the first check. To do this, position the active cell to row 6 and enter **/I R <RET>**. Fill in a description, date, and the starting balance. This might appear as follows:

```
   | A ||           B              ||   C    ||    D    ||    E    ||    F   ||    G   |
  1|Check Register
  2|
  3|Check                           Date          Amount       Acct
  4|Numb Description (Paid to)     Written     of Check    Balance
  5|=========================================================================================
  6|     STARTING BALANCE           8/1/83                   1850.00
  7| 101 A. B. Landlord Realty      8/1/83         500.00
  8| 102 Wild Fling Travel Agency   8/2/83         375.00
  9| 103 Specific Gas & Electric    8/5/83          40.00
 10| 104 T. P. C.                   8/15/83         32.30
 11| 105 Joe Turkey                 8/15/83         25.98
 12| 106 Roger Snyder
 13| 107
 14| 108
 15| 109
 16| 110
 17|
 18|
 19|
 20|
< E6          Form=1850.
Width:  9  Memory: 26 Last Col/Row:G17     ? for HELP
  1> █
```

To calculate the running account balance, enter **E6−D7** in cell E7 and replicate this down column E (**/R E7 , E8:E20**). Your model should now look like this:

```
   | A ||           B              ||   C    ||    D    ||    E    ||    F   ||    G   |
  1|Check Register
  2|
  3|Check                           Date          Amount       Acct
  4|Numb Description (Paid to)     Written     of Check    Balance
  5|=========================================================================================
  6|     STARTING BALANCE           8/1/83                   1850.00
  7| 101 A. B. Landlord Realty      8/1/83         500.00    1350.00
  8| 102 Wild Fling Travel Agency   8/2/83         375.00     975.00
  9| 103 Specific Gas & Electric    8/5/83          40.00     935.00
 10| 104 T. P. C.                   8/15/83         32.30     902.70
 11| 105 Joe Turkey                 8/15/83         25.98     876.72
 12| 106 Roger Snyder                                         876.72
 13| 107                                                      876.72
 14| 108                                                      876.72
 15| 109                                                      876.72
 16| 110                                                      876.72
 17|                                                          876.72
 18|                                                          876.72
 19|                                                          876.72
 20|                                                          876.72
^ E7          Form=E6-D7
Width:  9  Memory: 25 Last Col/Row:G20     ? for HELP
  1> █
```

Suppose you are entering last month's checks into the check register and you come upon a deposit slip. How do you record this in the check register? You might want to keep track of deposits in a separate column. To do this, simply insert a new column between the check column and the balance column and then change the formula in the balance column to add in deposits. This takes four steps.

First, insert the column with /**I C E <RET>** and title the column with the words "**Deposit** and "**Amount** in cells E3 and E4. Then format column E with the TextRight and Dollar options (enter /**F C E , TR $**). Now your display will appear as follows:

```
   | A ||              B             ||   C   ||   D   ||   E   ||   F   ||   G   |
  1|Check Register
  2|
  3|Check                               Date      Amount  Deposit      Acct
  4|Numb Description (Paid to)         Written   of Check   Amount  Balance
  5|===========================================================================
  6|     STARTING BALANCE               8/1/83                        1850.00
  7|  101 A. B. Landlord Realty         8/1/83      500.00             1350.00
  8|  102 Wild Fling Travel Agency      8/2/83      375.00              975.00
  9|  103 Specific Gas & Electric       8/5/83       40.00              935.00
 10|  104 T. P. C.                      8/15/83      32.30              902.70
 11|  105 Joe Turkey                    8/15/83      25.98              876.72
 12|  106 Roger Snyder                                                  876.72
 13|  107                                                               876.72
 14|  108                                                               876.72
 15|  109                                                               876.72
 16|  110                                                               876.72
 17|                                                                    876.72
 18|                                                                    876.72
 19|                                                                    876.72
 20|                                                                    876.72
v E4          Text="Amount
Width:  9  Memory: 25 Last Col/Row:H20     ? for HELP
  1> █
```

Second, position the active cell to cell F7 and edit the formula to include the deposit amount with the /Edit command. Enter /**E <RET>**. The formula now reads F6−D7. To include deposits, simply type the characters +E7 and press **<RET>**. The formula in cell F7 now reads F6−D7+E7, as shown in the following illustration:

```
  ! A !!          B              !!   C    !!   D    !!   E    !!   F    !!   G   !
 1!Check Register
 2!
 3!Check                          Date         Amount   Deposit      Acct
 4!Numb Description (Paid to)    Written     of Check   Amount    Balance
 5!==============================================================================
 6!     STARTING BALANCE         8/1/83                            1850.00
 7! 101 A. B. Landlord Realty    8/1/83        500.00              1350.00
 8! 102 Wild Fling Travel Agency 8/2/83        375.00               975.00
 9! 103 Specific Gas & Electric  8/5/83         40.00               935.00
10! 104 T. P. C.                 8/15/83        32.30               902.70
11! 105 Joe Turkey               8/15/83        25.98               876.72
12! 106 Roger Snyder                                                876.72
13! 107                                                             876.72
14! 108                                                             876.72
15! 109                                                             876.72
16! 110                                                             876.72
17!                                                                 876.72
18!                                                                 876.72
19!                                                                 876.72
20!                                                                 876.72
^ F7          Form=F6-D7+E7
Width:  9  Memory: 25 Last Col/Row:H20     ? for HELP
  1>
```

Third, replicate cell F7 down column F (enter **/R F7:F20 <RET>**).

Suppose you want to enter a deposit of $500 between checks 103 and 104. The easy way to do this is to enter 500 on the row for check 103 in cell E9. The hard way is to show the deposit on a separate line. If you want to do this, you will have to adjust the formulas in cells F10 and F11 after entering the formula because the /Insert command will disrupt the sequence of balance totals in column F. To do this, make the following entries:

Cell	*Entry*
	/I R 10 <RET>
B10	**"DEPOSIT**
C10	**"8/13/83**
E10	**500**
F9	**/R <RET> F10:F11 <RET>**

When you are finished, your screen should look like this:

```
   : A ::          B            ::   C   ::   D   ::   E   ::   F   ::   G  :
  1:Check Register
  2:
  3:Check                         Date       Amount  Deposit     Acct
  4:Numb Description (Paid to)    Written  of Check   Amount  Balance
  5:========================================================================
  6:     STARTING BALANCE         8/1/83                      1850.00
  7: 101 A. B. Landlord Realty    8/1/83     500.00           1350.00
  8: 102 Wild Fling Travel Agency 8/2/83     375.00            975.00
  9: 103 Specific Gas & Electric  8/5/83      40.00            935.00
 10:     DEPOSIT                  8/13/83            500.00   1435.00
 11: 104 T. P. C.                 8/15/83     32.30           1402.70
 12: 105 Joe Turkey               8/15/83     25.98           1376.72
 13: 106 Roger Snyder                                         1376.72
 14: 107                                                      1376.72
 15: 108                                                      1376.72
 16: 109                                                      1376.72
 17: 110                                                      1376.72
 18:                                                          1376.72
 19:                                                          1376.72
 20:                                                          1376.72
^ F9          Form=F8-D9+E9
Width:  9  Memory: 25 Last Col/Row:H21    ? for HELP
  1> █
```

Larger Applications

The check register model is fairly simple and has only one section in it; that is, it has one set of column or row headings and all the information appears under those headings.

A model for a large application may have several sections and LOOKUP tables, each having different column and row headings and showing different information. You might create a larger model out of several small ones using the smaller sections as "building blocks." By using the /Load command with the Part option, you can collect several sections together and locate the sections in different areas on the worksheet.

When you are building a model with several sections, it is important to maintain flexibility. As development of the model progresses, you will often find it necessary to add a row or column to a section. You can do this easily if you have laid out the sections properly.

But if you have not organized the sections properly, this will be difficult. If you place two or more sections of the model in rows adjoining each other horizontally, it becomes impossible to insert a new row into one section without affecting the other section. For instance, suppose you build one section from cells A1 to H20 and another section from cells K1 to P30. Inserting a new row at row 12 in the first section will also insert a blank row 12 in the middle of the other section.

In some cases, having a blank row in the middle of the section will cause only an aesthetic problem. In other cases it can destroy the operation of the model. A blank row in the middle of a LOOKUP table will definitely affect its operation.

Similarly, if you build a second section vertically below the first section in the same columns, inserting a column in one section will insert a column in the other. Additionally, you will often find that the column widths you have set for the first section are not suitable for other sections that you may want to build.

The way to avoid these problems is to build the model in a "stair-step" fashion, with each block lower and farther to the right than the one above it. Figure 11-2 illustrates this type of construction. A row or column can be added anywhere and not affect any of the other sections you have placed on the worksheet.

This sort of model design might waste a lot of memory with some spreadsheet programs, but SuperCalc only uses memory for occupied cells. The "stair-step" approach does not use up more memory or disk space. There is no penalty for designing a flexible model with SuperCalc.

A Production Model: Using the IF Function

Figure 11-2 shows a SuperCalc model for estimating costs in a machine shop. This model is shown in the middle of development. The three blocks of the model are "stair-stepped" down the worksheet for full flexibility. This particular shop has three machines that do the same type of work, but require different amounts of set-up time and have different production rates. The SuperCalc model calculates the cost of doing a given job on all three machines, and it selects and marks the most economical choice.

In order to use this model, you rate the difficulty of a job from 1 to 4, with 1 rated the easiest. This rating is entered in cell C5. You then enter the quantity of parts to be made in cell C6. When the model is finished, the minimum cost for the entered job will be displayed in cell H8, and the best machine for the job will be marked in column H.

The model operates in the following way. The block of cells from D8 to H15 contains all the formulas that make the calculations. Figure 11-3 shows the formulas for this part of the model. The formulas in column E look up the

```
  |  A   ||  B   ||C||  D  ||  E  ||  F  ||  G  ||  H   || I ||  J  ||  K  || L |
 1|A Production Model
 2|
 3|Description of Job
 4|-----------------------
 5|Difficulty Level.      1
 6|Quantity             100
 7|
 8|                          Minimum Cost . . . . . . . .     48.00
 9|
10|                          Machine  Setup    Run  Total Best Machine
11|                          Number    Cost   Cost   Cost For This Job
12|                          -----------------------------------------
13|                          #101     17.00  35.00  52.00
14|                          #102     24.00  24.00  48.00 *****
15|                          #103     12.00  60.00  72.00
16|
17|
18|
19|                                                         Costing Tables
20|
21|                                                         Machine #101
22|
23|                                                         Diff.     Setup  Diff. Unit
24|                                                         Level      Cost  Level Cost
25|                                                             1     17.00      1  .35
26|                                                             2     18.00      2  .40
27|                                                             3     19.00      3  .45
28|                                                             4     20.00      4  .50
29|                                                             5       N/A      5  N/A
30|
31|                                                         Machine #102
32|
33|                                                         Diff.     Setup  Diff. Unit
34|                                                         Level      Cost  Level Cost
35|                                                             1     24.00      1  .24
36|                                                             2     26.00      2  .26
37|                                                             3     28.00      3  .28
38|                                                             4     30.00      4  .30
39|                                                             5       N/A      5  N/A
40|
41|                                                         Machine #103
42|
43|                                                         Diff.     Setup  Diff. Unit
44|                                                         Level      Cost  Level Cost
45|                                                             1     12.00      1  .60
46|                                                             2     13.00      2  .65
47|                                                             3     15.00      3  .70
48|                                                             4     15.00      4  .75
49|                                                             5       N/A      5  N/A
```

Figure 11-2.

A production model

set-up cost for each machine based on the difficulty level of the work. The formulas in column F look up the unit cost of production and multiply it by the number of units to be produced. In column G these two values are added to give the total cost of production. Column H marks the lowest cost alternative given in column F. The formulas in column H use the IF function to compare the total cost for each machine with the minimum value from cell H8. The IF function returns a value of 5 if the adjacent value in column F is equal to the minimum value in column F, and a value of 0 if the adjacent value is not equal to the minimum. Cells H13 to H15 are in graphic format, so these cells display either five asterisks or none, giving a quick reference to the lowest cost alternative. To make this selection work correctly with no forward referencing, it is necessary to change the order of calculation to column order (by entering /G C) so that cell H8 is calculated after cells G13, G14, and G15.

Building In Error Messages

The LOOKUP tables in the block I19 to L49 of Figure 11-2 contain the set-up and unit costs for operating each machine. The four levels of difficulty of work are listed. A level of 5 returns a cost value of N/A (not available) if selected. This N/A will display in any cell that has a direct or indirect reference to this function. This is a planned error message to tell the person using the model that an invalid entry exists in cell C5 for level of difficulty. If you are using SuperCalc², you can improve this error message by making the following entries:

Cell	*Entry*
H29	**("Level")**
H39	**("Too")**
H49	**("High!")**

```
  ! D !!          E          !!          F          !!     G     !!       H        !
 8!Minimum Cost . . . . . . . . . . . . .                                MIN(G13:G15)
 9!
10!Machine              Setup                     Run          Total Best Machine
11!Number                Cost                     Cost          Cost For This Job
12!---------------------------------------------------------------------------------
13!#101     LOOKUP(C5,I25:I29)  LOOKUP(C5,K25:K29)*C6   SUM(E13:F13)   IF(G13=H8,5,0)
14!#102     LOOKUP(C5,I35:I39)  LOOKUP(C5,K35:K39)*C6   SUM(E14:F14)   IF(G14=H8,5,0)
15!#103     LOOKUP(C5,I45:I49)  LOOKUP(C5,K45:K49)*C6   SUM(E15:F15)   IF(G15=H8,5,0)
16!
17!
18!
```

Figure 11-3.

Formulas for the production model

Now if the user makes an invalid entry, cells E13, E14, and E15 will display an error message.

```
   :  A  ::  B  :: C:: D :: E :: F :: G ::  H  :: I ::  J  :
  1:A Production Model
  2:
  3:Description of Job
  4:----------------------
  5:Difficulty Level.    5
  6:Quantity           100
  7:
  8:                        Minimum Cost . . . . . . . .      N/A
  9:
 10:                        Machine  Setup    Run  Total Best Machine
 11:                        Number    Cost   Cost   Cost For This Job
 12:                        -----------------------------------------
 13:                        #101     Level    N/A    N/A      N/A
 14:                        #102     Too      N/A    N/A      N/A
 15:                        #103     High!    N/A    N/A      N/A
 16:
 17:
 18:
 19:                                                           Costing Tables
 20:
v A1          Text="A Production Model
Width:  9  Memory: 24 Last Col/Row:L49    ? for HELP
  1>
```

Avoiding Forward Referencing

As you develop applications, it is important to keep in mind the order of calculation to prevent forward references. In the production model it was necessary to change the order of calculation to column (/G C) to prevent a forward reference to cell H8. To be sure that no forward references have developed, change the input values and recalculate twice by pressing the exclamation point (!). If any of the values on the worksheet change the second time the worksheet is calculated, there is an incorrect forward reference. This means you are using a value in a formula and that value has not yet been calculated. At times this can be corrected by changing the order of calculation, but sometimes the positions of the formulas in the worksheet must be changed.

There is one convention you can use with the "stair-step" approach to help reduce forward referencing. This is to place the cells that you will frequently change the contents of in the upper left-hand section of the model. In this way formulas in other sections that use this information will be calculated in sequence. If you cannot eliminate forward references, you will have to remember to calculate the model twice by pressing the exclamation point.

While forward references to formulas cause problems, forward references to constants are fine. This means that LOOKUP tables that contain only constant values may be placed anywhere on the worksheet.

A Wholesale Pricing Model: Hiding Confidential Information

Figure 11-4 is a wholesaler's pricing model. This model shows the retail price, the wholesaler's purchase discount, the wholesaler's selling discount, gross profit, and the wholesale price. This is a useful way to begin a model for a wholesaler, since the model can be expanded to include other information like sales figures and dollar volumes.

The display shows the figures that the wholesaler must distribute to customers: the retail and wholesale product prices. But also on this sheet are many numbers that the wholesaler does not want customers to see, including the discount price that the wholesaler pays and the gross profit. SuperCalc provides two methods of printing out only the columns you want to publish. First,

```
  :          A          ::    B    ::    C    ::    D    ::    E    ::    F    :
 1:Wholesale Pricing Model
 2:
 3:
 4:                           Retail  Purchase   Selling      Gross Wholesale
 5:Product                     Price  Discount  Discount     Profit     Price
 6:-----------------------------------------------------------------------------
 7:Toaster Oven                49.95        55        45      12.36     27.47
 8:Food Processor             125.95        55        40      34.01     75.57
 9:Water Purifier              79.95        55        40      21.59     47.97
10:Blender                     23.95        60        30       6.71     16.77
11:Mixer                       15.95        60        30       4.47     11.17
12:Waffle Iron                 18.99        45        40       6.27     11.39
13:Crock Pot                   24.49        65        40       5.14     14.69
14:
15:
16:
17:
18:
19:
20:
v E7           Form=F7*(1-C7/100)
Width: 10  Memory: 25 Last Col/Row:F15      ? for HELP
 1>
```

Figure 11-4.

A wholesale pricing model

you can set the width of any columns that you don't want to print to zero. Figure 11-5 shows the same model with three of the columns set to zero width. Second, with SuperCalc², you can format a group of cells with the Hide option to make them invisible.

Using either of these methods, the wholesaler can publish the price list with no fear of error from incorrectly copying information; the published prices are the actual numbers calculated by SuperCalc. Yet the wholesaler is still able to maintain confidentiality where required.

Building Templates for Other Users

A *template* is a model prepared for general use by other people. It has headings and labels and all the formulas necessary to calculate the results, but it has no values entered. Templates are especially useful for repetitive functions, like a monthly inventory. The template is stored on disk and used as a "fill in the blanks" worksheet. The "MASTER" inventory model is a very simple example of a template.

```
   :          A           ::   B  ::    F  ::   G  ::   H  ::   I   :
  1:Wholesale Pricing Model
  2:
  3:
  4:                        Retail Wholesale
  5:Product                  Price    Price
  6:--------------------------------------------------------------------
  7:Toaster Oven             49.95    27.47
  8:Food Processor          125.95    75.57
  9:Water Purifier           79.95    47.97
 10:Blender                  23.95    16.77
 11:Mixer                    15.95    11.17
 12:Waffle Iron              18.99    11.39
 13:Crock Pot                24.49    14.69
 14:
 15:
 16:
 17:
 18:
 19:
 20:
< C7          Form=55
Width:  0  Memory: 25 Last Col/Row:F15    ? for HELP
  1>
```

Figure 11-5.

Confidential information in zero-width columns

Formatting a Template

Probably the most important factor in making your SuperCalc templates easy for other people to use is proper formatting of the display. The creative organization and display of worksheets can provide many interesting effects.

In the following example, we create a loan amortization model and then format it for another user. The user needs to enter the principal amount, the interest rate in percent, the term of the loan in years, and the number of payments per year. The model calculates the amount of each payment and then calculates a loan amortization schedule.

Figure 11-6 shows the formulas for the loan amortization model. The borders are on, the window is cleared, and some of the column widths have been changed. Use this figure to create the model on your computer. In cell B8 enter the following formula:

INT((B4/100*B3/B7)/(1−1/(B4/100/B7+)^(B7*B5)*100+.05)/100)

Enter the formulas in rows 14 and 15 and replicate row 15 to the rows below for as many payments as you wish to include. You need to ask for adjustment

```
  :  A   ::      B       ::     C    ::    D    ::     E    ::     F    :
 1:Loan Amortization
 2:
 3:Principal  5000
 4:Interest   18              %
 5:Years      5
 6:Payments
 7: Per Year  12
 8:Amount     INT((B4/100*B3/B7)/(1-1/(B4/100/B7+1)^(B7*B5))*100+.5)/100
 9:
10:=======================================================================
11:Payment  Interest         Cum.         Principal    Cum          Remaining
12:Number   Paid             Interest     Paid         Principal    Balance
13:-----------------------------------------------------------------------
14: A12+1   B3*B4/B7/100     C12+B14      B8-B14       E12+D14      B3-E14
15: A14+1   F14*B4/B7/100    C14+B15      B8-B15       E14+D15      B3-E15
16: A15+1   F15*B4/B7/100    C15+B16      B8-B16       E15+D16      B3-E16
17: A16+1   F16*B4/B7/100    C16+B17      B8-B17       E16+D17      B3-E17
18: A17+1   F17*B4/B7/100    C17+B18      B8-B18       E17+D18      B3-E18
19: A18+1   F18*B4/B7/100    C18+B19      B8-B19       E18+D19      B3-E19
20: A19+1   F19*B4/B7/100    C19+B20      B8-B20       E19+D20      B3-E20
> B11    TL      Text="Interest
Width: 15  Memory: 20 Last Col/Row:F47     ? for HELP
 1>
```

Figure 11-6.

Formulas for amortizing a loan

when replicating. For instance, to create 36 payment rows, enter **/R A15:F15 , A16:A46, A**. Answer the "Ask for Adjust" prompt as follows:

A14 **Y**	C14 **Y**	E14 **Y**
F14 **Y**	B15 **Y**	D15 **Y**
B4 **N**	B8 **N**	B3 **N**
B7 **N**	B15 **Y**	E15 **Y**

However, do not replicate the payment formulas in row 14. These formulas are different from the formulas in the rows below.

When you have entered all the labels and formulas, you can start formatting. Set the global format to dollars with text justified right (enter **/F G $ TR <RET>**). Set the format for column A to integers with numbers left and text left (enter **/F C A , I TL L <RET>**). Set the global column width to 12. Set column A to a width of 9. Format cells B5 and B7 to integer. After you set the display format for values again (**/G F**), your screen should look like this:

```
   !   A   !!      B      !!      C      !!      D      !!      E      !!      F      !
  1!Loan Amortization
  2!
  3!Principal      5000.00
  4!Interest            18 %
  5!Years                5
  6!Payments
  7! Per Year           12
  8!Amount          126.97
  9!
 10!=========================================================================
 11!Payment       Interest         Cum.   Principal          Cum   Remaining
 12!Number            Paid     Interest        Paid    Principal     Balance
 13!-------------------------------------------------------------------------
 14!        1        75.00        75.00       51.97        51.97     4948.03
 15!        2        74.22       149.22       52.75       104.72     4895.28
 16!        3        73.43       222.65       53.54       158.26     4841.74
 17!        4        72.63       295.28       54.34       212.60     4787.40
 18!        5        71.81       367.09       55.16       267.76     4732.24
 19!        6        70.98       438.07       55.99       323.75     4676.25
 20!        7        70.14       508.21       56.83       380.58     4619.42
 ^ A1           Text="Loan Amortization
Width:  9  Memory: 20 Last Col/Row:F47      ? for HELP
   1> ■
```

Now here is how to turn the model into a template. To begin, protect the entire worksheet by entering **/P ALL <RET>**, and then unprotect the input cells by entering **/U B3:B7 <RET>**. Move to cell A9 and enter **/WH** so that there are nine rows displayed in the upper window. You will now be positioned in the lower window. Place cell A11 in the upper-left corner of this window, and set a title lock at row 10. Move to cell B13 and lock the column headings on the screen with the /Title command (enter **/T H**). Turn off the borders by entering **/G B**.

Move to the upper window by pressing the semicolon (;). Enter /**G T** to turn on the tab mode in this window. Finally, turn off the borders in this window. The display should appear as follows:

```
    Loan Amortization

    Principal      5000.00
    Interest            18 %
    Years                5
    Payments
     Per Year           12
    Amount          126.97


    Payment        Interest         Cum.    Principal          Cum   Remaining
    Number             Paid     Interest         Paid    Principal     Balance
    --------------------------------------------------------------------------
               1      75.00        75.00        51.97        51.97     4948.03
               2      74.22       149.22        52.75       104.72     4895.28
               3      73.43       222.65        53.54       158.26     4841.74
               4      72.63       295.28        54.34       212.60     4787.40
               5      71.81       367.09        55.16       267.76     4732.24
               6      70.98       438.07        55.99       323.75     4676.25
               7      70.14       508.21        56.83       380.58     4619.42
< B3          Form=5000
Width: 12  Memory: 20 Last Col/Row:F47     ? for HELP
  1> █
```

By using the format and display capabilities of SuperCalc, you have built a good-looking template that can be used by even the most inexperienced SuperCalc users.

The column titles for the amortization schedule are locked with a title lock so that the payment detail can be scrolled up and down to check any individual payment. All cells in this template are protected except the four cells where the user needs to enter information: B3, B4, B5, and B7. Because the upper window is in tab mode, the active cell will only move to these four cells.

When you want to print out this worksheet, you must calculate the last row number to print. You only need to add 10 to the number of payments you wish to print since the first payment is in row 11. For example, if you wish to print 36 payments, set the range to A11 through F46.

Documenting a Template

Providing proper documentation for your templates is important for several reasons. With proper documentation, someone who has never seen the template will be able to use it more easily. Documentation will also help you to remember how to use a template that you have not used in some time.

An easy way to provide documentation of a SuperCalc template is to enter it on the worksheet. You can put all the documentation you need in an unused area of the worksheet. Since SuperCalc will display long lines of text in a single cell, it is easy to provide complete documentation.

Figure 11-7 shows a large template for estimating the cost of printing stationery.

Beginning at cell J2 is a full screen of instructions. To make a template most useful to users that are not familiar with it, save the template so that when it is loaded the documentation is the first thing that is seen. In addition, the last line of the instructions can tell the user how to move to the information entry section of the template (for instance, "To move to the estimate enter =A5 <RET>"). On the information entry section of the template you can even remind users how to get help for this specific template (for example, "Enter =J2 <RET> for HELP").

There are also other types of documentation you could include. LOOKUP

```
   | A || B  ||  C  ||  D  ||  E  ||  F  ||  G  ||  H  |
 24|
 25|Instaquote Worksheet - Revised 5/18/83
 26|For instructions enter: =J2 and press RETURN
 27|
 28|Wood and Jones Printers - Instaquote
 29|
 30|For: (Enter Customer Name here)              Date:      5/18/83
 31|
 32|ITEM PRODUCT      PAPER     QUAN   +COLOR   EMBOSS  EXTRA $     PRICE
 33| 1                    0        0        0        0        0       .00
 34| 2                    0        0        0        0        0       .00
 35| 3                    0        0        0        0        0       .00
 36| 4                    0        0        0        0        0       .00
 37| 5                    0        0        0        0        0       .00
 38| 6                    0        0        0        0        0       .00
 39|Extra-------------------------------------------------------------
 40|     Std Ink Spcl Ink Design $   Type $   #Dies Die size
 41|          0        0        0        0        0        0       .00
 42|------------------------------------------------------------------
 43|                                    Sub Total                  .00
 44|                                    Tax                        .00
 45|                                    ---------------------------
 46|                                    Total                      .00
```

Figure 11-7. (Part A)

A print shop application

```
  : J:: K  :: L:: M  :: N  :: O  :: P  :: Q  :: R  :
 2:Instructions for Stationery Quotation Worksheet
 3: o  To enter customer's name and date enter " as the first character
 4: o  Use the right arrow key to move from entry to entry
 5: o  To recalculate press the ! (exclamation) key
 6: o  To print enter: /ODA24:H47,P
 7:
 8:    After reading this, enter =A24 and press RETURN  to create estimate
 9:
10:Definitions:
11:    PRODUCT    =  1 = letterhead, 2 = envelopes, 3 = business cards
12:    PAPER      =  Paper class rating (Refer to paper class sheet)
13:    QUAN       =  Quantity ordered
14:    +COLOR     =  Additional ink colors (after the first)
15:    EMBOSS     =  Number of places this piece is embossed.
16:    EXTRA $    =  Extra costs associated with this piece (see below)
17:    PRICE      =  Calculated price for this piece
18:
19:    Std Ink    =  Standard colors (not black)
20:    Spcl Ink   =  Specially matched inks.
21:    Die area   =  Total area of all embossing dies (sq-in)
```

Figure 11-7. (Part B)

A print shop application

tables for rates or prices should have clear and complete titles. This makes it much easier to update these tables when prices change. And in cell A1 write the name of the template and the latest revision date. This is the entry that will show in a directory of SuperCalc files.

Using Separate Areas for Input and Output

Suppose you have a template with two areas that display the same information. In Figure 11-7, the block of cells A30:G41 is where the user enters information. In this block the information is in a very compact form so that it will all fit on the screen at one time. When the estimate is printed, however, the compact form does not provide a very readable report. Thus, you might set up another block such as T3:Z50 to provide a second copy of the same information in a less compact format for printing.

This results in one small problem. It is easy to provide a second copy of the numbers used in a worksheet by using cell references. But it is not so easy to repeat text entries like the customer's name and address. To solve this, when the report is printed you need to print it from two separate sections of the worksheet. First the block A30:H30 is printed for the report title, the customer's name and address, and the date. Then the block T3:Z50 is printed for the rest of the report. This makes printing the report somewhat complicated, but we will see how to make this easier by using the /eXecute command.

Making Templates Easy to Use With /eXecute

The template in Figure 11-7 is a good example of a model that can make good use of the /eXecute command. It is a fairly complicated model, it will be used often, and it is designed to be used by people that are not very familiar with SuperCalc.

We will develop a set of execute files for use with this model to make its operation even easier. The method that we will use with execute files can be used to operate many templates. In fact, it will provide a way to make the operation of many different models very consistent for the casual user.

The execute files that we will develop will load the template, print a report, and even provide help for users unfamiliar with the template.

This method assumes that to operate a template you have your SuperCalc program on a diskette in drive A and that you have only one template on the diskette in drive B. You can have other files on drive B, as long as they do not use this method. You will see why as the method is developed.

The first execute file we will create is the Help file. This file should be named B:HELP.XQT and should contain one line:

=J2

This is very simple, but it means that you do not have to remember where the documentation is on the worksheet. All you have to do to get help is to enter /XB:HELP.

To create this file, enter "**=J2** in cell A1. Then write this file to the diskette in drive B by entering the following:

/G B
/O D A1 , D B:HELP.XQT <RET>

The /Output command writes the contents of cell A1 in display format to the file B:HELP.XQT. However, you must turn the borders off before doing this. Otherwise the file will not work with the /eXecute command.

Next we create an execute file that will load the model. To do this, set the width of column A to 30 (enter **/F C A , 30**). Position to cell A1 and enter

"/LB:ESTIMATE , A. Finally, write this using **/O D A1 , D**. Call the file **B:LOAD.XQT**. Now all that the user needs to do to load the ESTIMATE worksheet is to enter /XB:LOAD.

To create the output execute file, make the following entries:

Cell	*Entry*
A1	**"/O D A30:H30 , P**
A2	**"/O D T3:Z50 , P**

This execute file will print the two sections of the model that make up the complete output report. Write this file to disk by entering **/O D A1:A2 , D** with the file name **B:PRINT.XQT**.

To obtain help, the user only needs to enter /XB:HELP. To load the ESTIMATE model the user enters /XB:LOAD, and to print a report the user enters /XB:PRINT.

Using /eXecute to Save Large Models

The same method of executing files can be used to save worksheets that are too large to fit on a single floppy disk. Each of the disks used to save the worksheet will have an execute file on it that will save a portion of the worksheet. The SuperCalc program disk will have an execute file that will use each of the files on the storage disks in turn.

As an example, assume the worst case: that you have a model that uses every cell of the worksheet; that is, the model starts in cell A1 and ends in cell BK254. Also assume that it will take three diskettes to completely store this model. The execute files required to do this are as follows:

Diskette	*Filename*	*Contents*
Model Disk 1	B:SAVE.XQT	"/SB:SECTION1,OPAA1:BK85
Model Disk 2	B:SAVE.XQT	"/SB:SECTION2,OPAA86:BK170
Model Disk 3	B:SAVE.XQT	"/SB:SECTION3,OPAA171:BK254

To create these files, load the first of the three diskettes that are to store the model in drive B. In cell A1 enter **"/SB:SECTION1,OPAA1:BK85**. Then write cell A1 to a file called B:SAVE.XQT with the /Output command.

The letter "O" that follows the comma in the /Save command in cell A1 means that the command will use the Overwrite option. This is necessary because the model file may occupy all of the space on the diskette and there would be no room for a back-up file. To maintain a back-up copy of these files, you would need a second set of diskettes.

Now load the second diskette in drive B; in cell A1 enter "/**SB:SECTION2, OPAA85:BK170**, and /Output cell A1 to the file B:SAVE.XQT. Finally, repeat this procedure for the third diskette.

When the user loads the first diskette in drive B and enters /XB:SAVE, the contents of cells A1 through BK85 will be saved into a file called B:SECTION1. Then the user loads the second diskette into drive B and enters /XB:SAVE again. Finally, the user loads the third diskette and repeats the procedure.

You can use a similar procedure to create a set of execute files that use the /Load command to reload the model sections from the storage disks.

WARNING: When you create templates or execute files for other users, carefully test them yourself first to see that they will work properly. Then give them to someone else to try. This will ensure that they work the way you expect them to and that someone else can understand them.

CHAPTER TWELVE

Using SuperCalc^3

Sorcim Corporation released SuperCalc^3 in October 1983 with several new features. These features include:

- Entering text without the double quote (").
- Graphics, including line, bar, and pie charts and variations on them.
- Graphics output for plotters and printers.
- Data management, including locating and selecting records from a block of cells.
- Several new financial functions, including Internal Rate of Return (IRR), Regular Payments on a Loan (PMT), Future Value of Payments (FV), and Present Value of Payments (PV).

This chapter explores these new capabilities in detail and gives useful examples for implementing them.

Entering Data

When you enter text in SuperCalc and SuperCalc², you begin with the double quote character ("). But with SuperCalc³ you do not need to include the double quote.

On a clear worksheet type in the letters **ABC** and press **<RET>**. Notice that the text ABC now appears in cell A1. The Active cell has moved to B1. Enter "**ABC** and press **<RET>**. The same text appears in cell B1. Now press the **LEFT ARROW** key and look at the prompt line. Cell B1 contains "ABC. Press the **LEFT ARROW** key again and look at the prompt line. The content of cell A1 is also "ABC.

What happens is that SuperCalc³ automatically inserts a double quote at the beginning of a text entry. To SuperCalc³ any data that it does not recognize as a number or as a valid formula is text. If you want to make a number into text, however, you can place a double quote in front of it. For instance, enter "**123** and press **<RET>**. Then enter **123** (without the initial quote) and press **<RET>**. Finally, press the **RIGHT ARROW** key and enter **A1+5**. These last entries are considered to be formulas, not text.

There are two things you should be aware of when you enter formulas using SuperCalc³. First, if you make a mistake while entering a formula, the formula will be considered text. To correct the formula you will need to either use the /Edit command (as explained in Chapter 4) or completely reenter the formula.

Second, when you edit the formula, you will need to eliminate the double quote that SuperCalc³ has inserted at the beginning of the entry. This is fairly simple to do if you have a BACK TAB key. Just press the BACK TAB key and then press the DOWN ARROW key, and the double quote will be eliminated.

For example, press the **RIGHT ARROW** key once, enter **A1*B1+**, and press **<RET>**.

```
    |  A   ||   B   ||   C   ||   D   ||   E   ||   F   ||   G   ||   H
  1|    123     126A1*B1+
  2|
  •
  •
  •
 19|
 20|
> D1
Width:  9  Memory: 66 Last Col/Row:C1      ? for HELP
  1>█
F1 = Help; F2 = Erase Line/Return to Spreadsheet; F9 = Plot; F10 = View
```

SuperCalc^3 has interpreted the data in cell C1 as text. The formula is almost correct; it is only missing a number or cell reference after the plus sign. But it only needs to be slightly incorrect for SuperCalc^3 to consider it text and not a formula. To correct the formula, press the **LEFT ARROW** key to move the active cell back to C1 and enter **/E <RET>**. The formula now appears on the entry line.

```
8>"A1*B1+█
```

To correct the formula, enter **25** so that it reads

```
10>"A1*B1+25█
```

To remove the double quote you need to back up the cursor by pressing the **LEFT ARROW** key to the double quote or pressing the **BACK TAB** key if you have one. With the cursor now placed on the double quote, press the **DOWN ARROW** key.

```
1>A1*B1+25
```

Press **<RET>** and the formula will be stored back in cell C1 as a formula.

SuperCalc^3 Graphics

Before you use the graphics capabilities of SuperCalc^3, you must perform several steps to tell the program about your computer and some of your preferences for graphics.

SuperCalc^3 supports several output devices including Hewlett-Packard, Strobe, and IBM plotters, and Epson FX-80 and MX-80 (with Graftrax) and MX-100 printers. The first step is to install the device that you are going to use for graphics output. You must use the install program that was furnished with SuperCalc^3 to install the proper device.

Once you have installed your output device, there are still several things you must tell SuperCalc^3 before you can begin. SuperCalc^3 has two new options on the /Global command that pertain to graphics: Global Graphics Install (/GGI) and Global Graphics Options (/GGO). We will start with the more permanent options since they should be selected first.

The Global Graphics Install option presents the menu screen shown in

```
GRAPHICS INSTALL OPTIONS:
To change current settings for FUTURE work sessions:
  1. Select new settings for future sessions.
  2. Perform  /Global,Graphics,Save  AND  /Quit

NOTE: Current settings on this screen remain in effect for this session.

MEMORY:  Select M for fastest response; more of the program is read into memory.
Select D for more spreadsheet space; more of the program remains on disk.
  Current setting:      M      Setting will be:     M

MONITOR:  If you have two monitors (monochrome and color), select 2 to see
spreadsheet on one and graph on the other.  Select 1 to use monochrome only.
  Current setting:      2      Setting will be:     2

AUTO REGRAPH: For two monitors, select A to automatically redisplay the current
graph each time a spreadsheet change is made.  Select M for manual redisplay.
  Current setting:      A      Setting will be:     A

IBM/COMPAQ: Select I for IBM.  Select C for best COMPAQ performance.
  Current setting:      I      Setting will be:     I
M(emory) or D(isk)?
 25>/Global,Graphics,Install
F1 = Help; F2 = Erase Line/Return to Spreadsheet; F9 = Plot; F10 = View
```

Figure 12-1.

The Global Graphics Install menu

Figure 12-1. To access this screen, enter **/GGI**. This menu allows you to specify several things about the way you want your system to operate. The first option is called "Memory". This option requires you to make a trade-off between the amount of memory used for the program and the amount reserved for the worksheet. You can select M (memory) for a quicker response or D (disk) for larger worksheets. The M option puts more of the program in memory. This speeds up the execution of the program because it reduces the number of times that the disk is used. The D option keeps more of the program on the disk, thereby reserving more memory for the worksheet. The M option always reserves at least 64K of memory for the worksheet, so if your worksheets are no larger than this, select the M option.

The next option, the "Monitor" option, is relevant if you have both a color and a monochrome display, each with its own adapter. If you have both, set this option to 2 so worksheets will be displayed on the monochrome monitor and graphs will be displayed on the color monitor. With this option set to 1 all displays will appear on the monochrome monitor. If you have a Compaq computer you can ignore this setting; both displays will be on the built-in screen with graphics also displayed on an external monitor if one is connected.

```
GRAPHICS AND DEVICE OPTIONS

Appearance Features:                       For graphics printers:
Grids              N                       Resolution          S
Axes               Y
Ticks              Y                       For pen plotters:
Graph Box          N                       Num. pens           1

For Pie, Bar and Stacked-Bar:              Plotter Interface:
Fill Type          S                       Use                 P

For Line, Hi-Lo, Area and X-Y:             Parallel Options:
Point Markers      Y                       Printer number      1
Lines              Y
                                           Serial Options:
GRAPHIC DEVICE SETTINGS:                   Com number          1
                                           Baud Rate        4800
Console:                                   Parity              N
Monitor            C                       Data bits           8
                                           Stop bits           1

H(orizontal), V(ertical), N(either) or B(oth)?
 25>/Global,Graphics,Options
F1 = Help; F2 = Erase Line/Return to Spreadsheet; F9 = Plot; F10 = View
```

Figure 12-2.

The Global Graphics Options menu

The last option on this screen tells SuperCalc³ whether you have an IBM or Compaq computer. Keep this set to I if you have an IBM or change it to C if you have a Compaq. The C setting increases the scrolling rate since the Compaq can scroll faster than the IBM.

Once you have made these selections, press **CTRL-Z** to return to the worksheet. Select the Global Graphics Save option by entering **/GGS**. This option makes your selections permanent. The /GGS option actually changes the SC3.COM program on the disk, but the changes don't take place until you enter /Quit and restart SuperCalc³.

The other options that you need to set are under Global Graphics Options. To access these, enter **/GGO**. This action presents the menu screen shown in Figure 12-2. You use this menu to tell SuperCalc³ about your graphics output device (printer or plotter) and its connection. There are only a few items on this screen that you should change at this time. You will learn about many of the others as you continue through this chapter and become more familiar with the graphics capabilities of SuperCalc³.

We will skip the first section of this screen that deals with the appearance of graphics displays. Press the **DOWN ARROW** key several times to move to the top of the second column of the menu. Then move down to the second item, "Num. pens". If you have a pen plotter, set this value to the number of pens that your plotter has. Move down to the "Plotter Interface:" entry and enter **P** if your plotting device is connected to the parallel printer port or **S** if it is connected to the serial port. Even if you are using a printer as a plotting device you must tell SuperCalc³ where it is connected with this entry.

If you entered P, SuperCalc³ will automatically advance you to the next entry "Printer number". This entry identifies which parallel port your plotting device is connected to. If you have only one parallel port, the chances are that it is number one, so enter a **1**.

If you entered S, SuperCalc³ will skip the next entry and advance you to the "Serial Options:" entries. These settings must conform to the configuration of your plotting device. The "Com number" refers to the number of the serial interface port that the plotting device is connected to. If you have only one serial port, chances are it is number one. This book cannot be specific about the other entries—you will have to check the manual of your plotting device to see how to set them.

This is all that needs to be set before you try to create graphics. Now press CTRL-Z to return to the worksheet. Use the Global Graphics Save option (**/GGS**) to save the changes that you have made. Finally, quit and restart SuperCalc³ (enter **/QT SC3 <RET>**) to use the program options that you selected.

Note: Only the options on the /GGI menu require that you quit and restart the program; the "Graphics and Device Options" that you changed in the /GGO menu will take effect immediately. However, they only become permanent after you save them by entering /GGS.

With the initial settings finished, let's see how to graph with SuperCalc³.

Creating a Simple Graph

To make a graph, you first need to create a model containing information to graph. Make the entries shown in Figure 12-3 to create this model.

This model shows the sales performance of three sales representatives over a three-month period. You will use this data to study the different ways that SuperCalc³ can graph.

The /View command controls most of the graphics functions of SuperCalc³. To make the simplest graph of the data, type **/V** to start the /View command.

```
|      |  A  ||  B  ||  C  ||  D  ||  E  ||  F  ||  G  ||  H
    1|
    2|National Distributing
    3|Sales Summary
    4|              Jan       Feb       Mar
    5|Smith         2546      3298      2267
    6|Jones         1876      2976      2754
    7|Brown         3165      2287      1949
    8|
    9|
   10|
   11|
   12|
   13|
   14|
   15|
   16|
   17|
   18|
   19|
   20|
  v D8
  Width:  9  Memory: 65 Last Col/Row:D7      ? for HELP
    1> █
  F1 = Help; F2 = Erase Line/Return to Spreadsheet; F9 = Plot; F10 = View
```

Figure 12-3.

Sales Summary model

The following prompt will appear:

```
#,?,D(ata),G(raph-Type),T(ime-Labs),V(ar-Labs),P(oint-Labs),H(eads), or O(pts)?
  7>/View, █
```

You can show several rows or columns of data at the same time with the /View command. In this example the performance of all three sales representatives is shown on one graph. Each row or column of data is called a *variable;* in this case, there will be three variables, one for each representative.

The /View command has many options, but the only one necessary to create a graph is the Data option. Type **D** for data, and you will see a prompt asking you to enter the range of data for variable A. You will be graphing three variables, which in this case are the sales figures for three sales reps. The range for the first sales rep would be B5:B7. You could define each sales representative's performance separately. To do this you would enter B5:B7, C5:C7, and D5:D7. But there's a shortcut for entering data ranges that you can use right now. Instead of entering three separate ranges for the three adjacent variables, you can just enter the block range that contains all three variables and SuperCalc[3] will assign them automatically. You may do this any time you want to graph two or more adjacent columns or rows of numbers. Enter **B5:D7** and press **<RET>**. SuperCalc[3] now knows what to graph; just press **<RET>** and the graph will be displayed on your screen.

How SuperCalc[3] displays the graph depends on the monitor and computer you have. SuperCalc[3] will display a graph, in some form, on any computer. If you have an IBM Monochrome Display Adapter (the IBM green screen), SuperCalc[3] will draw the graph using the available graphics characters since this adapter doesn't support true graphics.

If you have a Color/Graphics Monitor Adapter, SuperCalc[3] will use the capabilities of your system to create true graphic images. If you have both adapters, SuperCalc[3] will continue to display the worksheet on the monochrome monitor and display the graph on the color monitor. Figure 12-4 shows what this graph will look like.

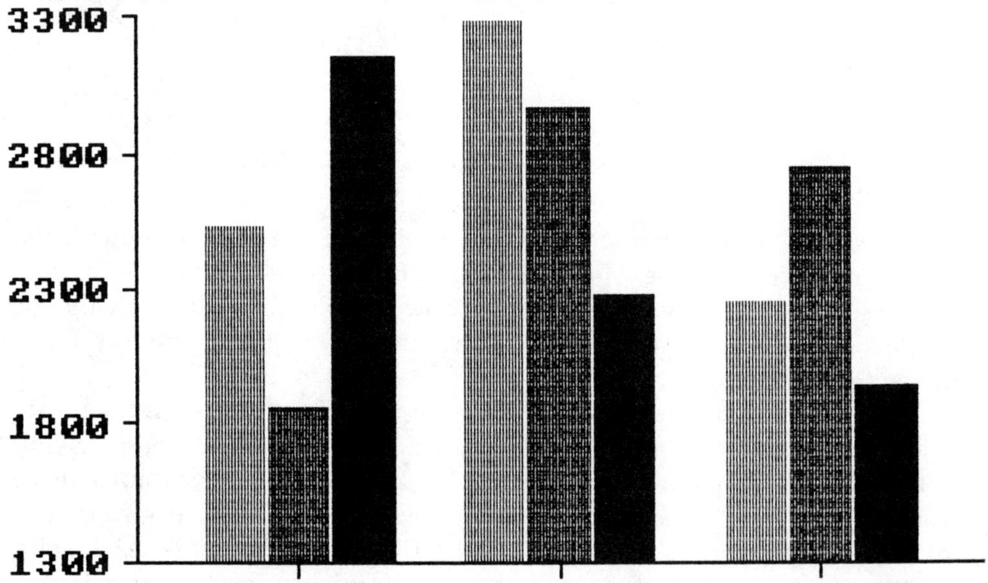

Figure 12-4.

Sales Summary bar graph

Take a moment to study this graph. On the left side, there are numbers from 3300 at the top to 1300 at the bottom. SuperCalc³ automatically sets the proper scale for the graph. The graph is made up of three groups of three bars, each a different shade (except on the monochrome monitor). Each group of bars represents the sales for one month; one bar represents each sales representative. The left bar in each group shows the sales of the first sales representative, and so on. This may be all the information that you want to graph, but you can't expect anyone else to know what it means without some text labels.

Labeling a Graph

The text labels that you need are already on the worksheet, so let's see how to include them on the graph. First return to the worksheet by pressing any key. Type **/V** to start the /View command. This time you will use two more of the options: the "T(ime-Labs) and V(ar-Labs)" options. Press the letter **T** to select the Time Labels option. You are prompted to "Enter Time-Label range." The names of the months that you are graphing are in cells B4 through D4, so enter **B4:D4** and press **<RET>**. The prompt will return to the beginning of the /View command.

Now type **V** to select the Variables Label option. We will label the variables with the sales representatives' names, which are in cells A5 through A7. Enter **A5:A7 <RET>**.

If your computer has function keys, press the **F10** function key. Otherwise press **<RET>**. The F10 key performs the same function that entering /V and pressing <RET> does: it displays the graph. You can use the F10 key any time except when you are in the middle of entering data into a cell. The graph will look like Figure 12-5. The text now makes it possible for others to use the information that you have graphed.

Adding Headings to a Graph

Suppose you want to include this graph in a presentation to someone outside your company. It should really identify the company and have a title as well. Let's add those two things. Press **<RET>** or any other key to return to the worksheet. Enter **/V** and press the letter **H** to select the H(eadings) option. SuperCalc³ will ask if you want "M(ain), S(ub), X(-axis) or Y(-axis)". Select **M** for a main heading and enter **A2 <RET>**. This defines the contents of cell A2 as the main heading. Next select **S** and enter **A3 <RET>** to define cell

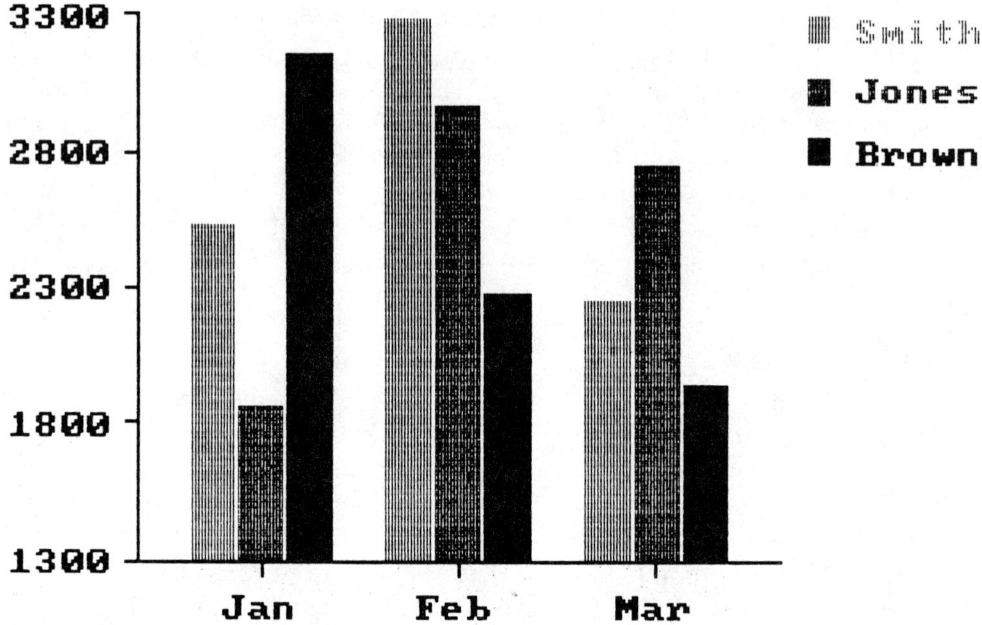

Figure 12-5.

Sales Summary bar graph with labels

A3 as the subhead. Now press the **F10** key to display the graph with headings. Figure 12-6 shows the graph as it now looks. Notice that as you add information to the graph SuperCalc^3 makes the graph smaller so that everything fits on the screen.

Resolution, Text Size, and Color

SuperCalc supports two graphics resolutions with the Color/Graphics Adapter. The resolution you select affects the character size shown in the graph. You can create graphs in color using large characters with only 40 text columns across the screen, or you can create black-and-white graphics with 80 text columns across the screen. You can select the one you want using the Global Graphics Options (/GGO) menu. You select B for a black-and-white monitor for 80 columns, or C for a color monitor for 40 columns (although it

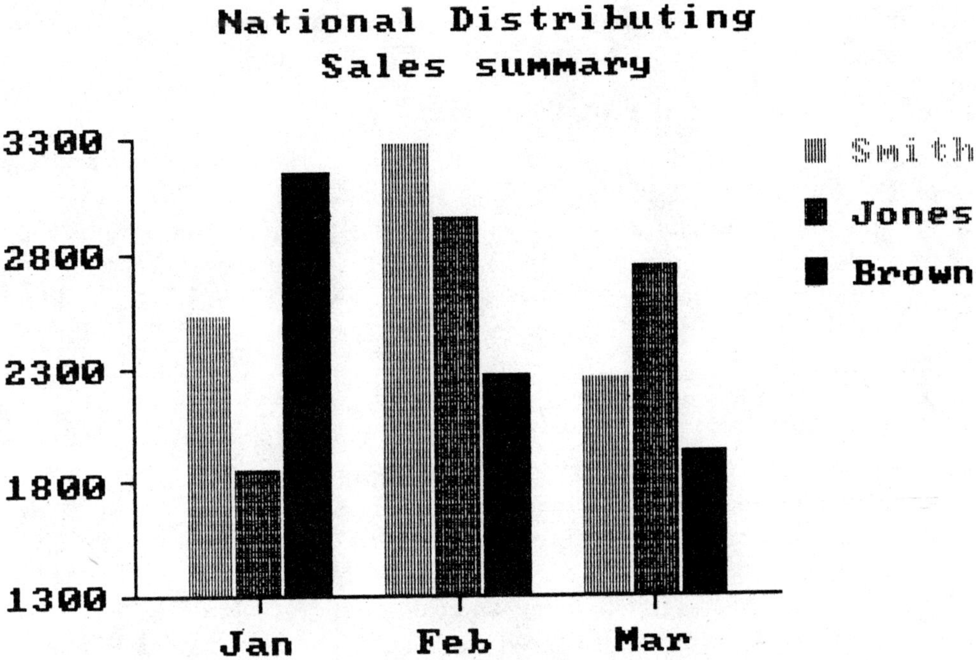

Figure 12-6.

Sales Summary bar graph with headings

really doesn't matter what kind of monitor you have, as long as it uses a Color/ Graphics Adapter).

If you select C, the filled areas on IBM PC-compatible computers appear in three colors: magenta, light blue, and white. These colors are used because they will not bleed or form jagged lines when placed next to each other. On the TI professional and other computers, additional colors are available. Selecting B causes the graph to appear in black-and-white. Filled areas are shown with different cross-hatched textures. You can also obtain cross-hatched textures in color by entering C for the "Fill Type" on the Global Graphics Options menu shown in Figure 12-2.

If you have a Compaq computer, SuperCalc³ uses the graphics capability of the built-in monitor and automatically switches back and forth between text and graphics modes as you switch from the worksheet to graphic displays. This graph displayed on a Compaq will look like Figure 12-4.

Creating Additional Graphs

You may have noticed that as you enter options to the /View command the SuperCalc^3 program inserts the number 1 in the entry line. This number is the graph you are working on. You can create as many as nine graphs with each worksheet. To change to a different graph, enter the number of the graph that you want to use after you enter /V to start the /View command. For example, you can switch to graph 2 by entering **/V 2 <RET>**. But you will see the error message "No Variable Defined". You have tried to draw a new graph which has not been defined yet. You could reenter the information that you used for the previous graph, but there is an easier way. You can use the /Copy command to copy the information you have defined for one graph to another graph. Clear the entry line and enter **/C *1 , 2 <RET>**. This copies the definition of graph number 1 to graph number 2. The asterisk (*) tells the /Copy command that you want to copy a graph definition and not a range of cells. Now press the **F10** function key, and the same graph that was defined as graph number 1 will be displayed as graph number 2. Finally, press **<RET>**.

Drawing Pie Graphs

Now let's change the type of graph. Enter **/V** and press **G** for Graph type. SuperCalc^3 gives you the option of choosing between seven different types of graphs. The first you are going to see is a pie graph, so press **P** for "Pie". Now press **<RET>** to display the graph. The pie chart produced looks like Figure 12-7.

This chart shows the sales for one of the salespeople for a three-month period. SuperCalc^3 also gives you the option of showing the sales for all of the salespeople for a one-month period as a pie chart. You can make this change by selecting the "O(pts)" option of the /View command. Press any key to return to the worksheet and then enter **/V O**. You will be prompted to select "F(ormat), E(xplosion), P(ie-mode) or S(caling)?". Press the letter **P** for the pie-mode option.

You will now see the prompt "O(ne) or A(ll) variables?" A pie graph shows a single cross section of the information you have defined with the View Data option. Normally, it includes all the data for one variable. However, you can

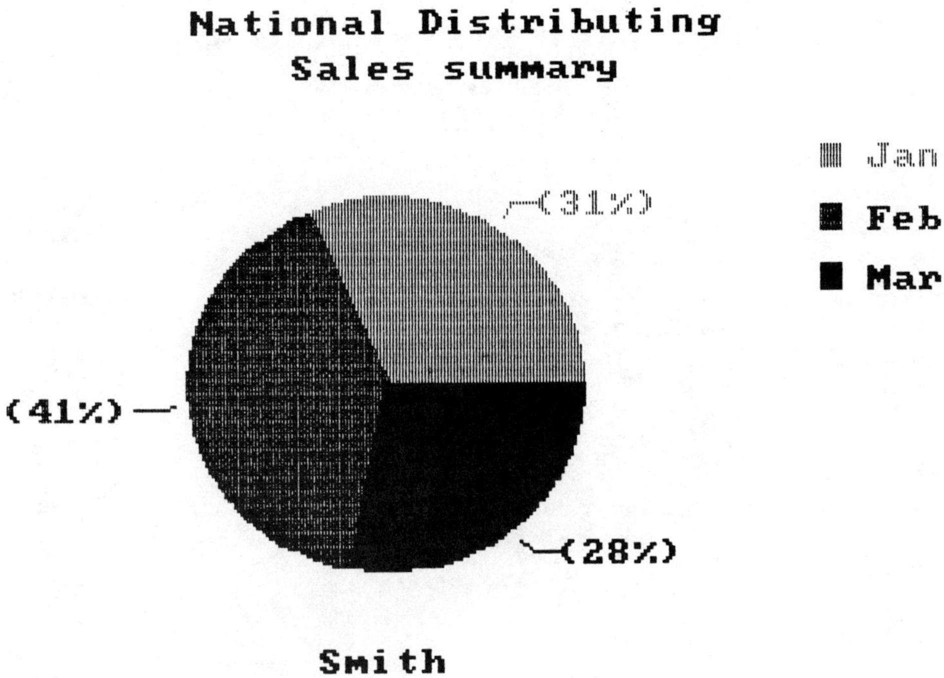

Figure 12-7.

Sales Summary pie chart

change the way that the pie graph selects information to show one time period for all variables. To select this option press **A** for "All variables". Next you need to select which month you want to graph. Enter **1 <RET>** to select the first month. Now press **<RET>** twice more (or press the **F10** key) to display the graph. It will look like Figure 12-8.

Drawing a Stacked Bar Chart

Let's create another type of graph using the same data. First copy the graph definition from graph 2 to graph 3 by typing **/C *2 , 3 <RET>**. Then enter **/V G S**. This changes the graph type to a stacked bar graph. Press **<RET>** and a stacked bar graph will be displayed on your screen.

A stacked bar graph puts the variables one on top of another so you can see

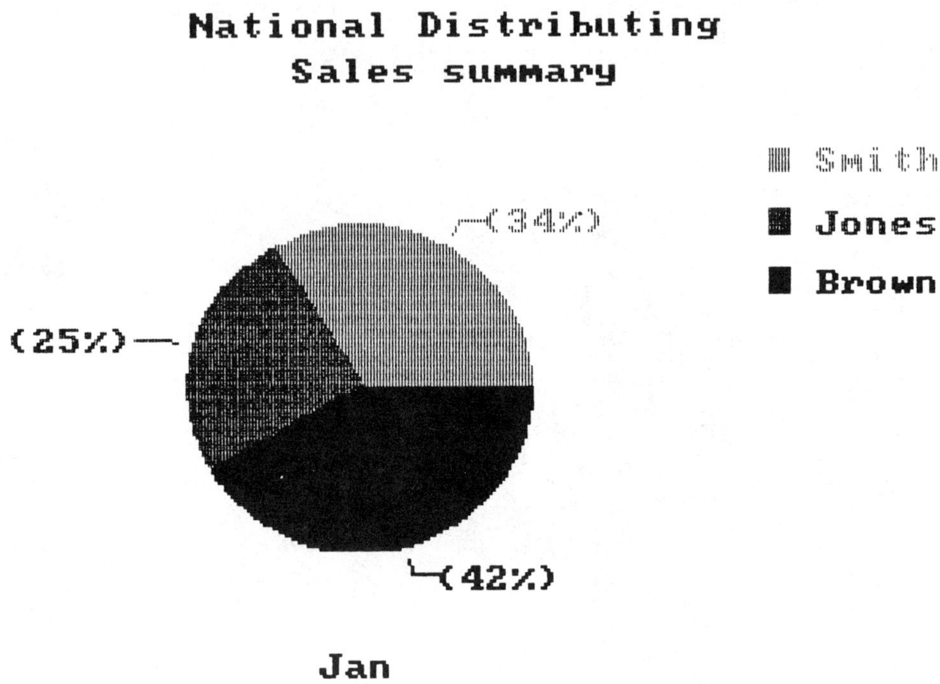

Figure 12-8.

Sales Summary pie chart with all variables

the total of all three variables. In this case you can see how each person's sales relate to the total sales.

Plotter and Printer Output

You have seen several of the graphics capabilities of SuperCalc[3] but still haven't put anything on paper yet. Before printing this graph, let's look at another of the Global Graphics options. Enter **/G G F** to select the Global Graphics Fonts option. This displays the screen shown in Figure 12-9. This option gives you the choice of eight different fonts for the different text elements on your graphs. For these graphs, set all the Headings to font number 3, which is "Roman, double-stroke", and leave all the labels as font number 1,

```
PLOTTER FONT SELECTIONS

Headings:                    Labels:
Main           3             Axis          1
Sub            3             Time          1
X-Axis         3             Vars          1
Y-Axis         3             Point         1

1 = Block,   single-stroke
2 = Block,   double-stroke
3 = Roman,   double-stroke
4 = Roman,   triple-stroke
5 = Italic,  double-stroke
6 = Italic,  triple-stroke
7 = Script,  single-stroke
8 = Script,  double-stroke


Font number <1-8>:
 23>/Global,Graphics,Fonts
F1 = Help; F2 = Erase Line/Return to Spreadsheet; F9 = Plot; F10 = View
```

Figure 12-9.

Plotter Font Selections menu

which is "Block, single-stroke." Make these changes on the screen and press F2 (or CTRL-Z) when you are done.

Now you are ready to print the graph. Be sure the printer or plotter is on-line and ready and then press F9 to start printing. If you are using a plotter, SuperCalc^3 will stop and tell you when to change pens. If you are using a printer, be patient since it takes a while to transform graphics information into data that your printer can understand. When the job is done, the graph will look like Figure 12-10.

Creating a Line Graph

The next type of graph to consider is a line graph. Use the "/View Graph-Type" option to change the graph type to line (enter **/V G L**). Press **<RET>** to display the graph. It will look like Figure 12-11.

The line graph shows the data points for each value of the variables connected with lines. The points are identified by different shapes and are keyed to a legend in the upper-right corner of the graph. For instance, each value of

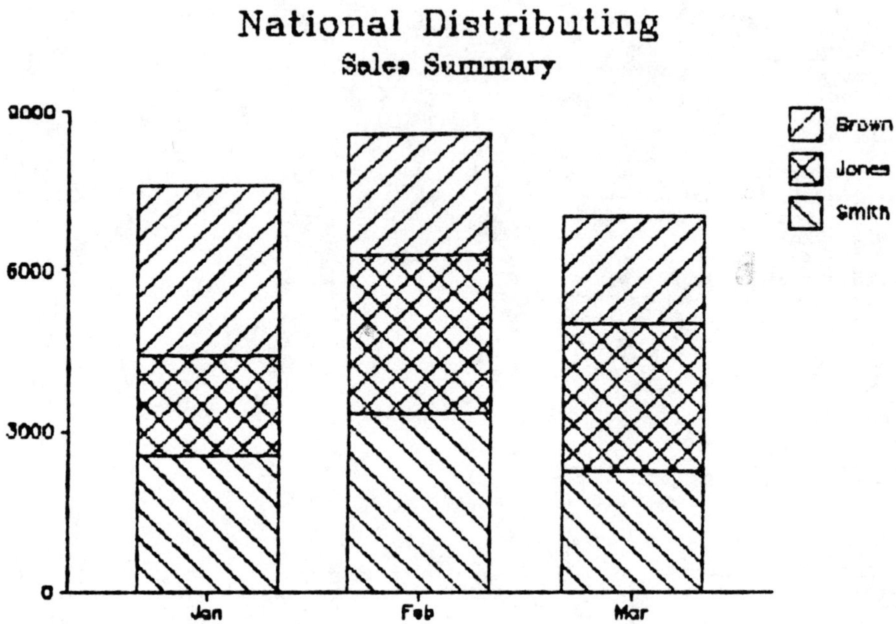

Figure 12-10.

Printout of Sales Summary stacked bar chart

Smith's sales is identified by a cross. The values on the left side of the graph form the scale that allows you to read the graph.

Area Graphs

Now change the graph type to *area* by entering **/V G A** and display the graph by pressing <**RET**>. This graph (Figure 12-12) is similar to the line graph that you just saw, but the scale up the left side is different and none of the lines cross. This is called an area graph because the value of the variables is represented by the area between the lines. The points plotted are the sum of the values of the variables that are previously plotted. The top value plotted is the total of the sales for the period. The area graph has the same relationship to the line graph as the stacked bar graph has to a regular bar graph. Both

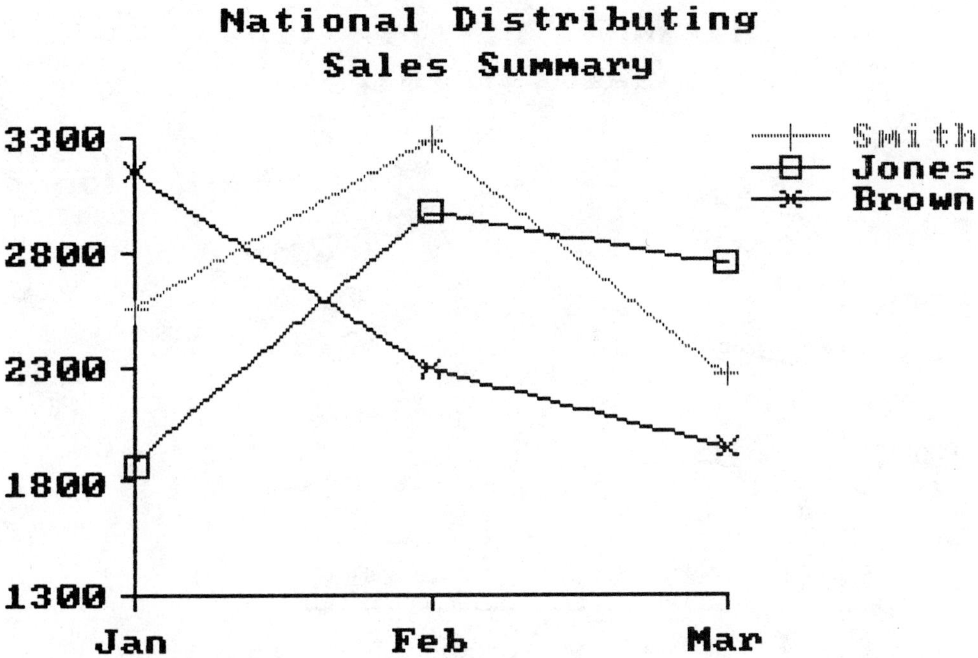

Figure 12-11.

Sales Summary line graph

the area graph and the stacked bar graph show the sum of the variables for each period.

Looking at the Settings for a Graph

SuperCalc³ provides you with a summary of the settings you have defined for a graph. To see the settings of graph number 2, enter /V 2?. The screen will change to show you a display like Figure 12-13. All the pertinent information about your graph is presented.

You have looked at five of the seven possible types of graphs. These types of graphs are normally used for displaying the values of variables with respect to time. The value of the variable is plotted on the vertical axis and time is

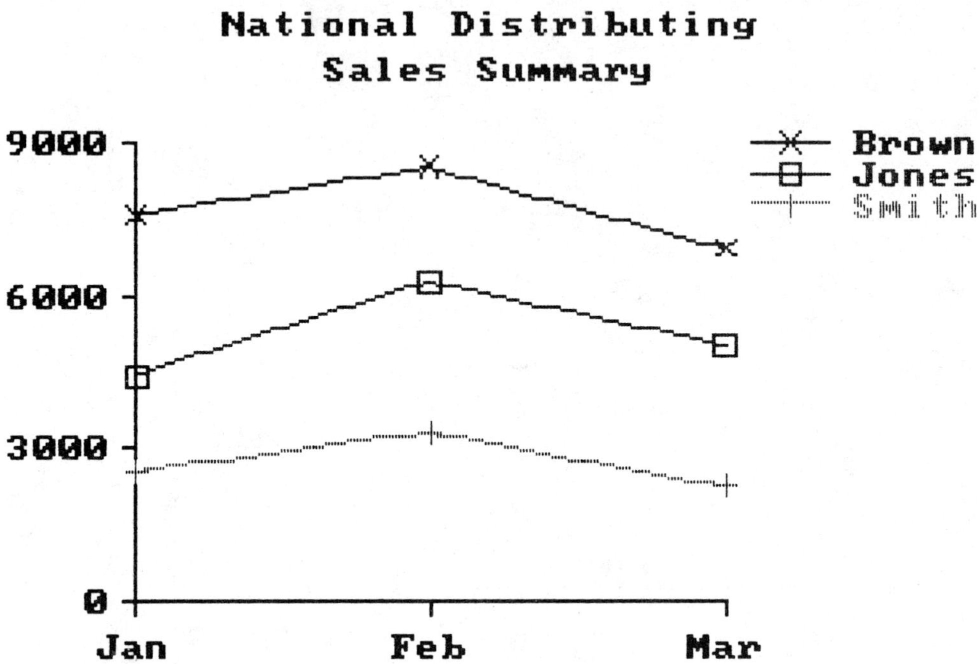

Figure 12-12.

Sales Summary area graph

```
Current Chart (#2) --> Pie

HEADINGS:                            SCALING:
Main:    (A2)                        Y-Axis: Auto
Sub:     (A3)                        X-Axis: Auto
X-Axis: (empty)
Y-Axis: (empty)

TIME LABELS: (B4:D4)

   Data              Pt-Labels       Var-Labels        FORMATS:
A: (B5:D5)           (empty)         (A5)              Axis:
B: (B6:D6)           (empty)         (A6)              Time:
C: (B7:D7)           (empty)         (A7)              Var:
D: (empty)           (empty)         (empty)           Point:
E: (empty)           (empty)         (empty)           % :
F: (empty)           (empty)         (empty)
G: (empty)           (empty)         (empty)
H: (empty)           (empty)         (empty)
I: (empty)           (empty)         (empty)
J: (empty)           (empty)         (empty)

PIE EXPLOSION: None                 MODE: All Variables (1)
F1 or <?> for AnswerScreen.
F1 = Help; F2 = Erase Line/Return to Spreadsheet; F9 = Plot; F10 = View
```

Figure 12-13.

Graph Definition screen

plotted on the horizontal axis (an exception being, of course, the pie graph). The two remaining types of graphs are for different applications.

Hi-Low Graphs

Hi-Low graphs are designed primarily for one application: tracking stocks. However, there are undoubtedly other applications for which they are useful as well. Enter the information shown in the following screen to provide some data to graph:

```
:       :  A    ::   B    ::   C   ::   D   ::   E   ::   F   ::   G   ::   H
     1:Portfolio Summary                                   Price
     2:Week of October 15, 1983                            Stock
     3:              High        Low     Close
     4:DEC        103.875         97     98.25
     5:IBM         134.25     130.75    131.75
     6:TI         124.375        115     120.5
     7:
     8:
     9:
    10:
    11:
    12:
    13:
    14:
    15:
    16:
    17:
    18:
    19:
    20:
  v D7
Width:  9  Memory: 65 Last Col/Row:F6      ? for HELP
   1>
F1 = Help; F2 = Erase Line/Return to Spreadsheet; F9 = Plot; F10 = View
```

Then make the following entries to define the graph:

Entry	*Function*
/V D B4:D7 <RET>	Enter data range
G H	Select the Hi-Low graph type
T A4:A6 <RET>	Assign Time labels
H M A1 <RET>	Set the Main heading
S A2 <RET>	Set the Subheading
<RET>	Exit from the Heads option
<RET>	Display the graph

The data range is entered with an extra row in it so that the variables will be in columns instead of rows. SuperCalc³ always creates the fewest variables possible, so a square data range should be extended to include a blank row.

Also notice that the "time labels" are *not* periods of time. SuperCalc³ calls these "time labels" because they are often used to represent time periods. There is no restriction on what you can use them for; in this case, they are used to label stocks.

You now need to add new elements to this graph, that is, headings to both the X-axis (horizontal) and the Y-axis (vertical). X-axis and Y-axis heads are defined just like the main heads and subheads; they are options on the same prompt. Our Y-head is in cell F1 and our X-head is in cell F2. Make the following entries to define these heads:

Entry	*Function*
/V H Y F1 <RET>	Enter the Y-head as cell F1
X F2 <RET>	Enter the X-head as cell F2
<RET>	Exit the heads sub-option
<RET>	Display the graph

Now you have labeled the two axes of the graph. One more thing that would make this graph clearer is to display the actual closing price of each stock on the graph. A label positioned at a point on the graph is called a *point-label.* You may have noticed that P(oint-Labs) is one of the options to the /View command. Select this option by entering **/V P**. The prompt now says "Var A: Enter Point-Label range (now empty), <space> to skip, <−> to clear". In plain language, this is asking you to enter the range of cells that contains the point labels for variable A. It also gives you the option of skipping to variable B by pressing the space bar. And you can clear the point-labels that you have already set for variable A by pressing the minus (−) key. If you had already set point-labels for this variable, the range would be indicated where the prompt says "(now empty)".

You want to define point-labels for the closing price, which is the third variable, or variable C. So skip variables A and B by pressing the **SPACE BAR** twice. Now enter **D4:D6** and press **<RET>**. This defines the cells that contain the closing prices as the point-labels. Notice that point-labels do not have to be text entries; numbers work just as well.

These closing values should include dollar signs so that there is no mistaking them. You can format label entries on a graph just as you format cell entries on the worksheet. Select the View Options Format option (enter **O F**). You will see the prompt "A(xis), T(ime), V(ar), P(oint) or % Labels". The labels that you have just defined are point-labels, so select **P** for point. Now you see the familiar /Format prompt. In this case we want User-defined format 1, so enter **U 1 <RET>**. Press the **F10** function key to display the graph; it

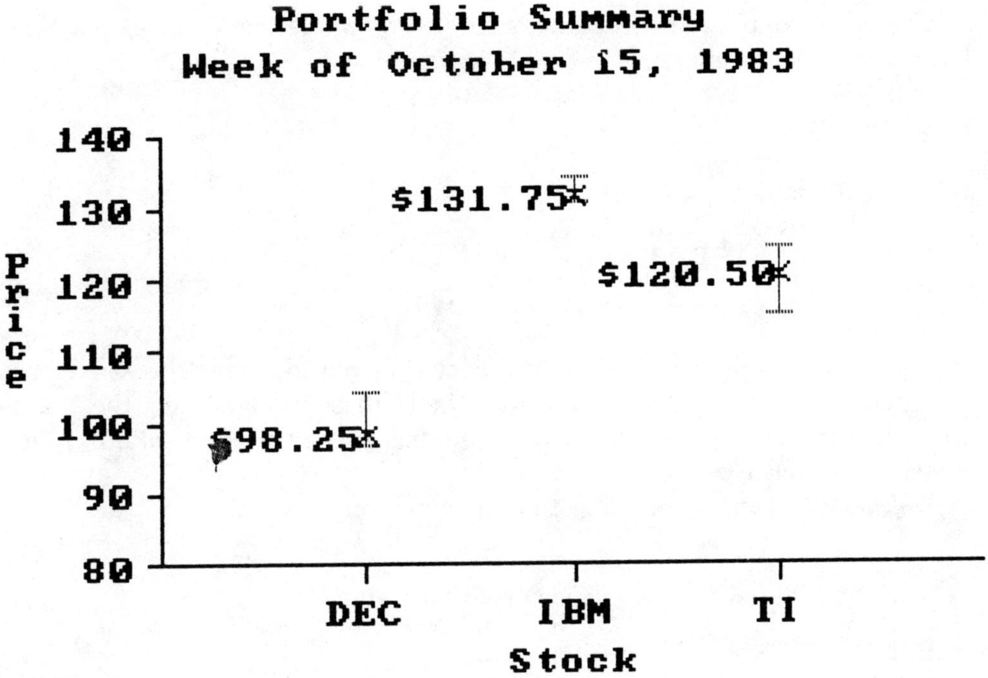

Figure 12-14.

Portfolio Summary hi-low graph

should look like Figure 12-14.

X-Y Graphs

The last type of graph shows the relationship between two numeric variables. Instead of one axis being time or some other non-numeric value, both axes of an X-Y graph represent numbers. The graph is used to show the relationship of the two numbers. For example, the X-axis might represent earnings, and the Y-axis might represent tax rates. The graph would show how tax rates increase with respect to earnings. This type of graph is used extensively in economics, physical science, and engineering.

For this example you will graph a sine wave. Make the following entries to create the data to graph:

Cell	*Entry*
A1	**0**
A2	**A1+.2512**
B1	**SIN(A1)**
	/R A2 , A3:A26
	/R B1 , B2:B26
D1	**Sine**
D2	**Radians**

The values in column A are values that will be plotted along the X-axis, and the values in column B are the values that will be plotted along the Y-axis. (Remember that SuperCalc works in radians, so the values in column A represent a complete circle.)

Define the graph by making the following entries:

Entry	*Function*
/V D A1:B26 <RET>	Define data range
G X	Set the graph type to X-Y graph
H Y D1 <RET>	Y-axis label
X D2 <RET>	X-axis label
<RET>	Exit Heads option
<RET>	Draw the graph

This graph should look like Figure 12-15.

Data Management (//Data)

SuperCalc^3 provides a command you can use to search for and select information from a block of cells. It is called the //Data command. You might note that the //Data command looks a bit unusual; it is the only command you start by entering two slashes. If you enter only one slash followed by the letter D you will be using the /Delete command, not the //Data command.

With the //Data command you specify what data to look for by entering *criteria* on the worksheet. You then request the program to search for information based on this criteria. You must also specify a block that you want to be searched. This block is called the *Input Area*. SuperCalc searches the

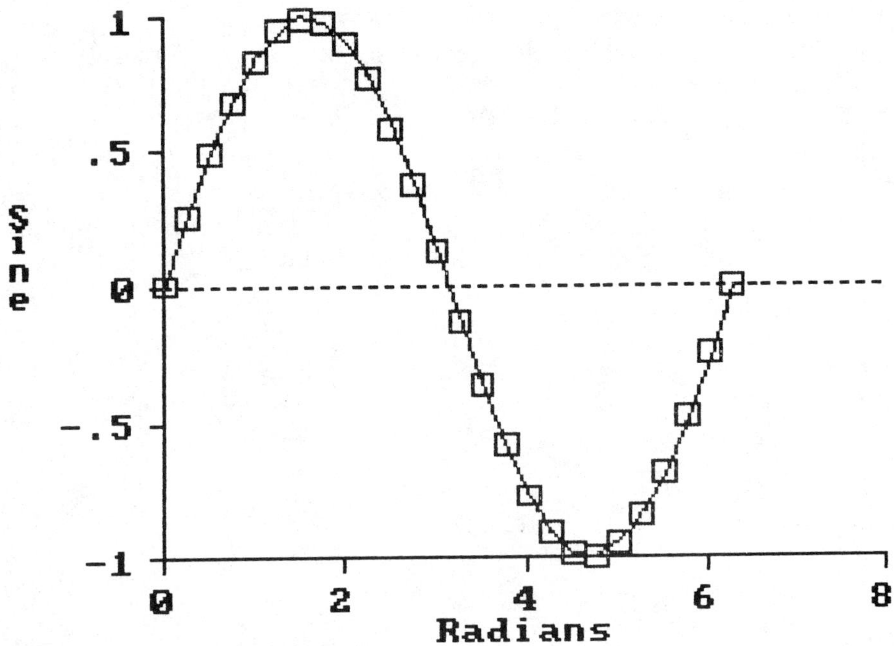

Figure 12-15.

Sine wave X-Y graph

Input Area row by row.

The //Data command has three options for locating information: "Find, Select, and Extract". When you use the Find option, SuperCalc points to and highlights each row that contains data matching what you have asked it to look for.

You can also copy rows or portions of a row from the Input Area to another block that you define on the worksheet as the *Output Area*. To do this you can use either the Extract or Select option. Using the Extract option, SuperCalc finds rows with matching data and then copies the designated columns from the Input Area to the Output Area.

The Select option does the same thing, except that when a matching row is found, it asks you whether you want to copy it or not. You then press **Y** (for yes) if you want it copied or **N** (for no) if you don't want to copy the data. The data you decide to copy is placed into the Output Area.

The Find option is the simplest to set up, so it will be demonstrated first. Reload the file B:NLWEST, which you saved in Chapter 7 (enter **/L B:NLWEST , A**). When using //Data, the first row of the Input Area must contain column headings. You should have the first row of data just below the column headings with no rows between. So enter **/D R 6 <RET>** to delete row 6. To make this a little more interesting, insert columns for the state and attendance to date for each team. Enter the following:

Cell	*Entry*	*Cell*	*Entry*
	/I C C:D <RET>	D4	**To Date**
C5	**St**	D5	**Attendance**
C6	**Ga**	D6	**1400000**
C7	**Ca**	D7	**1600000**
C8	**Ca**	D8	**1000000**
C9	**Ca**	D9	**800000**
C10	**Oh**	D10	**700000**
C11	**Tx**	D11	**1100000**

Now make row 5 the top row on the screen by entering **=5 <RET> =<RET>**. Finally, move the Los Angeles Dodgers to row 10 by entering **/M R 8 , 10 <RET>**. The screen should now appear as follows:

```
  !      A        !!   B    !!  C  !!    D    !!   E   !!   F   !!   G   !
 5!City            Team      St       Attendanc     Won     Lost     Back
 6!Atlanta         Braves    Ga         1400000      62       43        0
 7!San Diego       Padres    Ca         1600000      63       44        0
 8!San Francisco   Giants    Ca          800000      57       49      5.5
 9!Cincinnati      Reds      Oh          700000      40       67       23
10!Los Angeles     Dodgers   Ca         1000000      65       47       .5
11!Houston         Astros    Tx         1100000      35       72       28
12!
13!Total                                            322      322
14!
15!
16!
17!
18!
19!
20!
21!
22!
23!
24!
> A5          Text="City
Width: 15  Memory: 61  Last Col/Row:I13    ? for HELP
 1>█
F1 = Help; F2 = Erase Line/Return to Spreadsheet; F9 = Plot; F10 = View
```

Defining the Input Area

Suppose you want to find all the teams located in California. In this example, the Input Area to search will be the block from row 5 through row 12 and columns A through G. To tell SuperCalc this, enter **//D** to start the //Data command. You will see the following prompt:

```
I(nput), C(riterion), O(utput), F(ind), E(xtract), S(elect), R(emain)?
  8>//Data,█
```

To specify the Input Area, press the letter **I**. SuperCalc will ask you to enter the "Input range." Enter **A5:I12**. Then press **<RET>**, but don't press any other keys yet.

Defining the Criteria

To tell the //Data command what you want to look for, you enter one or more search criteria into a separate block on the worksheet called the *Criteria Area*. You can define the search criteria in many different ways, but the Criteria Area must contain at least two rows. Like the Input Area, the first row of the Criteria Area is used for column headings. The rows below the column headings may contain one or several of the following:

- Text strings to match in a particular column
- Text strings to match from any column
- Logical tests to match.

You need to tell the //Data command where the Criteria Area is. You can place the Criteria Area anywhere on the worksheet. In this example, the criteria will be placed in the block from A14 to C15. While still in the //Data command press the letter **C** for Criteria. SuperCalc³ will again ask you for a range. Enter **A14:C15** and press **<RET>**. Then press **<RET>** again to exit from the //Data command.

Now enter the criteria as follows:

Cell	*Entry*	*Purpose*
A14	**St**	This is the heading of the column you want to search.
A15	**Ca**	This is the data you want to match.

This criteria will match all rows that contain the text string "Ca" in the column headed by "St" (in other words, all the teams in California).

Finding Data

Now you are ready to use the Find option. Enter **//D F** and watch what happens. SuperCalc now highlights the row containing the San Diego Padres.

```
  :      A        ::    B    ::    C    ::    D     ::    E    ::    F    ::    G    :
 5:City            Team       St          Attendanc       Won        Lost       Back
 6:Atlanta         Braves     Ga            1400000        62          43          0
 7:San Diego       Padres     Ca            1600000        63          44          0
 8:San Francisco   Giants     Ca             800000        57          49        5.5
 9:Cincinnati      Reds       Oh             700000        40          67         23
10:Los Angeles     Dodgers    Ca            1000000        65          47         .5
11:Houston         Astros     Tx            1100000        35          72         28
12:
13:Total                                                  322         322
14:St
15:Ca
16:
 .
 .
 .
24:
v A7             Text="San Diego
Next record: \/ or /\ , Next field: <-- or -->
 12>//Data,Find █
F1 = Help; F2 = Erase Line/Return to Spreadsheet; F9 = Plot; F10 = View
```

Press the **DOWN ARROW** key. The highlighting moves to the row containing the San Francisco Giants. Press the **DOWN ARROW** key once more. This time the highlighting skips down to the row containing the Dodgers. Press the **DOWN ARROW** key again. This time the highlighting doesn't move, and SuperCalc displays the message "No more matching records."

```
  :      A        ::    B    ::    C    ::    D     ::    E    ::    F    ::    G    :
 5:City            Team       St          Attendanc       Won        Lost       Back
 6:Atlanta         Braves     Ga            1400000        62          43          0
 7:San Diego       Padres     Ca            1600000        63          44          0
 8:San Francisco   Giants     Ca             800000        57          49        5.5
 9:Cincinnati      Reds       Oh             700000        40          67         23
10:Los Angeles     Dodgers    Ca            1000000        65          47         .5
11:Houston         Astros     Tx            1100000        35          72         28
12:
13:Total                                                  322         322
14:St
15:Ca
16:
 .
 .
 .
24:
v A10            Text="Los Angeles                    No more matching records
Next record: \/ or /\ , Next field: <-- or -->
 12>//Data,Find █
F1 = Help; F2 = Erase Line/Return to Spreadsheet; F9 = Plot; F10 = View
```

The Find option has done all that it is able to do. Now press the **UP ARROW** key and the highlighting moves back up to the Giants, bypassing the rows that do not match. Press **<RET>**. This cancels the Find option but leaves you in the //Data command.

Extracting Data

Now we will use the Extract option to copy information from the Input Area to another area on the worksheet called the Output Area. To tell the //Data command where you want the output to go, press the letter **O**. SuperCalc prompts you for a range. Enter **A18:H25** and press **<RET>**. The Output Area need not have the same number of rows or columns as the Input Area does. Like the Input Area and Criteria Area, the first row of the Output Area is used for column headings. Now press **<RET>** again to exit from the //Data command. Make the following entries to specify that you want to extract the team name, state, and games won:

Cell	*Entry*
A18	**Team**
B18	**St**
C18	**Attendance**

Enter //**D E**, and watch what happens.

```
  :       A        ::   B    ::  C  ::    D    ::   E   ::   F   ::   G   :
 5:City             Team      St      Attendanc      Won      Lost     Back
 6:Atlanta          Braves    Ga        1400000       62        43        0
 7:San Diego        Padres    Ca        1600000       63        44        0
 8:San Francisco    Giants    Ca         800000       57        49      5.5
 9:Cincinnati       Reds      Oh         700000       40        67       23
10:Los Angeles      Dodgers   Ca        1000000       65        47       .5
11:Houston          Astros    Tx        1100000       35        72       28
12:
13:Total                                            322       322
14:St
15:Ca
16:
17:
18:Team             St        Attendance
19:Padres           Ca          1600000
20:Giants           Ca           800000
21:Dodgers          Ca          1000000
22:
23:
24:
> A18           Text="Team
I(nput), C(riterion), O(utput), F(ind), E(xtract), S(elect), R(emain)?
 8>//Data,█
F1 = Help; F2 = Erase Line/Return to Spreadsheet; F9 = Plot; F10 = View
```

Now press <**RET**>.

The Extract option has selected the three teams that are located in California and copied them to the Output Area. However, only those columns you requested have been copied. It is even easier to copy all the information on each row. First, enter /**B 18** to blank out the column headings in row 18. Now enter //**D E** again.

```
  !       A        !!   B    !!  C  !!    D    !!   E   !!   F   !!   G   !
 5!City              Team      St      Attendanc      Won      Lost     Back
 6!Atlanta           Braves    Ga        1400000       62        43        0
 7!San Diego         Padres    Ca        1600000       63        44        0
 8!San Francisco     Giants    Ca         800000       57        49      5.5
 9!Cincinnati        Reds      Oh         700000       40        67       23
10!Los Angeles       Dodgers   Ca        1000000       65        47       .5
11!Houston           Astros    Tx        1100000       35        72       28
12!
13!Total                                              322       322
14!St
15!Ca
16!
17!
18!
19!San Diego         Padres    Ca        1600000       63        44        0
20!San Francisco     Giants    Ca         800000       57        49      5.5
21!Los Angeles       Dodgers   Ca        1000000       65        47       .5
22!
23!
24!
> A18
I(nput), C(riterion), O(utput), F(ind), E(xtract), S(elect), R(emain)?
 8>//Data,█
F1 = Help; F2 = Erase Line/Return to Spreadsheet; F9 = Plot; F10 = View
```

This time all the information on each matching row is copied to the Output Area.

Summary

Here is a summary of what has been covered so far. To find matching rows in the Input Area, perform the following steps:

1. Load a model file or enter data into a block of cells on the worksheet to use as an Input Area. Enter column headings in the first row of the Input area.
2. Create another block of cells to use as criteria. Place the column headings for the columns you want to search in the first row of the Criteria Area. Then enter the search criteria on the second row.
3. Enter //**D** to begin the Data command.

4. Press **I** and define the Input Area as a block of cells on the worksheet.
5. Press **C** and define the block where the Criteria Area is.
6. Press **F**. Press the **DOWN ARROW** key to advance the highlighting to the next row. Press **<RET>** to stop the Find option.

To Extract rows from the Input Area into an Output Area:

1. Press **O** and define the Output Area as the block where you want to send the output.
2. Press **E**. Press **<RET>** to leave the //Data command.

To Extract specific columns into the Output Area:

Enter the headings for columns you want to extract into the top row of the Output Area and enter //**D E** again.

Searching for Numerical Values

When you want to match numerical values, you set up a logical formula in the Criteria Area that checks for the numerical values you want. You write the formula so that it checks the first data row in the Input Area. When you use the Find, Extract, or Select options, SuperCalc automatically adjusts this formula as it looks at each row.

Blank out the Criteria Area (enter **/B A14:A15 <RET>**) and then enter **E6>60** in cell C15. This formula returns a value of 1 if the value in E6 is greater than 60. The number of games won by the Atlanta Braves is in cell E6. Notice that cell C15 now displays the value 1. This is because the Atlanta Braves have won more than 60 games and the formula E6>60 is true.

Now here is what this formula will do as a search criteria for the //Data command: The number of games won by each team is in column E. The Atlanta Braves are in the first data row in the Input Area on row 6. As the //Data command runs, it adjusts this formula to look at the cell in column E on each row. So for row 7 it will check cell E7, for row 8 it will check cell E8, and so on.

Now enter //**D E**.

```
    !       A       !!    B    !!  C   !!    D    !!    E   !!    F   !!    G   !
   5!City            Team      St        Attendanc       Won       Lost      Back
   6!Atlanta         Braves    Ga          1400000        62         43         0
   7!San Diego       Padres    Ca          1600000        63         44         0
   8!San Francisco   Giants    Ca           800000        57         49       5.5
   9!Cincinnati      Reds      Oh           700000        40         67        23
  10!Los Angeles     Dodgers   Ca          1000000        65         47        .5
  11!Houston         Astros    Tx          1100000        35         72        28
  12!
  13!Total                                               322        322
  14!
  15!                               1
  16!
  17!
  18!
  19!Atlanta         Braves    Ga          1400000        62         43         0
  20!San Diego       Padres    Ca          1600000        63         44         0
  21!Los Angeles     Dodgers   Ca          1000000        65         47        .5
  22!
  23!
  24!
< A18
I(nput), C(riterion), O(utput), F(ind), E(xtract), S(elect), R(emain)?
  8>//Data,█
F1 = Help; F2 = Erase Line/Return to Spreadsheet; F9 = Plot; F10 = View
```

All of the teams that have won more than 60 games have been extracted to the Output Area. Note that when you want to search for numerical values you do not need to specify a column heading over the formula in the Criteria Area.

Adding More Criteria

Up to now we have only used two rows for the Criteria Area. The first row contains column headings you want to search for text matches. The second contains text information or logical formulas to match.

You may also use additional rows to define criteria. If you add a third row of criteria, the //Data command will locate any record that matches the criteria on either the second row or the third row. You may also specify more than one criterion on the same row. If you enter two criteria on one row, SuperCalc will locate only the rows in the Input Area that match both criteria.

Clear the entry line (**CTRL-Z**) and enter the following:

Cell	*Entry*
B14	**City**
B16	**Houston**

The criteria in row 15 is still checking for all teams that have won more than 60 games. The criteria in row 16 now checks for teams located in Houston.

Make the following entries:

Entry	*Function*
//D	Begin the //Data command
C A14:C16 <RET>	Include row 16 in the criteria
E	Start the extract option

```
   :      A       ::   B    ::  C  ::    D    ::   E   ::   F   ::   G   :
  5:City           Team      St        Attendanc     Won     Lost     Back
  6:Atlanta        Braves    Ga          1400000      62       43        0
  7:San Diego      Padres    Ca          1600000      63       44        0
  8:San Francisco  Giants    Ca           800000      57       49      5.5
  9:Cincinnati     Reds      Oh           700000      40       67       23
 10:Los Angeles    Dodgers   Ca          1000000      65       47       .5
 11:Houston        Astros    Tx          1100000      35       72       28
 12:
 13:Total                                            322      322
 14:               City
 15:                               1
 16:               Houston
 17:
 18:
 19:Atlanta        Braves    Ga          1400000      62       43        0
 20:San Diego      Padres    Ca          1600000      63       44        0
 21:Los Angeles    Dodgers   Ca          1000000      65       47       .5
 22:Houston        Astros    Tx          1100000      35       72       28
 23:
 24:
< A18
I(nput), C(riterion), O(utput), F(ind), E(xtract), S(elect), R(emain)?
  8>//Data,█
F1 = Help; F2 = Erase Line/Return to Spreadsheet; F9 = Plot; F10 = View
```

This time both the teams that have won more than 60 games as well as the team located in Houston are copied to the Output Area.

You can use information you have extracted to create a separate report or in any other way you like. For instance, you can use this information to draw a graph. To do this enter the following:

Cell	*Entry*	*Purpose*
A17	**Astros vs. Leaders**	Heading
	/V	Begin /View command
	D D19:D25 <RET>	Data to be graphed
	T B19:B25 <RET>	Team name labels
	H M A17 <RET>	Main heading
	S C5 <RET> <RET>	Subheading
	O F T 5 <RET>	Set team name width to 5
	<RET>	Draw the graph
	<RET>	

Notes

1. In this graph, the "time labels" are actually team names. You can use any information you want as time labels for a graph.
2. After you have used the //Data or /View command, be careful when you move, rearrange, or delete rows or columns. If you change the order of rows or columns you have used as a range for //Data Input, Output, Criteria, or /View Data, you will need to reestablish these ranges again before searching or graphing.

SuperCalc³ Financial Functions

SuperCalc³ includes three new financial functions.

Internal Rate of Return (IRR)

Internal rate of return (IRR) accounts for how fast an investment will pay back. The higher the internal rate of return, the faster an investment will pay back. IRR can be used to compare two investments in the same way that net present value (NPV) does. Both IRR and NPV account for the decrease in the value of money over time by discounting future returns on an investment. However, IRR is a rate of return and thus accounts for the amount of time in which you have invested more money than you have received, while net present value tells you how much the investment is worth.

Formally defined, the internal rate of return on an investment is equal to the discount rate for which the net present value of the investment would be equal to zero. You *could* calculate internal rate of return using the NPV function. You would keep altering the cell that contained the discount rate until the NPV function evaluated to zero. This is exactly what you would do if you have an older version of SuperCalc. If you have SuperCalc³ you don't need to do this any more. You can use the IRR function instead.

To use the IRR function, you first set up a model that finds the future earnings on an investment over time. Then enter the IRR function to evaluate the earnings. The format is

IRR(*guess*,*range*)

Guess is a value which you think approximates the internal rate of return. By entering an approximate value, you can make the IRR function run slightly faster. However, you may enter zero if you prefer. The *range* is a partial column or partial row that contains earnings from the investment you are evaluating.

The example used is the same one used in Chapter 10 for the NPV function. To apply the IRR function, reload the file B:NPV and add the following entries:

Cell	*Entry*
A21	**Internal Rate of Return**
D21	**IRR(0,D6:D16)**

```
 :  A  ::  B  ::  C  ::  D  ::  E  ::  F  ::  G  ::  H
 3:Discount Rate:        .055
 4:
 5:                      Year    Amount
 6:Annual Earnings:      1984    -10000
 7:                      1985      1500
 8:                      1986      1500
 9:                      1987      1500
10:                      1988      1500
11:                      1989      1500
12:                      1990      1500
13:                      1991      1500
14:                      1992      1500
15:                      1993      1500
16:                      1994      1500
17:                   ==================
18:Total Earnings                  5000
19:
20:Net present value            1238.33
21:Internal Rate of Return      .0814417
22:
> D21          Form=IRR(0,D6:D16)
Width:  9  Memory: 65 Last Col/Row:E21     ? for HELP
 1>
F1 = Help; F2 = Erase Line/Return to Spreadsheet; F9 = Plot; F10 = View
```

The result is .0814417, or approximately 8.1%. Try entering this number as the discount rate in cell C3. Note that the resulting net present value is very close to zero. If you enter a discount rate which is lower than the IRR, the resulting Net Present Value will be greater than zero. For discount rates higher than the IRR, the Net Present Value will be negative.

Regular Payments on a Loan (PMT)

SuperCalc³ also provides a function that calculates regular payments on a loan. The PMT function can be used in place of the complex formula used in

Chapter 4. The format of the PMT function is

PMT(*Principal,Periodic Interest,Number of Payments*)

The input values for the PMT function are similar to but not exactly the same as the entries for the example in Chapter 4. The *Principal* is the amount of the loan; *Number of Payments* is the total number of payments for the entire loan. If you have a 5-year loan and make monthly payments, the number of payments would be 60. *Periodic Interest* is the interest rate per payment period, not the annual interest rate. If you make monthly payments and you know the annual interest rate, you need to calculate the periodic interest rate as shown in the following example. Clear the worksheet (/**ZY**) and enter the following:

Cell	*Entry*	*Cell*	*Entry*
			/FE C9,$
A4	**Principal**	C4	**10000**
A5	**Annual Interest**	C5	**.125**
A6	**Years**	C6	**5**
A7	**Payments/Year**	C7	**12**
A8	**Periodic Interest**	C8	**(1+C5)^(1/C7)−1**
A9	**Payment Amount**	C9	**PMT(C4,C8,C6*C7)**

```
  :  A  ::  B  ::  C  ::  D  ::  E  ::  F  ::  G  ::  H
 1:
 2:
 3:
 4:Principal            10000
 5:Annual Interest       .125
 6:Years                    5
 7:Payments/Year           12
 8:Periodic Interest .0098636
 9:Payment Amount      221.62
10:
11:
12:
13:
14:
15:
16:
17:
18:
19:
20:
v C9    $        Form=PMT(C4,C8,C6*C7)
Width:  9  Memory: 65 Last Col/Row:C9      ? for HELP
 1>
F1 = Help; F2 = Erase Line/Return to Spreadsheet; F9 = Plot; F10 = View
```

In this example, the formula in cell C8 calculates the monthly interest rate. This is then used in the PMT function in cell C9.

Present Value of Payments (PV)

The Present Value function looks at a regular loan payment from the viewpoint of the investor. The Present Value of regular payments (also called Present Value of an *Annuity*) is the same as the Net Present Value; it calculates the amount a single payment would have to be in today's money to be equivalent to the periodic payments. However, the calculation for the present value is less involved than that for the more general NPV function. You do not have to put in all the earnings as you do with NPV; you only enter one payment. The PV function assumes all payments are equal. The format of the PV function is

PV(*Principal,Periodic Discount Rate,Number of Payments*)

Assuming the discount rate is 10% and using the previous model, you can solve for the present value by entering the following cells:

Cell	*Entry*	*Cell*	*Entry*
A10	**Discount Rate**	C10	**.10**
A11	**Periodic Rate**	C11	**(1+C10)^(1/C7)−1**
A10	**Present Value**	C10	**PV(C9,C11,C6*C7)**

```
   |  A  ||  B  ||  C  ||  D  ||  E  ||  F  ||  G  ||  H
  1|
  2|
  3|
  4|Principal              10000
  5|Annual Interest         .125
  6|Years                      5
  7|Payments/Year             12
  8|Periodic Interest   .0098636
  9|Payment Amount        221.62
 10|Discount Rate             .1
 11|Periodic Rate       .0079741
 12|Present Value       10535.39
 13|
  .
  .
  .
 19|
 20|
> C12           Form=PV(C9,C11,C6*C7)
Width:  9  Memory: 65 Last Col/Row:C12    ? for HELP
  1>■
F1 = Help; F2 = Erase Line/Return to Spreadsheet; F9 = Plot; F10 = View
```

Future Value of Payments (FV)

The Future Value of regular payments calculates the total compound value of all payments that will be made over a specified period. The format of the FV function is

FV(*Principal,Periodic Interest,Number of Payments*)

Suppose you plan to deposit $1000 at the end of each year in a savings account that earns 7.5% per year. The amount you would have at the end of three years would be **FV(1000,7.5,3)**. Enter this formula into cell C7. Suppose you want to know what your balance will be at the end of each of the next ten years. You can calculate this by entering the following:

Cell	*Entry*	*Cell*	*Entry*	*Cell*	*Entry*
	/ZY		**/FR2,TR**		**/FCC,8**
A1	**Deposit:**	B1	**1000**	C1	**"/year at**
D1	**.075**	E1	**Interest**		
B2	**Period**	C2	**Balance**		
B3	**1**	C3	**FV(B1,D1,B3)**		
B4	**B3+1**	C4	**FV(B1,D1,B4)**		

/R B4:C4, B5:B12, A Y N N Y

```
  :   A    ::    B    ::    C    ::    D    ::    E    ::    F    ::    G    ::    H
 1:Deposit:        1000/year at:       .075 interest
 2:                Year  Balance
 3:                   1  1000.00
 4:                   2  2075.00
 5:                   3  3230.63
 6:                   4  4472.92
 7:                   5  5808.39
 8:                   6  7244.02
 9:                   7  8787.32
10:                   8 10446.37
11:                   9 12229.85
12:                  10 14147.09
13:
14:
15:
16:
17:
18:
19:
20:
> C4              Form=FV(B1,D1,B4)
Width:  9  Memory: 65 Last Col/Row:E12    ? for HELP
 1>█
F1 = Help; F2 = Erase Line/Return to Spreadsheet; F9 = Plot; F10 = View
```

For more information on financial measures and their use, it is worthwhile to refer to a book on financial management such as *Essentials of Managerial Finance*, 6th Edition, by J. Fred Weston and Eugene F. Brigham, 1982, CBS College Publishing, Dryden Press.

APPENDIXES

Appendix A

SuperCalc Commands

This appendix describes all the commands for the SuperCalc program. The commands are listed in alphabetical order. The questions SuperCalc asks and what you need to enter are described, and simple examples are included. References are provided to show you where you can find examples in the text of how to use each command.

Certain conventions are used in the descriptions. Anything that appears in **boldface** is what you actually type in. Items shown in *italics* refer to information that you must supply. The italicized terms used are described in Table A-1.

The prompts shown are for SuperCalc^2. To use some of the commands and options, you must have SuperCalc^2 or Version 1.10 of SuperCalc. This is noted in parentheses where applicable. (For explanations of /View and //Data, see Chapter 12.)

Italicized Terms	***Meaning***
cell name	The name of a particular cell, such as A5.
column letter	A letter from A to Z or letter pair from AA to AZ or BA to BK that indicates the column you want to use.
column range	A pair of column letters separated by a colon, such as B:E, meaning from column B through column E.
file name	The name of a file on disk, consisting of no more than eight characters, preceded by the disk drive and a colon and followed by a period and an extension of no more than three characters, such as B:GEORGE.CAL.
range	Any kind of range you want to use: a single cell, a series along a row or column, or a block.
row number	A number from 1 to 254 that indicates the row you want to use.
row range	A pair of row numbers separated by a colon, such as 8:10, meaning row 8 through row 10.
series range	A range that is a series of cells along a row or column, such as A1:A5 (along column A) or B2:K2 (along row 2).
width	A number from 0 to 127 that represents the width you want a column to be.

Table A-1.

Terms Used in Appendix A

/Arrange

Sorts the worksheet or a portion of the worksheet into a new sequence according to a row or column (Requires SuperCalc² or later versions).

You enter: /**A**

SuperCalc asks: R(ow) or C(olumn)?

If you enter: **R**

SuperCalc asks: Enter Row Number, then Return; or "," for options

You enter:

row number	Row to sort on

and then enter:

<RET>	To sort entire worksheet
or	
,	To select options (recommended)

If you press comma to select options:

SuperCalc asks: Enter Column Range

You enter:

column range ,

If you enter: **C**

SuperCalc asks: Enter Column Letter, then Return; or "," for options

You enter:

column letter	Column to sort on

and then enter:

<RET>	To sort entire worksheet
or	
,	To select options (recommended)

If you press comma to select options:

SuperCalc asks: Enter Row Range

You enter:

row range ,

Then, if you have selected either row or column options:

SuperCalc asks: A(scending) or D(escending)?

You enter:

A	Sorts in ascending sequence
D	Sorts in descending sequence

SuperCalc asks: Adjust? Y(es) or N(o)

You enter:

Y	All formulas are adjusted
N	No adjustments are made (recommended)

Examples:

/A R 10 , B:D , A Y	Sorts columns B through D in ascending sequence according to row 10, with all formulas adjusted.
/A C B, 5:15 , D N	Sorts rows 5 through 15 in descending order according to what is in column B. Formulas are not adjusted.
Reference:	Chapter 7.

/Blank

Erases (blanks) the contents and clears the format of a cell or range of cells.

You enter: **/B**

SuperCalc asks: Enter Range
You enter:

<RET>	To blank the active cell only
or	
range **<RET>**	To blank the specified range

Examples:

/B <RET>	Blanks the active cell.
/B B1:C2 <RET>	Blanks the block containing cells B1, C1, B2, and C2.
/B*2 <RET>	Blank graph number 2 (SuperCalc^3)
References:	Chapter 1. Blanking a single cell. Chapter 4. Blanking a range of cells.

/Copy

Makes a single copy of a cell, a series of cells, or a block of cells.

You enter: **/C**

SuperCalc asks: From? (Enter range)

You enter:

range ,

SuperCalc asks: To? (Enter Cell), then Return; or "," for options

You enter:

cell name	Upper left-hand corner of destination range

and then enter:

<RET>	To copy with formula adjustment

or

,	To select options

If you select options:

SuperCalc asks: N(o Adjust), A(sk for Adjust), V(alues only), +, −, *, /

You enter:

N	No adjustment is made.
A	SuperCalc requests adjustment for each cell reference.
V	Only values are copied.

With SuperCalc², you can also select:

+	Values in source range are added to values in destination range.
−	Values in source range are subtracted from values in destination range.
*	Values in destination range are multiplied by values in source range.
/	Values in destination range are divided by values in source range.

Examples:

/C A1:B5 , D1 <RET>	The block from cell A1 to cell B5 is copied to cells D1 through E5 with formula adjustment.
/C A1:B5 , D1 , +	The values in the block from A1 to B5 are added to the cells D1 through E5 (SuperCalc²).
Reference:	Chapter 6.
	Chapter 12. Copying a graph.

//Data

Searches an area on the worksheet and selects information. With //Data you define an input area to search and then locate or extract information from the input area. The selection is based on criteria that you define on the worksheet. (SuperCalc^3)

Reference: Chapter 12.

/Delete

Deletes an entire row or column. /DC deletes a column, while /DR deletes a row. In SuperCalc^2, you can delete several rows or columns at once by specifying a row range or column range. /DF erases a file from a disk.

You enter: **/D**

SuperCalc asks: R(ow), C(olumn) or F(ile)?

If you enter: **R**

SuperCalc asks: Enter Row Range
You enter:

<RET>	To delete row where the active cell is located
row number **<RET>**	To delete row specified
row range **<RET>**	To delete rows specified (SuperCalc^2)

If you enter: **C**

SuperCalc asks: Enter Column Range
You enter:

<RET>	To delete column where active cell is located
column letter **<RET>**	To delete column specified
column range **<RET>**	To delete columns specified (SuperCalc^2)

If you enter: **F**

SuperCalc asks: Enter File Name (or <RETURN> for directory)
You enter:

<RET>	To display Disk Directory Menu

or

file name	To erase specified file

Examples:

/D R 10 <RET>	Deletes row 10
/D C E:F <RET>	Deletes columns E through F (SuperCalc^2)
/D F B:GEORGE.CAL <RET>	Erases the file GEORGE.CAL on drive B
Reference:	Chapter 7.

/Edit

Allows you to edit the data you have already entered into a cell on the worksheet. This command places the contents of a cell on the entry line where you can edit them. When you are finished, the results are stored in the active cell.

You enter: **/E**

SuperCalc asks: From? Enter cell

You enter:

<RET>	To place data from the active cell on entry line.
or	
cell name **<RET>**	To place data from another cell on entry line.

Examples:

/E <RET>	Edits the active cell.
/E A1 <RET>	Edits the contents of cell A1 into the active cell.
Reference:	Chapter 4.

/Format

Sets the display format for numbers and text entries in a cell or group of cells. /FE sets the format for a range of cells. /FR formats an entire row, and /FC formats an entire column. /FG sets the default format for the whole worksheet. In SuperCalc^2, /FD allows you to define your own special formats.

You enter: **/F**

SuperCalc asks:

Enter Level: G(lobal), C(olumn), R(ow), E(ntry) or D(efine)

You enter: **G** To format the whole worksheet

You enter: **C** To format a column

SuperCalc asks: Enter Column Range
You enter:

<RET> For the column containing the active cell

column letter **<RET>**

column range **<RET>** (SuperCalc^2 or later versions)

Then, if you have selected either /FG or /FC:

SuperCalc displays:
Define Formats: (I,G,E,$,R,L,TR,TL,*,U(1-8),H,D, column widths)

You enter: **R** To format a row

SuperCalc asks: Enter Row Range
You enter:

<RET> The row containing the active cell

row number **<RET>**

row range **<RET>** (SuperCalc^2 or later versions)

You enter: **E** To format a cell or group of cells

SuperCalc asks: Enter Range
You enter:

<RET> To specify the active cell

or

range **<RET>** To specify a range of cells

Then, if you have selected either /FR or /FE:

SuperCalc displays:
Define Formats: (I,G,E,$,R,L,TR,TL,*,U(1-8),H,D,column widths)

You enter: **D** To define a user format (U1 through U8)

SuperCalc displays: the User-Defined Format menu
You select the options by:

moving the cursor with the arrow keys and entering the settings you want for each format.

If you selected /FG, /FC, /FR, or /FE:

You may enter one or several of these formats:

I	Displays numbers as Integers.
G	Displays numbers in General format.
E	Displays numbers in Exponential format.
$	Displays numbers with two decimal places.
R	Displays numbers right-justified.
L	Displays numbers left-justified.
TR	Displays text right-justified.
TL	Displays text left-justified.
U1-U8	User-Defined Formats (SuperCalc^2).
*****	Displays numbers in Graphic format (*).
H	Hides information in cells (SuperCalc^2).
D	Default.
0-127	Sets width of column or columns (/FC, /FG only).

and then press **<RET>**.

Examples:

/F G $ <RET>	Sets the Global format to dollars (two decimal places).
/F R 4 <RET> TR <RET>	Sets row 4 to right-justified text.
/F C A , 12 <RET>	Sets the width of column A to 12 characters.
/F C B:G , 5 <RET>	Sets the width of columns B through G to 5 (SuperCalc^2).

References:

Chapter 4. General information on the /Format command.

Chapter 8. User-Defined formats.

Chapter 11. Example with /Format Hide option.

/Global

Changes global display or data entry and calculation options.

You enter: **/G**

SuperCalc asks:

F(orm.), N(ext), B(order), T(ab), R(ow), C(ol.), M(an.), A(uto.)

You enter:

F	To turn on/off display formulas instead of results.
N	To turn off/on automatic advance of active cell.
B	To turn off/on borders.
T	To turn on/off restriction of movement of active cell.
R	To calculate row by row.
C	To calculate column by column.
M	To turn on manual recalculation.
A	To turn on automatic recalculation.
G	For graphics option. (SuperCalc^3)

Example:

/G R	Changes order of calculation to row by row
References:	Chapter 8. Global formula and border options
	Chapter 9. All other Global options
	Chapter 12. Graphics options (SuperCalc^3)

/Insert

Inserts an entire new row or column. /IC inserts a column, while /IR inserts a row. In SuperCalc^2, you can insert several rows or columns at once by specifying a row range or column range.

You enter: **/I**

SuperCalc asks: R(ow) or C(olumn)?

If you enter: **R**

SuperCalc asks: Enter Row Range
You enter:

<RET>	To insert a row above the active cell
row number **<RET>**	To insert the specified row
row range **<RET>**	To insert the specified rows (SuperCalc^2)

If you enter: **C**

SuperCalc asks: Enter Column Range
You enter:

<RET>	To insert a column to the left of the active cell.
column letter **<RET>**	To insert the specified column.
column range **<RET>**	To insert the specified columns (SuperCalc^2).

Examples:

/I R <RET>	Inserts a row above the active cell.
/I C E:F <RET>	Inserts two new columns to the left of column E (SuperCalc^2).
Reference:	Chapter 7.

/Load

Loads a SuperCalc model file or portion of a model from disk into the computer's memory.

You enter: **/L**

SuperCalc asks: Enter File Name (or <RETURN> for directory)
You enter:

<RET>	Displays directory menu

or

file name **<RET>**

SuperCalc asks: A(ll), P(art) or C(onsolidate)?
You enter:

A	To load entire model file
C	To consolidate values from model file
P	To load a portion of model file

If you select the Part option:

SuperCalc asks: From? (Enter Range)
You enter:

range ,	Group of cells to load

SuperCalc asks:
To? (Enter Cell), then Return; or "," for Options
You enter:

cell name	Upper left-hand corner

and then enter:

<RET>	To adjust cell references

or

,	To select options

If you select options:

SuperCalc asks:
N(o Adjust), A(sk for Adjust), V(alues only), +, −, *, /
You enter:

N	No adjustment of cell references.
A	SuperCalc requests adjustment for each cell reference.
V	Only values are copied from the file.

With SuperCalc², you can also select:

+	Values in file are added to worksheet cells.
−	Values in file are subtracted from worksheet cells.
*	Worksheet cells are multiplied by values in file.
/	Worksheet cells are divided by values in file.

Examples:

/L B:MASTER , A	Loads the file MASTER from disk B.
/L B:AUG-DATA , C	Loads AUG-DATA and consolidates its cells with the information in the cells on the worksheet (SuperCalc²).
/L B:MODEL1 , P C1:D20 , F31 <RET>	Loads and adjusts all cell references from file MODEL1 cells C1:D20 into the block F31 to G50 on the worksheet (SuperCalc²).
/L B:LASTWEEK , P A20:G20 , A5 , V	Takes the results from row 20 in the file called B:LASTWEEK and inserts them in row 5 on the worksheet (SuperCalc²).

References: Chapter 3. Loading with All option.
Chapter 9. Consolidation and partial loads.
Chapter 11. Loading the worksheet from several diskettes.

/Move

Moves an entire column or row to a new position on the worksheet.

You enter: **/M**

SuperCalc asks: R(ow) or C(olumn)?

If you enter: **R**

SuperCalc asks: From? Enter row range
You enter:

row number ,

or

<RET> to specify the row containing the active cell.

SuperCalc asks: To? Enter row number
You enter:

row number **<RET>**

If you enter: **C**

SuperCalc asks: From? Enter column range
You enter:

column letter ,

or

<RET> to specify the row containing the active cell.

SuperCalc asks: To? Enter column letter
You enter:

column letter **<RET>**

Examples:

/M C B , A <RET> Moves column B to column A. This also pushes the old column A over to the right and it becomes the new column B.

/M R 5 , 8 <RET> Moves row 5 to row 8. The old row 8 becomes new row 7, old row 7 becomes new row 6, and old row 6 becomes new row 5.

Reference: Chapter 7.

/Output

Prints the worksheet or the contents of each cell on the printer, to the console, or to a disk file which may be read by a word processor. Also sends setup control codes to the printer.

You enter: **/O**

SuperCalc asks: D(isplay) or C(ontents) report?
You enter:

D — For a report like you see on the screen

or

C — For a listing of the model cell by cell

SuperCalc asks: Enter Range
You enter:

range

SuperCalc asks:
Enter Device: P(rinter), S(etup), C(onsole), or D(isk)

If you enter:

P — SuperCalc prints model on printer

C — SuperCalc prints model on console

If you select P or C:

SuperCalc will begin to print and will display:
Enter CTRL-Z to STOP print

At the end of each page SuperCalc will display:
More ... ('return' to continue or CTRL-Z to stop).
You enter:

<RET>

When the report is complete, SuperCalc will display:
End of Report ... Type any key to return to worksheet.
You enter:

any key

D — SuperCalc outputs file to disk

SuperCalc asks: Enter File Name (or <RETURN> for directory)
You enter:

file name **<RET>**

S	For Printer Setup

SuperCalc displays the Printer Setup Menu
You enter:

L	To change page length
W	To change page width
A	For automatic form feed
D	To double space
S	For setup codes

If you press S:

SuperCalc asks:
Enter codes (CR when done)
You enter:

codes to control printer **<RET>**

and then enter:

P	To print the report

Examples:

/O D All , P	Prints entire worksheet on printer.
/O C All , P	Lists cell contents on printer.
/O D All , D B:XYZ<RET>	Writes a report to disk file called B:XYZ.PRN.
/O D All , S W 132 <RET> P	Sets printer width to 132 characters and then prints report.

References:

Chapter 3. Printing a simple report on the printer.
Chapter 8. Writing a report on disk.
Chapter 9. Creating an execute file on disk.
Chapter 11. Printing a report in sections.

/Protect

Protects cell contents and formats from being changed.

You enter: **/P**

SuperCalc asks: Enter Range

/

You enter:

<RET>	To protect the active cell
or	
range **<RET>**	To protect a range of cells

Example:

/P C5:F8<RET>	Protects the block of cells bounded by columns C and F and rows 5 and 8.
Reference:	Chapter 5.

/Quit

Leaves SuperCalc and goes to another program or back to the operating system.

You enter: **/Q**

SuperCalc asks: EXIT SuperCalc? Y(es), N(o) or T(o)
You enter:

Y	To clear the worksheet and leave the program.
N	To cancel the /Quit command.
T	To allow you to leave SuperCalc^2 and enter another program.

If you select To (SuperCalc^2 only):

SuperCalc asks:
Enter file name (or <RETURN> for directory)
You enter:

program name **<RET>**	To clear the worksheet, leave SuperCalc, and start the requested program.

Examples:

/Q Y	Exits SuperCalc.
/Q T PROGRAM <RET>	Exits SuperCalc and enters the program PROGRAM.COM.
Reference:	Chapter 3.

/Replicate

Makes from one to several copies of a cell or series of cells.

You enter: **/R**

SuperCalc asks: From? (Enter Range)
You enter:

cell name **<RET>**	To copy one cell
or	
series range **<RET>**	To copy a series of cells

SuperCalc asks: To? (Enter Range), then Return; or "," for options
You enter:

cell name	To make a single copy
or	
series range	To make multiple copies

and then enter:

<RET>	To copy with formula adjustment
or	
,	To select options

If you press comma:

SuperCalc asks:
N(o Adjust), A(sk for Adjust), V(alues), +, −, *, /
You enter:

N	For no adjustment of cell references.
A	For SuperCalc to request adjustment for each cell reference.
V	For only values to be copied to destination range.

With SuperCalc^2, you can also select:

+	Values in source range are added to destination cells.
−	Values in source range are subtracted from destination cells.
*	Destination cells are multiplied by values in source range.
/	Destination cells are divided by values in source range.

Examples:

/R A1 , D1 <RET>	Cell A1 is copied to cell D1 with formula adjustment.
/R A1 , B1:D1 <RET>	Cell A1 is replicated to cells B1, C1, and D1 with formula adjustment.
/R A1:A5 , B1 <RET>	The series A1, A2, A3, A4, and A5 are copied to cells B1, B2, B3, B4, and B5 with formula adjustment.
/R A1:A5 , B1:D1 <RET>	The series A1, A2, A3, A4, and A5 are replicated into rows B, C, and D with formula adjustment.
/R A1:A5 , B1 , V	The numerical values from series A1, A2, A3, A4, and A5 are copied to cells B1, B2, B3, B4, and B5 (SuperCalc^2).
/R A1:A5 , B1 , +	The numerical values from series A1, A2, A3, A4, and A5 are added to the values of cells B1, B2, B3, B4, and B5. Any formulas in B1:B5 are converted to numerical totals (SuperCalc^2).
References:	Chapter 2. Replicating single cells: numbers and formulas. Chapter 6. Replicating a series. Replicating text. Ask for Adjustment option.

/Save

Saves the worksheet or portion of the worksheet into a file on disk. The /Save Part option is available in SuperCalc Version 1.10, SuperCalc^2, and later versions.

You enter: **/S**

SuperCalc asks: Enter File Name (or <RETURN> for directory)
You enter:

<RET> — To display directory menu

or

file name **<RET>**

SuperCalc asks: A(ll), P(art) or V(alues)
You enter:

A	To save entire model in file.
V	To save only values in file.
P	To save a portion of model in file. (Requires SuperCalc version 1.10 or later version.)

If you select the Part option:

SuperCalc asks: A(ll) or V(alues)
You enter:

A	For partial save with formulas
V	For partial save of values only

SuperCalc asks: From? (Enter Range)
You enter:

range ,	Group of cells to save

If the file already exists on disk:

SuperCalc asks:
File already exists: C(hange name), B(ackup), or O(verwrite)?
You enter:

C	To go back and change the file name
B	To back up the file (recommended)
O	To write over the previous file

Examples:

/S B:BUDGET.CAL, A, B	Saves and backs up all of the file BUDGET.-CAL on disk B.
/S B:PARTLOAN.CAL, P, V, C8:J21 <RET>	Saves only the values in the range C8:J21 of the current worksheet in a new file called PARTLOAN.CAL on disk B. (Requires Super-Calc Version 1.10, or later version.)
References:	Chapter 3. Saving with the All option.
	Chapter 9. Saving with the Values and Part options.
	Chapter 11. Saving a large model on several diskettes.

/Title

Locks a row, a column, or a row and a column on the display screen so that they are always visible.

You enter: **/T**

SuperCalc asks: H(oriz.), V(ert.), B(oth), or C(lear)?
You enter:

H	To lock on screen rows from the active cell upward.
V	To lock on screen columns from the active cell left.
B	To lock both rows upward and columns to the left.
C	To clear title locks.

Example:

/T V	Produces a vertical title lock to the left of the active cell.
References:	Chapter 7. General information on /Title.
	Chapter 11. Locking titles within a window.

/Unprotect

Removes protection from specified cells.

You enter: **/U**

SuperCalc asks: Enter Range
You enter:

range **<RET>**

Example:

/U E15:G19 <RET>	Unprotects the block of cells bounded by columns E and G and by rows 15 and 19.
Reference:	Chapter 4.

/View

Draws a graph of data from the worksheet. Using /View you can choose from seven types of graphs and you can create up to nine different graphs for each worksheet. The graphs can be displayed on the screen, drawn on a plotter, or printed on a graphics printer. (SuperCalc^3)

Example:

/V D A10:B20 <RET><RET>	Display a bar graph of two variables extending from A10:A20 and B10:B20.
Reference:	Chapter 12.

/Window

Splits the display screen horizontally into an upper and lower window or vertically into a left and right window.

You enter: **/W**

SuperCalc asks:

H(oriz.), V(ert.), C(lear Split), S(ynch.) or U(nsynch.)

You enter:

H	To split the screen into upper and lower windows.
V	To split the screen into right and left windows.
C	To clear any existing windows.
S	To synchronize scrolling in existing windows.
U	To cancel sychronized scrolling.

Examples:

/W V	Creates a left and a right window on the screen.
/W S	Synchronizes scrolling in existing windows.
References:	Chapter 7. General information on /Window.
	Chapter 11. Using windows to view two sections of a model simultaneously.

/eXecute

Executes a series of SuperCalc commands that have been written into a disk file. (Requires SuperCalc Version 1.10 or later version.)

You enter: /**X**

SuperCalc asks: Enter File Name (or <RETURN> for directory)
You enter:

<RET>	To display directory menu
or	
file name **<RET>**	

Example:

/X B:LOADMEM <RET>	Executes the file LOADMEM.XQT on disk B.
References:	Chapter 9. Using /eXecute to load part of a model file. Creating an execute file with the /Output command.
	Chapter 11. Using /eXecute to load and print and to help users. Using /eXecute to save on multiple diskettes.

/Zap

Clears the worksheet. Returns all formats and options to their initial (default) settings.

You enter: /**Z**

SuperCalc asks: /Zap-ENTIRE-Worksheet Y(es), N(o) or C(ontents)?
You enter:

Y	To clear the worksheet.
N	To cancel the /Zap command and let the information on the worksheet remain.
C	To clear all contents and formats but leave user-defined formats intact (SuperCalc^2).

Example:

/Z Y	Erases all information from worksheet
Reference:	Chapter 3

Appendix B

SuperCalc Functions

This appendix describes the functions that are built into the SuperCalc program. These functions are grouped into five sections: arithmetic functions, trigonometric functions, date functions, relational operators and logical functions, and special functions.

Terms that are shown in *italics* refer to information you must supply to use the function. The italicized terms used are described in Table B-1.

Arithmetic Functions

The arithmetic functions are described in Chapter 5.

ABS(*value*)

The ABS (absolute value) function returns the absolute value of the argument *value*. The absolute value of a number is always greater than or equal to zero and represents the magnitude of the number. ABS does not change *value* if *value* is positive or zero, but it changes the sign of *value* if *value* is negative. For instance, ABS(−8) would display (8).

AVERAGE(*list*)

The AVERAGE function returns the arithmetic mean of the non-blank entries in the *list*. The average is the sum of the items divided by the number of items. It is important to note the difference between a blank entry and an entry with a value of zero. A blank entry, which is either an empty cell or one with a text entry, is completely ignored by the AVERAGE function, while a cell with a value of zero is included in the average. For example, AVERAGE(C1:C20) would average the contents of cells C1 through C2O.

Italicized Terms	Meaning
value	A number, cell reference, or formula. A value can be a simple number such as 3, a cell reference such as A5, or a formula such as A5/2+3.
range	A range can be a single cell, a series along a row or column, or a block.
list	One single value or range, or several values and/or ranges separated by commas. The following are examples of lists and are shown used in the SUM function. SUM(A1) — a value SUM(A1,A2,D3,3) — several values SUM(A1:A5) — a range SUM(A1:A5,D1:F5) — several ranges SUM(A1,A3,A5,D1:F5,B20:G20) — values and ranges
series range	A range that is a series of cells along a row or column, such as A1:A4 (along column A) or B2:K2 (along row 2).
logical value	An input value to a logical function or to the IF function. A logical value is usually the result of logical functions or relational operators such as A1<A3, AND(B1,C1). In SuperCalc a logical value is always evaluated as zero or non-zero. Zero means False and non-zero means True.
date value	The value of a cell which is the result of using the DATE function. For instance, if you enter **DATE(10,31,83)** into cell A1, then cell A1 contains a date value. If you then enter **A1+3** into cell A2, then cell A2 will also contain a date value because its formula refers to the date value in cell A1.

Table B-1.

Terms used in Appendix B

COUNT(*list*)

The COUNT function returns a count of the non-blank entries in the *list*. It is important to note the difference between a blank entry and an entry with a value of zero. A blank entry, which is either an empty cell or one with a text entry, is not counted by the COUNT function, while a cell with a value of zero is included in the count. For example, COUNT(B1:D10) would count all the non-zero cells in the block B1 through D10.

EXP(*value*)

The EXP (exponential) function raises the constant "e" to the power *value*. "e", which is approximately 2.71828, is the base used in natural logarithms. This function finds the antilogarithm of a natural logarithm. To see this, try entering EXP(LN(30)).

INT(*value*)

The INT (integer) function returns the whole number portion of *value*. This means that *value* is truncated at the decimal place, and only the whole number to the left of the decimal is returned. *value* is not rounded. Do not confuse this function with the integer display format or with the ROUND function. INT(2.6) would be 2.

LN(*value*)

The LN (natural log) function returns the natural logarithm of *value*. This is the power that "e" (approximately 2.71828) must be raised to in order to equal the input value.

LOG10(*value*)

The LOG10 (common log) function returns the common or base 10 logarithm of *value*. This is the power that 10 must be raised to in order to equal *value*. The antilogarithm of a common logarithm can be found by raising 10 to the power of the logarithm. For example, LOG10(10^4.5) is 4.5.

MAX(*list*)

The MAX (maximum) function returns the maximum value in the *list*. If cell C1 contains 3, cell C2 contains 7, and cell D3 contains 9, then MAX(C1,C2,D3) would be 9.

MIN(*list*)

The MIN (minimum) function returns the minimum value in the *list*. This function considers a blank cell or a text entry to have a value of zero. For this function to return relevant results you must be sure there are no blank cells or text entries in the defined range.

MOD(*value1,value2*)

The MOD (modular) function returns the remainder that results from dividing *value1* by *value2*. For example, MOD(5,4) would return 1. (SuperCalc^2 only.)

ROUND(*value1,value2*)

The ROUND function returns *value1* rounded to *value2* decimal places. If *value2* is negative, then *value1* is rounded *value2* places to the left of the decimal place. For example, ROUND(2.46,1) would be 2.5 (SuperCalc^2 only).

SQRT(*value*)

The SQRT (square root) function returns the square root of *value*. This is a simple way to get a square root, but it is restricted to square roots only. It is possible to get other roots with SuperCalc by raising the value you want the root of to the power of the reciprocal of the root you want. For example, to take the cube root of 27 you could enter the formula 27^(1/3).

SUM(*list*)

The SUM function returns the sum of all the items in the *list*. Blank cells and text entries are ignored by this function. For example, SUM(D1:D5) adds the contents of cells D1 through D5.

Trigonometric Functions

All the trigonometric functions use angles in radians. There are 2*PI radians in a circle. To convert angles to radians you must multiply by 2*PI and divide by 360 (radians = degrees*PI/180). To convert radians to degrees, multiply by 360 and divide by 2*PI (degrees = radians*180/PI).

NOTE: The tangents of PI/2 and 3*PI/2 radians (90 degrees and 270 degrees) are infinity and will display "ERROR".

For more information on trigonometric functions see Chapter 5.

SIN(*value*)

The SIN (sine) function returns the sine of the radian angle *value*. SIN(30*PI/180) would be the sine of 30 degrees, which is equal to 0.5.

COS(*value*)

The COS (cosine) function returns the cosine of the radian angle *value*. Try COS(30*PI/180), which is approximately 0.866.

TAN(*value*)

The TAN (tangent) function returns the tangent of the radian angle *value*. TAN(30*PI/180) is approximately equal to .5774.

ASIN(*value*)

The ASIN (arcsine) function returns the radian angle of the sine *value*.

ACOS(*value*)

The ACOS (arccosine) function returns the radian angle of the cosine *value*.

ATAN(*value*)

The ATAN (arctangent) function returns the radian angle of the tangent *value*.

PI

The PI function returns the mathematical constant *pi*, correct to 16 significant digits. The value returned is always 3.141592653589793. Since this is a constant, there is no argument required.

Date Functions

SuperCalc^2 has a built-in calendar that covers the period from March 1, 1900 to February 28, 2100. This calendar is a Modified Julian Calendar that numbers the days during this period from 1 to 73049.

There are two types of SuperCalc date functions: those that display a date and those that require a date as an argument. The date functions are explained in Chapter 10.

DATE(*value1,value2,value3*)

The DATE function is used to enter a date value. The date value is displayed in the format *value1, value2,* and *value3,* which are values for the month, day, and year respectively. A date entered with the DATE function can be used in date calculations. If the column width is less than 11, the date will be displayed with two digits for the year. A four-digit year is displayed if the column width is 11 or greater. For instance, DATE(8,22,83) will display as 8/22/83 if the column width is 9, and as 8/22/1983 if the width is set to 11.

TODAY

The TODAY function displays today's date value in the active cell. If you have not entered the date into your system, the TODAY function will display N/A or an incorrect date. A date entered with the TODAY function can be used in date calculations. The TODAY function looks for the current system date each time the worksheet is recalculated.

DVAL(*value*)

The DVAL (date value) function takes a Modified Julian Date *value* such as 30560 and returns a date value such as 10/31/83. The input value must be an integer between 1 and 73049. A date returned by the DVAL function can be used in date calculations. DVAL is the opposite of JDATE, which takes a date and returns an integer.

DAY(*date value*)

The DAY function returns the number of the day of the month of *date value*. The number returned will range from 1 to 31. For instance, if cell A1 contains DATE(10,31,83), then DAY(A1) will return 31.

MONTH(*date value*)

The MONTH function returns the number of the month of *date value*. 1 is for January, 2 is for February, and so on to 12 for December. If cell A1 contains DATE(10,31,83), then MONTH(A1) will return 10.

YEAR(*date value*)

The YEAR function returns the number of the year of *date value*. The number returned is the actual calendar year. If cell A1 contains DATE(10,31,83), then YEAR(A1) would be 1983.

WDAY(*date value*)

The WDAY (weekday) function returns the Julian number of the day of the week of *date value*. 1 is for Sunday, 2 is for Monday, and so on to 7 for Saturday. If cell A1 contains DATE(10,31,83), then WDAY(A1) will return 2 because 10/31/83 falls on a Monday.

JDATE(*date value*)

The JDATE (Julian Date) function returns the Modified Julian Date of *date value*. The number returned will range from 1 for March 1, 1900, to 73049 for February 28, 2100. JDATE is the opposite of DVAL. If cell A1 contains DATE(10,31,83), then JDATE(A1) will return 30560.

Relational Operators and Logical Functions

The relational operators and logical functions are described in Chapter 10. The relational operators are used to compare two values. They return a 1 if the comparison is true or a 0 if it is false. Table B-2 shows the relational operators used in SuperCalc. In the example column, A1=3 and A2=2.

The relational operators are often used as logical values in arguments to the IF function.

IF(*logical value1,value2,value3*)

logical value1 is the logical expression that is evaluated in order to choose whether *value2* or *value3* will be returned.

value2 is returned by the IF function if *logical value1* is non-zero.

value3 is returned by the IF function if logical *value1* is zero.

Suppose cell A1 contains 3 and A2 contains 2. Then IF(A1>A2,5,4) will result in 5. *value 2* is chosen because A1>A2 is True (non-zero).

AND(*logical value1,logical value2*)

logical value1 and *logical value2* are both logical expressions. The AND function returns a value of 1 if both expressions are non-zero. If either expression is zero, the AND function returns a zero. Like the relational operators, the AND function can be used in an IF function. For example, if cell A1 contains 3 and A2 contains 2, IF(AND(A1>A2,A1=3)5,1) will return 5 since both A1>A2 and A1=3 are True (non-zero).

OR(*logical value1,logical value2*)

Operator	Description	Example	Result
=	is equal to	A1=A2	0
<>	is not equal to	A1<>A2	1
<	is less than	A1<A2	0
<=	is less than or equal to	A1<=A2	0
>	is greater than	A1>A2	1
>=	is greater than or equal to	A1>=A2	1

Table B-2.

The Relational Operators

logical value1 and *logical value2* are both evaluated. The OR function returns a value of 1 if either expression is non-zero. If neither logical value is non-zero, the OR function returns a zero.

NOT(*logical value*)

If *logical value* is non-zero, the NOT function returns a zero. If *logical value* is zero, the NOT function returns a 1.

Special Functions

SuperCalc has several special functions that don't fit into a distinct category. These functions are further described in Chapter 10.

ERROR

The ERROR function will display the word "ERROR" in any cell that evaluates the ERROR function. This function is usually used as one of the results of an IF function to report an incorrect entry or invalid result.

ISERROR(*value*)

The ISERROR function returns a logical value of 1 if *value* is ERROR; otherwise it returns a zero.

LOOKUP(*value,series range*)

value is used as an index into a table.
series range defines a range of cells containing the index to a table of values.
The LOOKUP function performs a search through the *series range*. When

the last entry less than or equal to *value* is found, the LOOKUP function returns the value of the cell adjacent to the match cell. If the series range is along a column, the value returned is that of the cell directly to the right of the match cell. If the series range is along a row, the value returned is that of the cell directly below the match cell. For example, if cells C1 through C5 contain 1, 2, 3, 4, 5, and cells D1 through D5 contain 5, 8, 13, 21, 34, then LOOKUP(2,C1:C5) will return 8.

NA

The NA (not available) function will display "N/A" in any cell that evaluates the NA function. This function is often used as one of the results of an IF function to report an incorrect entry or invalid result.

ISNA(*value*)

The ISNA (is not available) function returns a value of 1 if *value* is N/A otherwise it returns a zero.

NPV(*value,series range*)

value is a discount rate. *series range* is a group of cash earnings on an investment, at equal intervals (usually years).

The NPV (Net Present Value) function returns the present value of the group of cash earnings at the given discount rate. The discount rate must be entered as a decimal fraction, not a percentage (for example, .10, not 10%).

The NPV function accumulates the earnings in the series range, discounting the first value once, the second value twice, and so forth. For example, if C1 contains .12 and D1 through D3 contain 1000, 1000, and 1000, then NPV(C1,D1:D3) performs the following calculation:

$$\frac{1000}{1.12} + \frac{1000}{(1.12)\hat{}2} + \frac{1000}{(1.12)\hat{}3}$$

Appendix C

Hard Disk and RAM Disk

SuperCalc can be used with a hard disk or a disk that is "emulated" by your computer's memory, also called *RAM* (Random Access Memory). Either of these allows SuperCalc to operate much faster than it does from floppy disks.

A hard disk is a high-speed storage device that stores much more information than a floppy disk and can retrieve that information much faster. A RAM disk emulator is a program that sets aside some of your computer's memory to act like a disk. The information in a RAM disk emulator is available almost instantly because it is already contained in your computer's memory.

SuperCalc is a large program; it is not all loaded in the memory of your computer at the same time. Instead, it repeatedly reads parts of the program from the disk as you use certain commands or mathematical functions. You may be aware of this from watching the indicator lights on your disk drives as the program runs.

If you place the SuperCalc program files on a hard disk or a disk emulator, it can more quickly read the parts of the program that it requires. This makes SuperCalc operate faster, especially when you are using many different commands.

The SuperCalc program consists of three parts: the main program file, the overlay file, and the help file. These files are shown in Table I-1 in the Introduction. All of these files must be on the *default drive* for SuperCalc to operate.

To operate SuperCalc from a hard disk or a disk emulator, these three files must be copied from the floppy disk. This is not a problem with a hard disk—you do it once. But with a disk emulator, you must do this each time you turn on the computer or initialize the disk emulator. The file names make it easy; they all start with SC. Thus, you can copy all of them with a single operating system command. If you are using MS-DOS the command is **COPY SC*.* C:**. If you are using CP/M or CP/M-86, you enter **PIP C:=SC*.***. This assumes that the SuperCalc files (and for CP/M, PIP.COM) are on the current default drive and drive C is your hard disk or disk emulator.

Once the three files are on this drive, just make it the default drive (in the example, enter **C:<RET>**), and then start SuperCalc as you normally would, by typing **SC<RET>**.

You should not store SuperCalc model files on a RAM disk emulator. The disk emulator is not permanent storage, and it will probably not save much time since SuperCalc loads and saves worksheets quite rapidly. It is better in the long run to store model files directly on a real disk.

Appendix D

Glossary

Active cell. The highlighted cell location on the worksheet where data that you enter will be placed. (Chapter 1)

Application. One of the uses to which a program may be put. For instance, one of the applications for a spreadsheet program might be to keep track of your household budget. (Chapter 11)

Argument. The input value to a function on which the function operates. An argument is always enclosed in parentheses. For example, in the formula SQRT(2), the 2 is the argument to the square root function. (Chapter 5)

Arithmetic operator. One of five symbols that you may use in a formula to calculate a value. These symbols are

Symbol	*Meaning*
+	Addition
−	Subtraction
*	Multiplication
/	Division
^	Exponentiation

SuperCalc evaluates formulas in regular mathematical order from left to right with exponentiation first, multiplication and division next, and then addition and subtraction. This order of precedence can be changed if you add parentheses. For example, the formula A1*A2−3 multiplies the value of cell A1 by the value of cell A2 and then subtracts 3, but the formula A1*(A2−3) subtracts 3 from the value of cell A2 and then multiplies the result by the value of cell A1. (Chapter 5)

Arrow keys. The four keys on a terminal marked with up, down, right, and left arrows. These keys are used to move the active cell from location to location on the worksheet and also provide editing capabilities on the entry line. If the terminal you are using does not have arrow keys, you need to use the CONTROL (CTRL) key with the letter E to move the active cell up, X to move down, D to move right, and S to move left. (Chapter 1)

Backup. This word has two related meanings in SuperCalc. Backup is an option to the /Save command that allows you to save an updated model without erasing the original model saved on disk. The original is automatically given the file name extension .BAK to distinguish it from the newer version. (Chapter 3) The second meaning refers to the recommended practice of making a copy of a disk in order to ensure that the information on the disk is not inadvertently lost or destroyed. This can be done with a command provided by your computer's operating system. (Chapter 11)

Block. A rectangular group of cells on the worksheet. You can specify a particular block by naming the cell in the upper left-hand corner followed by a colon and then the cell in the lower right-hand corner. For instance, the formula SUM(C5:F10) totals all the values in the cells on rows 5 through 10 in columns C through F. (Chapter 4) You may specify a block as a range for any function that can operate on lists (Chapter 5) and also for the /Blank, /Copy, /Load, /Save, and /Format commands. (Chapters 4, 6, and 9)

Built-in. A built-in feature is one that is an integral part of a program. The square root function (SQRT) is an example of this. You do not have to create such a feature to be able to use it.

Calendar functions. Functions built into SuperCalc^2 that you can use to put dates in a model and to solve scheduling problems. The calendar functions are based on a modified Julian calendar, which starts with March 1, 1900 (represented as 1) and goes to February 28, 2100 (represented as 73049). (Chapter 10)

Cell. A particular location on the worksheet. The name of a cell is made up of both the column and the row in which it appears. Cell C3, for instance, is at the intersection of column C and row 3. (Chapter 1)

Cell contents. Information that has been entered into a cell. A cell may contain text, a number, or a formula. (Chapter 1)

Cell reference. The use of the contents of a particular cell by a formula in another cell. For instance, the formula B3−5+A2 contains references to cells B3 and A2. This formula subtracts 5 from the value of cell B3 and then adds the value of cell A2 to the result. (Chapter 2)

Circular reference. A situation where the formula in a particular cell refers to itself or when the formula in one cell refers to a second cell that contains a reference to the first. (Chapter 9)

Column. A vertical arrangement of cells on the spreadsheet. There are 63 columns on the SuperCalc spreadsheet, which are designated by the letters A to Z, AA to AZ, and BA to BK. (Chapter 1)

Command. An instruction to SuperCalc to perform a particular operation. All commands begin with a slash (/). See Appendix A for a complete list of SuperCalc commands. (Chapter 4)

Coordinate. Another word for cell. Coordinate refers to the fact that cells are named by the letter and number of the column and row that form them. In effect, this system uses a cell's coordinates to locate it within the grid of the spreadsheet. (Chapter 1)

.CSV. The file name extension that is given to SuperCalc files prepared by the SuperData Interchange program to be readable by a BASIC program. This extension is an abbreviation for Comma Separated Value format. (Chapter 9)

CTRL key. A key on the keyboard which is also called the CONTROL key. To use this key, you press it simultaneously with another key in order to make the other key perform an alternate function. For example, pressing CTRL with E, S, D, or X will make these keys work like the arrow keys, and pressing CTRL with Z will erase all of the data on the entry line. (Chapter 1)

Current cell. The cell on the spreadsheet that the active cell is currently occupying.

Current cell key. The ESCAPE (ESC) key is called the current cell key when it is used to place the address of the current cell on the data entry line. When you are entering a formula or a range to complete a command, pressing the ESC key will allow you to move the active cell around on the worksheet with the arrow keys. The address of the active cell is displayed on the data entry line. When the active cell is on the cell address you need, just press the ESC key again and that address will remain on the data entry line. This method is sometimes called "pointing to" a cell address. (Chapter 3)

Cursor. The small highlighted rectangle on the last status line where the next character you enter is placed. (Chapter 1)

Cursor diamond. The letters E, S, D, and X, which function like the arrow keys when pressed simultaneously with the CTRL key. (Chapter 1)

Default drive. The disk drive that the disk containing the SuperCalc program is in. In this book the default drive is assumed to be drive A. (Introduction, Chapter 3, Appendix C)

Default value. The original setting of an option or format that the SuperCalc program assumes when first turned on. You can change these settings by entering a command to tell SuperCalc to use a different value. For instance, the default column width is 9 characters, but you can make a column from 0 to 127 characters wide with the /Format command. (Chapter 4)

Destination range. A series or block of cells into which information will be placed when you complete the /Copy, /Load, or /Replicate command in progress. The destination range for the /Copy or /Load commands can be a single cell, a partial row or column, or a block. For /Replicate, the destination range can be either a single cell or a partial row or column. See also "Range." (Chapters 3 and 6)

Directional indicator. An arrow-shaped character, displayed at the left of the first status line, that shows the direction the active cell will move when you press <RET>. (Chapter 1)

Directory. The list of files that are stored on a disk. (Chapter 3)

Disk drive. An electro-mechanical device that is used in conjunction with a computer to store information on and retrieve information from a magnetic storage disk (either a floppy diskette or a hard disk). (Chapters 3 and 11)

Disk emulator. A program that allows you to use part of your computer's memory as if it were a diskette for temporary information storage. (Appendix C)

Diskette. A floppy diskette, which is a flexible, magnetic medium used for information storage. Floppy diskettes come in several sizes, including 3 1/2, 5 1/4 and 8 inches in diameter.

Display screen. The area of your terminal where you view the visible portion of the SuperCalc worksheet. (Chapter 1)

Documentation. Information, explanations, and instructions that are included in a particular applications model to allow someone unfamiliar with the model to use it effectively and to allow the author to recreate his or her original reasoning during the development of the model. (Chapters 8 and 11)

Execute file. A file saved on a disk that contains a sequence of SuperCalc commands that are read and executed when you use the /eXecute command. The purpose of such a file is to perform a repetitive task or to make it easy for someone unfamiliar with SuperCalc to use applications models correctly and effectively. Execute files should have the file name extension .XQT. (Chapter 9)

Exponential notation. A way of writing numbers (also called scientific notation) that shortens very large and very small numbers so they can be displayed in a narrow column width. Exponential notation places the decimal point after the first digit of a number and raises that number to the appropriate power of 10. (SuperCalc has a limit of plus or minus the 63rd power of 10.) An "e" is inserted between the number and its power of 10. For example, the number 8,714,000 becomes 8.714e6 in exponential notation. You can specify that the values in any part of your worksheet be displayed in exponential notation with the Exponential option of the /Format command. (Chapter 4)

File. A group of related information that is stored together under one name on a disk. In SuperCalc, a file usually contains a single applications model. (Chapter 3)

File name. The name given to a file to differentiate it from other files on the same diskette. A file name should be in the form THISFILE.EXT; it can have as many as eight characters in the main name and an extension after the period of as many as three characters. SuperCalc files have the default file name extension .CAL, which is used unless you specify a different extension. (Chapter 3)

Floating dollar sign. A user-defined format option that puts a dollar sign to the left of the first digit of a displayed value, regardless of the magnitude of the value. See also "User-defined format." (Chapter 8)

Format of a cell. /Format command allows you to specify how the information in the cells on your worksheet will appear. In addition to the built-in formats, SuperCalc^2 allows you to define eight of your own formats with the User-defined options of the /Format command. (Chapters 4 and 9)

Format (initialize). To prepare a new diskette to store information in a way your computer understands. This must be done with your computer's operating system; the SuperCalc program does not format diskettes. (Chapter 3)

Formula. A calculation. In SuperCalc, a formula is an algebraic expression that can contain numbers and refer to other cells. For example, the formula A6/12+B4 divides the value in cell A6 by 12 and then adds the value in cell B4 to the result. If the values in cells A6 or B4 change, the value calculated by this formula will change accordingly. (Chapter 3)

Formula ERROR. A message displayed at the right of the first status line when you try to enter a formula that does not conform to the rules for using formulas in SuperCalc. These rules specify that a formula must begin with a number, an arithmetic operator, a cell reference, or a function, and can be 116 characters in length. Numbers (in both regular and exponential format) can be 16 digits in length plus a decimal point. Text entries must be preceded by a double quote ("). Any deviation from these rules will result in a formula error. (Chapter 1)

Forward reference. A situation where a formula in a cell contains a reference to a cell whose value has not yet been calculated. Forward references can be checked for by calculating a model twice (press the exclamation point (!) once if your worksheet is in automatic recalculation mode and twice if it is in manual recalculation mode). If anything changes the second time, there is a forward reference in the model. Often such a problem can be corrected by changing the model's order of calculation with the /Global command. (Chapter 9)

Function. A built-in mathematical calculation. All SuperCalc functions (except the PI function) perform their calculations on at least one input value enclosed in parentheses. (Chapters 5, 10, and 12)

Go to command. The name given to the equal sign (=) when it is used as a command to jump to a cell on the worksheet. To use the Go to command, enter an equal sign (=) onto the blank entry line, followed by the coordinate to which you want the active cell to be moved; then press <RET>. (Chapter 1)

Integer. A whole number with no digits to the right of the decimal point. You can specify that the values in any part of your worksheet be displayed as integers with the Integer option of the /Format command. You can also display the result of a formula as an integer with the INT function. (Chapters 4 and 5)

LOOKUP function. A built-in function that finds a specified value in a table. The LOOKUP function requires an input value and a range in which to look for that value. When the function finds the last value in the range that is less than or equal to the input value, it returns the value of the cell adjacent to the matching cell. (Chapter 10)

Memory (RAM). Random-access memory (RAM) is the part of a computer where information that you are working on is temporarily stored. This memory can be both read from and written to, and all information stored there is equally easy to get to, which is why it is called random-access.

Menu. A screen display that shows you a list of options for a particular part of the SuperCalc program. For instance, pressing the question mark (?) at a time when you are entering data or a command shows you a Help menu, which explains what the prompts mean or what command options are available to you at that point. See also "Setup menu." (Chapter 1)

MOD function. A function built into SuperCalc^2 that returns only the remainder of a division, not the entire result. See Appendix B for an explanation of how to use this function. (Chapter 5)

Model. A part of the SuperCalc worksheet that you have set up to perform calculations and display values for a single application. A model will usually contain labels, formulas, working values, and some sort of documentation showing how to use the model. One model usually corresponds to a single file on a diskette, and the name of that file often describes the purpose of the model. (Chapter 11)

Natural logarithm (LN function). A logarithm to the base *e*, as opposed to common logarithms, which are to the base 10. *e* is a mathematical constant (sometimes called Euler's constant) that equals approximately 2.718. SuperCalc's LN function will return the natural logarithm of its argument. (Chapter 5)

Nesting. Using one or more functions as the argument to another function. For instance, INT(SQRT(10)) is a nested function because the SQRT function forms the argument to the INT function. (Chapters 5 and 10)

NPV function. A built-in function that calculates the present value of money you will receive in the future. The NPV (Net Present Value) function uses a value called the discount rate to do this. The discount rate, which you must supply, is the amount that money will be devalued in the future. This function is useful for comparing possible investments and taking inflation into account in your long-term financial plans. For more information, see Appendix B. (Chapter 10)

Overwrite. An option of the /Save command that tells the SuperCalc program to retain on disk only the newest version of the file you are saving. This option destroys the original file, so it should be used with caution. (Chapter 3)

Prompt. A question, appearing on the second status line, that asks you to enter the next piece of information necessary to complete a command. (Chapter 1)

Protected entry. The /Protect command protects the contents and format of cells from being changed. When a cell is protected, you cannot enter new data into it, and you cannot edit or delete the information it already contains. If you try to do so, you will see the message "Protected entry" at the right end of the status line. However, a cell's protection can be easily removed with the /Unprotect command. See Appendix A for more information. (Chapter 4)

Range. A range tells the SuperCalc program which cells you want to be affected by the command you have entered. A range can be a cell, a partial column, a column, a column range, a partial row, a row, a row range, or a block, depending on the command you are using. A range is defined by first entering its upper-left cell, then a colon (:), and then its lower-right cell. You can also use the current cell key to point to the cell addresses you want to enter. An example of how ranges are used in a command is /R , A12 , A14:A20. This command replicates the contents of cell A12 (the source range) into cells A14 through A20 (the destination range). (Chapter 3)

Range ERROR. This message is displayed at the right end of the status line if you attempt to enter an incorrect range. See "Range" for rules to enter the ranges that are allowed by SuperCalc. (Chapter 3)

Relational operator. A symbol that compares two values and returns a True or False answer, depending on the values it is comparing. A True answer has a numerical value of 1, while False has a numerical value of 0. The relational operators are

Symbol	*Meaning*
=	Equal to
>	Greater than
<	Less than
<>	Not equal to
>=	Greater than or equal to
<=	Less than or equal to

The relational operators are often used with the logical functions (AND, IF, NOT, and OR) to make conditional calculations. For example, the formula IF (A3<>B7,100,0) first compares the values in cells A3 and B7 to see if they are equal or not. If they are not equal, the IF function returns a value of 100, but if they are equal, it returns 0. (Chapter 10)

Repeating entry. A special entry that repeats itself to the right of the cell it was entered into until it reaches a non-blank cell. Repeating entries are preceded by a single quote (') and are usually used to make lines to mark off different sections of a model. You can stop a repeating entry by entering a double quote (") into the cell to the right of where you want the repeating entry to end. (Chapter 2)

Replication. The process of making a copy of something. In SuperCalc, replication is done with the /Replicate command, which is especially useful for making multiple copies of a cell, a partial column, or a partial row. The /Copy command is used to make one copy of a single cell or block of cells. (Chapter 3)

<RET>. In this book, the symbol <RET> indicates the RETURN key. On some computer keyboards, the RETURN key may be identified with the word ENTER or NEW LINE or with a down and left arrow. (Introduction, Chapter 1)

Row. A horizontal arrangement of cells on the spreadsheet. Rows in SuperCalc are designated by the numbers 1 through 254. (Chapter 1)

Scrolling. When you move the active cell with the arrow keys to a cell that was not visible when you started, your display screen appears to move across the spreadsheet grid to show you a previously invisible part of it. This apparent movement is called scrolling. (Chapter 1)

SDI. An abbreviation for the SuperData Interchange program, which is used to copy SuperCalc files into a form that is readable by both BASIC programs and SuperCalc-compatible programs. (Chapter 9)

Setup menu. A menu of options displayed when you choose the Setup option of the /Output command. With these options you can change the format of a printed report and send special instructions to the printer. (Chapter 8)

Setup string. A series of characters the printer understands as special control codes. (Chapter 8)

Sorting. Arranging a list of data into alphabetical or numerical order. This can be done in SuperCalc with the /Arrange command, which allows you to sort entries listed in a row or column in either ascending or descending order. (Chapter 7)

Source range. A cell or cells from which information will be duplicated when you complete the /Copy, /Load, or /Replicate command in progress. The source range for the /Copy and /Load commands can be a single cell, a partial column or row, or a block of cells. For /Replicate, the source range can be a single cell or a partial column or row. See also "Range." (Chapter 3)

Spreadsheet. The grid used by a spreadsheet program like SuperCalc. This grid is arranged into columns and rows, and data can be entered into cells that occur at the intersections of these columns and rows. These cells are usually designated by the names of the rows and columns where they occur.

Stair-step approach. A method of developing an applications model that allows you to expand the model at any point in its development without disrupting its function. This is done by positioning each new section of the model below and to the right of the previous sections, provided you started at cell A1. This arrangement allows you to insert, delete, or copy rows or columns without affecting any of the formulas you have already developed. (Chapter 11)

Status line. The first line below the worksheet area on the display screen that gives you the status line is called the Active Cell line, because it shows you the address of the active cell, the directional indicator, the data type and contents of the current cell, and error messages as needed. (Chapter 1)

Template. A model from which working values have been removed. Templates are designed to be used as models for a repetitive function and are especially good for use by people who are unfamiliar with SuperCalc. For example, a good application for a template would be a monthly inventory for a small business. After you developed the template, you or another user could simply load it into memory, fill in a month's inventory figures, and save it under the name of the month. Then you could use the template again for each successive month, saving each model under the month's name. Someone unfamiliar with SuperCalc could fill in the working values as easily as the author, provided that the template was well documented. (Chapter 11)

Terminal. A single desktop unit that contains a display screen and a keyboard for use with a computer. (Chapter 1)

Title lock. A situation where one column or row of a model is always visible, even if you scroll away from it. The /Title command allows you to make either horizontal (row) or vertical (column) locks, or both. A locked row will scroll horizontally but not vertically, and a locked column will scroll vertically but not horizontally, while a column-row lock will not scroll at all. You cannot move the active cell into a locked area with the arrow keys; you must use the Go to command (=) to do this. Title locks are removed with the Clear option of the /Title command. (Chapter 7)

Unprotect. The /Unprotect command reverses the /Protect command, which protects the contents and format of cells from being changed or deleted. (Chapter 4)

User-defined format. The User option of the /Format command, which is available only in SuperCalc^2, allows you to define eight special formats for use in each model. You define these formats by choosing different combinations of the seven format options in the User-defined format table, which appears when you select the User option. The format options in this table are floating dollar sign, embedded commas, minus in parentheses, zero as blank, percent, decimal places, and scaling factor. (Chapter 8)

Window. The /Window command creates a division in the display screen that allows you to see two separate portions of the spreadsheet at one time.

These portions are called windows. With the /Window command you can create either a horizontal or a vertical division. You use the semicolon (;)—not the arrow keys or the Go to command (=)—to move back and forth from one window to another. (Chapter 7)

Worksheet. Another word for spreadsheet, which is the electronic grid produced by a spreadsheet program such as SuperCalc. See also "Spreadsheet." (Chapter 1)

INDEX

ABOUT THE AUTHOR

Chris Wood has written several manuals and user guides for Epson. In addition, he is the Production Manager of Wood & Jones, a commercial printing plant where he provides technical supervision for the data processing functions. He holds a B.S. degree in Mechanical Engineering from California State Polytechnic College in San Luis Obispo, CA.